LKJ

LINTON KWESI JOHNSON

AND THE DENNIS BOVELL DUB BAND

Time Come

SELECTED PROSE

Time Come

SELECTED PROSE

Linton Kwesi Johnson

WITH AN INTRODUCTION
BY PAUL GILROY

PICADOR

First published 2023 by Picador
an imprint of Pan Macmillan
The Smithson, 6 Briset Street, London EC1M 5NR
EU representative: Macmillan Publishers Ireland Limited, 1st Floor, The Liffey Trust
Centre, 117–126 Sheriff Street Upper, Dublin 1 D01 YC43
Associated companies throughout the world
www.panmacmillan.com

ISBN 978-1-0350-0632-8

The acknowledgements on pages 295–8 constitute an extension of this copyright page.

1 3 5 7 9 8 6 4 2

A CIP catalogue record for this book is available from the British Library.

Typeset in Janson Text by Palimpsest Book Production Ltd, Falkirk, Stirlingshire
Printed and bound by CPI Group (UK) Ltd, Croydon, CR0 4YY

Visit **www.picador.com** to read more about all our books
and to buy them. You will also find features, author interviews and
news of any author events, and you can sign up for e-newsletters
so that you're always first to hear about our new releases.

To Sharmilla

What use immortal fame
to mortal body?

(Du Fu, 'Winding River', trans. by Andrew Neilson
in *Modern Poetry in Translation* no.1, 2022)

Contents

Paul Gilroy – Introduction: Culture as a Vital Force   xv

1. 'REGGAE SOUNDS' – MUSIC

Jamaican Rebel Music   3
Race & Class XVII 4, 1976

The Reggae Rebellion   29
New Society, 10 June 1976

The Year of Reggae   35
Melody Maker, 25 December 1976

Marley at the Polls   43
Melody Maker, 5 February 1977

Bob Marley and the Reggae International   49
Race Today, June/July 1977

'Blackbeard' in Profile: Laying the Foundations   57
Race Today Review, December 1981/January 1982

Exodus: The Poetry of Exile   69
The Independent, 1 June 2007

African Consciousness in Reggae Music: 75
Some Examples
Lecture, July 2013

The People Speak   87
  Introduction to *So Much Things to Say*
  by Roger Steffens, 2015

The Upsetter   93
  Introduction to *People Funny Boy*
  by David Katz, 8 September 2021

2. 'STORY' – LITERATURE

The Swamp Dwellers by Wole Soyinka   99
  Race Today, September 1975

Caribbean Chronicles   103
  Times Literary Supplement, 25 March 1977

Echo by Orlando Wong   105
[the former name of Oku Onuora]
  Race Today, September 1977

Language as Power: 111
Decolonising the Mind by Ngũgĩ wa Thiong'o
  Race Today, December 1986

Searching for Answers: 115
Caryl Phillips in Conversation
  Race Today Review, 1987

Speaking in Tongues: 129
Dictionary of Caribbean English Usage
  The Guardian, 19 April 1996

Writing Reggae: 133
Poetry, Politics and Popular Culture
  Jamaica Journal, December 2010

I & I: The Natural Mystics by Colin Grant   163
   Wasafiri, July 2011

3. 'DI ANFINISH REVALUESHAN' – POLITICS

Jamaica Uncovered: *Life and Debt*   171
   The Guardian, 28 February 2002

We Have Not Forgotten   175
   Prologue to *The New Cross Massacre Story*,
   New Beacon Books and the George Padmore
   Institute, 2011

Riots, Rhyme and Reason   181
   Local Brixton speech, 24 March 2012

Thatcher and the Inner-City Riots   189
   LKJ Records blog, 14 April 2013

South African Connections   193
   Honorary doctorate acceptance speech,
   April 2017

4. 'TINGS AN TIMES' – PLACES AND MOMENTS

Introduction   203
   Race Today Review, 1986

Introduction   207
   Race Today Review, 1987

South London Calling   213
   Time Out, 23 March 2000

Reunited: Shocking with Such Glee 219
Times Higher Education Supplement, 24 September 2004

Amsterdam: Places, People and Beginnings 223
Amsterdam event speech, September 2014

Acceptance Speech to the University 233
of the West Indies
Honorary doctorate acceptance speech,
19 October 2021

5. 'BEACON OF HOPE' – PEOPLE

Martin Carter: Give Thanks 239
All are Involved: The Art of Martin Carter,
ed. Stewart Brown, written 12 December 1997

Remembering Michael Smith: 241
Mikey, Dub and Me
Lecture, 4 August 2005

Mutabaruka: Cutting Edge of Dub 257
The Guardian, 27 August 2005

Obituary: John La Rose 265
The Guardian, 4 March 2006

Obituary: Louise Bennett, Voice of the People 271
Wasafiri, October 2006

Remembering Andrew Salkey 277
Speech at the University of Glasgow, October 2014

Don Mattera and James Matthews: A Tribute 283
Speech in South Africa, May 2019

Jean 'Binta' Breeze: A Tribute 287
 George Padmore Institute website, 21 June 2021

Linton Kwesi Johnson's prose in chronological order 291

Acknowledgements and permissions 295

Index 299

Introduction:
Culture as a Vital Force

It is mistaken to think of Linton Kwesi Johnson only as the sometime Poet Laureate of black Britain, the role for which he is best known in the mainstream. Johnson's output of cultural commentary, journalistic and critical writing about politics, music, literature and drama is extensive and far from familiar. The contents of this rich anthology are drawn from a wide variety of publications and contexts. Johnson's writing has been salvaged and recycled from ephemeral publications: *Melody Maker*, *Race Today* and *New Society*. Forgotten and overlooked statements have been combined with talks, speeches, reviews and dialogues from book festivals, activist rallies, memorial and ceremonial meetings here, in Europe, the Caribbean and South Africa.

This is all firmly analogue writing which, for the most part, cannot be found anywhere online. Brought together in this way, the material painfully conveys the contraction and diminution of the public world of ideas created by combative, radical interests during almost five decades. The resulting patchwork of lectures, talks, eulogies and expository essays is therefore more than merely a counterpoint to Johnson's poetic chronicling of the life of his generation of settlers from the Caribbean and the locally born sufferers with whom they made common cause. His commentaries, observations and insights derive from and operate within the wide, transnational geography of the twentieth century's black freedom movement. However, they are energized by the poet's local affiliations with London and his neighbourhood as well as the various activist groups to which he has belonged. Among them were the Race Today Collective and the arts organisation Creation For Liberation, which operated in alliance with the Black Parents Movement, the Black Youth Movement and associated groups outside London.

The bulk of the writing here addresses the intercultural, creolized, diasporic and Caribbean dimensions of Johnson's signature predicament. He is affiliated to several locations, all of which make claims upon him and all of which he claims in return, because they accent different features of a complex, anti-/postcolonial formation. This material shows how Johnson has repeatedly turned that vexed position into a creative opportunity.

His cultural and geopolitical ties supply a heavy bass line here. It is heard in a framework supplied by irreducibly human tones which are audible on another frequency. Their strength and appeal derive equally from Johnson's rebel disposition and his abiding attachment to universalizing themes rendered in the language of freedom-seeking tradition to which he subscribes. It has been nobly augmented by the poetic idiom he created. This material insists upon the truth, value of art, the inevitability of social struggle and the eternal necessity of pursuing justice, equality and peace. Johnson's righteous endorsement of those time-worn demands is greatly amplified by the manner in which they have been mutually articulated.

—

It is well known that Johnson worked as a librarian at the fabled Keskidee Centre on north London's Caledonian Road. That role highlights his distinctive generational position. His creative life extends back into the sophisticated anticolonial furnace of the Caribbean Artists Movement, where he was mentored by the likes of Andrew Salkey, John La Rose and others. Under the impact of Black Power and in solidarity with national liberation struggles, that formation morphed into a distinctive Black Arts Movement contoured by local conflicts and conditions somewhat different from the situations found in the Caribbean and the United States.

Johnson's history of frontline activism is manifest in the choice of topics covered here and in the angles of interpretative vision that he adopts to unlock them. His recurrent focus on insurgent culture encompasses a shadow political history of the Caribbean region during the later stages of the Cold War – the pivotal decade between the electoral victory of Jamaican Michael Manley's PNP and the overthrow of the Grenadian revolution in 1983.

Johnson speaks from the Left, but not in a doctrinaire or formulaic way. His distinctive critical voice has, he tells us, been 'achieved on my own terms from a position of cultural autonomy'. Black expressive cultures are carefully historicized, explicated and enthused over. The work of critique is undertaken thoughtfully and appreciatively. The influence of Frantz Fanon and Amilcar Cabral was among the important ancestral guidance that Johnson absorbed as a young militant. Their impact is evident in the distinctive way that he presents culture as a vital force endowed with revolutionary potential, especially in the petrified, segregated worlds colonialism made.

Taken together, these pieces compose a fragmentary but tenaciously Caribbean-centric history of the transnational black movement. Johnson's commentaries are spiced with a scattering of autobiographical detail that will help to secure the attention of younger readers for whom Ethiopianism, Black Power and revolutionary, tropical socialism are distant spectacles remote from the compass of lived experience.

Johnson's path-breaking essay 'Jamaican Rebel Music' was published in *Race & Class* in 1976. Related pieces on the same topic are included here, having originally appeared in the pages of *New Society* and later, in *The Independent*. After all this time, it is difficult to convey the signal importance of those historic interventions. They fostered and inspired many others, like myself, who were emboldened and excited by the way that Johnson approached Caribbean popular culture seriously and employed methodical analysis of it to open up some of the most important historical and political questions of that time. His later pieces on aspects of music show that Johnson remains a knowledgeable and astute observer of reggae's history and its evolving social and cultural scenes. There are portraits of key figures like Maestro Dennis Bovell and Lee Perry – 'the Dalí of Reggae' – as well as detailed presentations on the art, music and literature produced by his poetic peers.

INTRODUCTION

The overall effect is to situate Johnson's own work carefully. He locates himself almost inadvertently by praising the writers like Louise Bennett, Bongo Jerry and Kamau Brathwaite who inspired him and, with humility and generosity, hailing his fellow 'dub poets' Mutabaruka and Oku Onuora, Mikey Smith, Noel Walcott, M'bala and Jean Binta Breeze. Their insurgent lyricism and command of the vernacular tones and rhythms of Jamaican speech consolidated novel forms and performance styles into an aesthetic breakthrough that subsequently acquired a planetary reach.

This scandalously overdue volume will no doubt add a lot to the way Johnson's poetry is understood, but that is not its primary significance. These useful fragments convey the fluctuating pulse of the movement from which they sprang. The author's contingent judgements may be compelling, but this is an invitation to know the history of that movement as well as to see how learning about it might furnish a different picture of political culture: ceaselessly moving, insurgent and mutable.

Paul Gilroy, May 2022

Time Come

1.
'REGGAE SOUNDS' – MUSIC

Jamaican Rebel Music (1976)

Sometimes I cry
when I see my people
and ooe
pure pain and poverty
we black people
suffering so
and yet I know
history will show
how long we suffer so[1]

LEROY SIBBLES

The popular music of Jamaica today is a music whose pulse is 'the ground-beat of survival itself'.[2] It is a 'music of the blood/ black reared/ pain rooted/ heart geared', a music 'all tensed-up in the bubble and the bounce and the leap and the weight drop'.[3] It is a music that is at once violent and awesome, forceful and mighty, aggressive and cathartic. It is a music that beats heavily against the walls of babylon,* that the walls may come a-tumbling down; a music that chucks a heavy historical load that is pain that is hunger that is bitter that is blood, that is dread. Yes the popular music of Jamaica is full of dread for it is dread down Jamaica way this day; it is red down there I say.

---

* Rastafarian word meaning police, oppressor, land of oppression.

Jamaica is red with the blood of innocents who are daily slaughtered by babylon; red with the blood of repression and rebellion that floods the streets of Kingston as the guns rage in the noonday sun, as the guns bark throughout the troubled nights; red with the fratricidal blood of the oppressed. And it is this tale that the musician, singer and the dub-lyricist tells.* They tell of the burden of the history of oppression, rebellion and repression; of the 'tribal wars', the political skank,† the despair and desperation. Not only does the poetry of Jamaican music lament the suffering of the 'sufferers', it also asserts their strength and their determination to struggle on relentlessly, and prophesies the coming Armageddon wherein 'only the fittest of the fittest shall survive' and 'no weak heart shall prosper', because 'it dread down a babylon! dreaaaad'.[4]

Jamaican music embodies the historical experience of the Jamaican masses – it reflects, and in reflecting, reveals the contemporary situation of the nation. He who feels it knows it, the saying goes, and it is the sufferer from the urban ghettoes, the 'creation rebel' who has 'travelled up that old rough road' to find his bread who really has the say as to what is happening down Jamaica way today. So forward we now go with this musical exploration, the 'creation rebel' will guide us on our way.

---

* The 'dub-lyricist' is the deejay turned poet. He intones his lyrics rather than sings them. Dub-lyricism is a new form of (oral) music-poetry, wherein the lyricist overdubs rhythmic phrases onto the rhythm of a popular song. Dub-lyricists include poets like Big Youth, I Roy, U-Roy, Dillinger, Shorty the President, Prince Jazzbo and others.
† Jamaican Creolism meaning 'to fool around, to fool someone or to play the fool for the purpose of deception'.

I shall say it again: the popular music of Jamaica, the music of the people, is an essentially experiential music, not merely in the sense that the people *experience* the music, but also in the sense that the music is true to the historical experience of the people, that the music reflects the historical experience. It is the *spiritual* expression of the *historical* experience of the Afro-Jamaican. In making the music, the musicians themselves enter a common stream of consciousness, and what they create is an invitation to the listeners to be entered into that consciousness – which is also the consciousness of their people. The feel of the music is the feel of their common history, the burden of their history; their suffering and their woe; their endurance and their strength, their poverty and their pain. This is precisely what Leroy Sibbles of the Heptones means when he says of 'dub' or 'drum and bass music', the music of Jamaica today: 'Well . . . it signifies some kind of African feeling, the beat and the drum and the bass. We are all black and we have Africa deep within us. Yea we feel it. It's cultural and you just got to get with it because you feel it. Deep down inside, from you hear it, you feel it.'[5] You feel it because the 'bad bass bounce' is your 'blood a leap an pulse a pounce',[6] you feel it because this 'rhythm of a tropical electrical storm',[7] 'rhythm cuttin sharp so' cuts at your hurt; you feel it for the 'bass history is a moving/ is a hurting black story';[8] you feel it because it is your pain; you feel it because it is your hunger. Deep down inside, from you hear it, you feel it, for it is your heart-song and it touches your soul's senses. The youth who live in the ghettoes and shanty towns of Jamaica describe the music in terms of their own existence, which is basically a rebel existence: they call the music rebel music. According to Leroy Sibbles, 'they use the way they *feel* to describe the music', and this is so precisely because the music is expressive of how they 'feel'.

The musician, singer and dub-lyricist are mostly 'sufferers'. Through music, song and poetry, they give spiritual expression to their own inner beings, to their own experience. But in so doing, they are also giving spiritual expression to the collective experience of sufferation that is shared by all sufferers. Perhaps Toots and the Maytals' 'Time Tough' will help us to explain the reciprocal relationship between the spiritual expression of experience by the artist on the one hand, and the *experiencing* of this spiritual expression by the people on the other hand. In this song, the lyricist is lamenting the hardships of life, the bitterness of life.

> I go to bed
> but sleep won't come
> get up in the night
> couldn't stand my *feeling*
> early in the morning
> it's the same situation
> then come the landlord
> just a knock knocking upon my door
> I've got four hundred month rent to pay
> and I can't find a dollar[9]

Here the lyrics are sung in the first person, so that it is the individual experience, the personal situation, that informs the song. But the individual experience is the experience of all:

able "MPLA." Hoo Kim's list of success includes the Mighty Diamonds " Right Time ", Dillinger's CB200 album and scores of singles including Earth and Fire's " Time To Come ".

It has also been another creative and fruitful year for the energetic producer, Lee Perry, the Upsetter, a leading exponent of another style of 'rockers,' with achievements like Junior Murvin's ever-popular " Police And Thieves," Max Romeo's single and album " War In A Babylon ", and what is undoubtedly the greatest achievement of nemesis in dub music yet, Perry's own super " Super Ape." The only other memorable dub album of '76 is " Raas Claat Dub " a spill-over of '75 rhythms into '76.

" Dis yah music yah, a strickly roots music yaah; strictly rockers music wi a deal wid oll over di world, yu se'it." So says Johnnie Clarke from the title track of his most stylistically accomplished album yet, " Rockers Time," a part of the " Virgin Rockers " output.

Virgin Records, who have certainly benefited from Islands' experience, made history this year by showing us how a rock company becomes a rock and reggae company almost overnight with almost a dozen albums in something like eight months, including the Mighty Diamonds' "Right Time " and the Gladiators' "Trenchtown Mix-up," the cream of their crop.

Virgin have spent a lot of money on promotions and spent it wisely with their cheap promotional album, " The Front Line," making the Top 20 album charts and, moderately successful promotional tours by U Roy and the Diamonds. By the end of the summer, Virgin rockers were selling as well as, and in some cases even better than Virgin's rock.

With the Virgin promotional machinery behind him and rockers rhythms to jive-talk in, U Roy, the veteran deejay dub-lyricist, has achieved a level of popular response in Britain this year with "Dread In A Babylon" and "Natty Rebel " which no other deejay/dub-lyricist has matched.

Dillinger, during the year, also added considerably to his reputation as one of the fore-

DELROY WASHINGTON: the British experience / PETER TOSH: anticlimax / MIGHTY DIAMONDS: on Jo Jo Hoo Kim's success list

Cutting from Christmas Day's *Melody Maker*, 1976.

time tough
everything is out of sight
it is so hard so hard
everything is going higher and higher[10]

Every sufferer is experiencing the hardness of the time. 'Sister Lee cannot bear it/ and brother Lee can hardly stand it/ they're crying night and day/ nobody to help them in their way'.[11] So when Toots, with so much pain in his parched voice, sings: 'from I was a little boy/ I keep on feeling it feeling it now',[12] 'Sister Lee' feels it, and 'brother Lee' feels it too; immersed in music and song, everyone feels it for they immediately recognize the pain in this song as their own pain as the music takes them to the very depths of their being.

Music totally encompasses the lives of the oppressed in Jamaica this day. From the old and disillusioned to the young and rebellious, music is the 'food of love', their spiritual and cultural nourishment. For through music, their dreams are unveiled, their souls exorcized, their tensions canalized, their strength realized. In the Afro-Jamaican churches, men, women and children gather together to rid themselves of their pain and their agony in a remorseful outpouring of the souls as they sing those mournful songs, bleeding on the cross, stretching forth their cupped hands, reaching, reaching out for the 'new Jerusalem'.

The dances which complement the popular music – the ska, the rock steady, the reggae, the skank and the chucky – are at once erotic and sensual, violent, aggressive and cathartic. The music invokes what psychiatrist and political philosopher Frantz Fanon calls the 'emotional sensitivity' of the oppressed and gives vent to it through dance.[13] As Fanon puts it: 'The native's relaxation takes precisely the form of muscular orgy in which the most acute aggressivity and the most impelling violence are transformed and conjured away'.[14] 'There are no limits – for in reality your purpose in coming together is to allow the accumulated libido, the hampered aggressivity to dissolve as in a volcanic eruption. Symbolic killings, fantastic rites, imaginary mass murders – all must be brought out'.[15]

But it so happens that, at times, the catharsis does not come through dance, for the violence that the music carries is turned inwards and personalized, so that for no apparent reason, the dance halls and yards often explode into fratricidal violence and general pandemonium. Whenever two rival sound systems meet, violence often erupts between the rival supporters, so the deejay is often both the musical pace-setter and the musical peace-keeper. He tells the dancers, 'those who deal in violence shall go down in silence'. Similarly, the dub-lyricist who has developed the deejay talk into a form of music-poetry tells his listeners that they are invited to a musical happening, but he warns them, 'when you come/ I don't want you to bring your skeng/ 1 want you to leave your skeng at home'.[16] Big Youth tells his listener:

> you should make a love not war
> cause war is ugly love is lovely
> cause if it's war then you'll be double double ugly
> and if it's love then you'll be a double double lovely[17]

Jamaica, that 'Caribbean island paradise in the sun', is one of the most violent places under the sun. This is not surprising when we recall that Jamaican society, like all colonial societies, is one which was founded upon, and is maintained through, violence. Gordon Rohlehr, the West Indian literary critic, has commented on the fierceness of the 'forces of despair and erosion' that permeate Jamaican society and culture, and its relation to the music. 'Each new weight of pressure' in the society, says Rohlehr, 'has its corresponding effect on the music, and the revolution is usually felt first as a perceptible change in the bass, the basic rhythm, the inner pulse whose origin is in the confrontation between the despair which history and iniquitous politics inflict, and the rooted strength of the people'.[18] The music responds to changes in the society, so that as the society becomes more violent, more dread, more tense, the beat becomes more dread and the rhythm more taut. The bass and the rhythm are the city's 'grounded heart beat', as Rohlehr puts it, and the beat of the music 'dominates the city'. So 'when the rhythm goes dread, the whole society *feels* the tension, and why not? After all it was the cruel tension which determined that the beat should go dread in the first place'.[19]

And every sufferer, from the old to the young in Jamaica today, wears the look of dread, a permanent grimace, a 'permanent screw'.[20] This look of dread testifies to the inner tension they feel, an agony that is real. I Roy's 'screw-face man'[21] is the 'mafiah', the 'dread', the man who has completely internalized the historical experience of violence and the violence of his existence, and acts out this violence through an existence of violence; for 'screw face carrying skeng/ and a screw-face carrying bucky'.* Bob Marley's 'Talkin' Blues' is here enlightening. Marley writes:

> I've been down on the rock for so long
> I seem to wear a permanent screw[22]

In this song, Marley is talking about a bitter existence in babylon which is 'blues'. He is 'saying talkin' blues' because 'cold ground' was his bed last night 'and rock was my pillow too'.[23] The permanence of this blues experience and existence is the historical experience that is facially expressed in the 'permanent screw'. But, along with this 'blues' feeling, this inner agony and outer look of dread, there is an urgent desire to tear down the walls of babylon:

> But I'm gonna stare in the sun
> let the rays shine in my eyes
> I'm gonna take just one step more
> for I feel like bombing a church[24]

So that when Laxton Ford implores his listeners to: 'take some time and learn to smile/ it's a better way to stay', we immediately understand his meaning.[25]

The historical experience of the Jamaican masses, part of the wider Caribbean experience of colonialism and neo-

---

* 'Skeng' is a Jamaican Creolism meaning pistol, and 'bucky' means shotgun, often homemade.

colonialism, is one that began with slavery. The barbarity of the slave-masters and slave-drivers has been well documented and does not have to be repeated here. Neither do we have to recall the raping, plunder and murder. Sam Clayton's words will suffice:

Jamaica is an island in the Caribbean – they say Caribbean but if I remember clearly it has carried us beyond our borders, not by freewill but by force, force! Like in 1565 when John Hawkins was given a Royal Charter from Her Majesty, Queen Elizabeth the first of England, and her personal ship, the SS Jesus of Lubek to transport slaves from Africa to the West Indies. As the history states, his methods were crude though effective. He just landed on the Guinea coast, seized three hundred Negroes and prepared for the Caribbean with his human cargo. They call us human cargo, but I say that is infra dig.[26]

It was a violent and bloody beginning, a brutal and trau-matic beginning. Slavery was the name and capital accumulation the game. And although it is four hundred years hence, the violence of the people's existence persists like a naked light in a house full of dynamite. And the blood has not ceased to gush, but continues to flow over. And the brutality is intensified under a different name. And the orig-inal trauma is the cause of the protracted drama that threatens the rule of a ruthless native bourgeoisie. For the wounds of history have not yet healed, but fester in the hot sun from day unto day so they multiply. So, for the oppressed Jamaican, history is not a fleeting memory of the distant past, but the unbearable weight of the present. That as captives they came and as captives they remain is the veritable tale their history tells. And the people, they still feel the terrible sting of the whip of oppression, of poverty, of fruitless toil, and that is why the singerman sings:

> four hundred years
> we have been here as a slave
> now I an' I
> must find a way
> of not being enslaved
>
> no shackles on our feet
> no whip on our back
> Yet I an' I
> must realize
> we're still being enslaved[27]

Chattel slavery was finally abolished in 1838 in Jamaica, but already with the introduction of the system of apprenticeship in 1833 the slaves could sing: 'we free!/ Lawd we free!'[28] But it did not take the people long to realize that 'the jangling chains', as Jamaican author Andrew Salkey puts it, were 'replaced by different noises'; it did not take the ex-slaves long to realize that 'freedom is as freedom does/ and it did not accomplish much'.[29] So it is no wonder that Winston Rodney – better known by the stage name Burning Spear – should ask 'do you remember/ the days of slavery?' He implores us to try to remember the days of slavery when they 'beat us/ when they use us/ till they refuse us'[30] for it was then . . . it was then that it all began. And ever since then, ever since that terrible day when 'they took us away from civilization' and 'brought us slave on this plantation',[31] they have been asking: 'how long must we wait for repatriation',[32] and the Afro-Jamaican has been praying: 'O father free us from/ the chains of babylon/ and let us live to walk in zion/ for we are pressurized just like the Israelites'.[33] Ever since the days of slavery, my people have been singing this sad, sad song:

> took us away
> in captivity
> and brought us down here
> where we can't be free
> I wanna know how long
> how long
> how long shall evil rage
> evil rage over my people[34]

The image of slavery persists in the mind of the Afro-Jamaican, and the conditions of slavery weigh down his existence. Though it was his sweat, blood and tears that built Jamaica, he shares no part of it. All he knows is 'pure pain and poverty' and all he sees around him is despair and sufferation and hopelessness. So the Rastafarian refuses to accept this barren existence in a 'foreign land'. He has never renounced his African citizenship, for he has never been given a citizenship, and so he sings this song of despair, dreaming of the day when he will 'sail/ on the *Black Star Line*/ homeward bound'.[35]

> I just can't take it no more
> I just can't stand it no more
> So let me go home to Ethiopia land[36]

The Rastafarian's demand of repatriation back to Africa, then, is not unreasonable but legitimate. And it is the historical experience which legitimizes this demand. In fact, it was the same hopelessness and despair which substantiates the Rastafarian's demand that led to mass emigration since the turn of the twentieth century to places like Cuba, Panama, North America and the UK. As one lyricist explains:

> the time is getting hard boy
> we've got to travel on
> the time is getting hard boy
> we've got to leave this land
> a man can't stay where nothing goes right
> and everything goes wrong
> I've got to find somewhere else
> where I can help myself[37]

From the days of slavery unto this day, the history of the Jamaican masses has been a tumultuous one. It has been a history of unrelenting struggle against slavery, colonialism and neo-colonialism. It is a history characterized by slave uprisings and repression; riots and repression; betrayal, rebellion and repression. Between 1664, the year of the first civil administration, and 1838, the year of the abolition of chattel slavery, there were no less than twelve reported slave uprisings. There were also the Maroon Wars of 1729–39 and 1760–95 and 'the Second Maroon War' of 1795. In 1831, two years before the apprenticeship act, 'the signal was given for the launching of the greatest slave rebellion in all of the British Caribbean'.[38] The leaders of this 'Emancipation Rebellion', as Richard Hart calls the pro-emancipation revolts, were a group of black Baptist church leaders: Thomas Burchell, George Taylor, Robert Dove, Robert Gardiner, Sam Sharpe, the main organizer, and others. A major riot was to occur thirty-four years later, nearly three decades after the abolition of chattel slavery, led again by a black Baptist preacher named Paul Bogle, wherein a police station was attacked, a courthouse set on fire and several whites killed. This was the famous Morant Bay Rebellion of 1865, which was brutally put down by the establishment. After 1865 there were at least three reported riots, in the years 1902, 1912 and 1924. Then there was the spontaneous mobilization of the oppressed throughout the Caribbean in 1938, a year of rioting and labour disputes. It was out of the struggle of 1938 that Norman Washington Manley and the People's National Party and Alexander Bustamante and the Jamaican Labour Party emerged. Between 1944 and 1962 Jamaica passed from what political scientist Dr Trevor Munroe calls 'constitutional apprenticeship' to political independence; colonialism stepped out and neo-colonialism stepped in.[39]

The granting of independence in 1962, which marked a turning point in the history of decolonization in Jamaica, instead of bringing the long-awaited change has brought the people from 'hope to hopelessness', lawlessness and despair. The truth is that, as Joseph Ruglass puts it:

> Four hundred years of colonial reign
> Has brought the people misery
> It has left them such pain
> The talk is now of independence you see
> Seems it wasn't meant for you or for me[40]

The discontent of the disinherited Jamaican masses was to burst into revolutionary activity in 1968, only six years after the new dependence, by which time the fact that 'independence' would not bring the long awaited change had been well realized. The famous 'Rodney riots' were sparked off by the banning of Guyanese historian Dr Walter Rodney from his lecturing position at the University of the West Indies by the repressive Hugh Shearer administration in October 1968. At least '50 buses were overturned and burnt. 14 major fires were started in different parts of the city; certain known enemies of the people were spat upon, dragged out of their cars and beaten, shop windows were wrecked'.[41] As Rodney himself has said, the riots had only 'marginal significance' as far as his ban was concerned, but were more fundamentally a 'part of a whole social malaise, that is revolutionary activity'.[42]

This brief sketch then provides the historical perspective which informs the music of Jamaica today. The people have come a long way since their historical journey was begun. It has been a long arduous journey, a long unending journey:

Linton Kwesi Johnson

Photo Credit: Dennis Morris March 1979

Island Records' publicity photo of LKJ from 1979.

journey journey journey
journey journey journey journey
journey journey journey
journey journey journey
journey
journey
journey journey journey journey
long long journey[43]

Yes they have been 'travelling/ for more than 2000 miles' up the old rocky road, through the gates of hell, down the valley of the shadow of death and they can't get no . . . 'can't get no shady tree to res'/ and the sun is red-hot/ hotter than hot – red-hot', their own thought being 'we must, we will, go on'.[44]

In the same way as the musicians have responded to the changes in Jamaican society, incorporating the new pressures and tensions into the music, giving spiritual expression to the historical experience of oppression and rebellion, the singer and dub-lyricist likewise have given lyrical expression to this experience. The lyricism of Jamaican music, which is a part of, as well as being informed by, the wider Jamaican oral tradition, gives poetic or lyrical expression to what the music expresses. It is a lyricism which laments the human suffering, the terrible torments, the toil, a lyricism whose imagery is that of blood and fire, apocalyptic and dread – images that are really pictures of a brutal existence in the 'land of Sodom and Gomorrah'. Songs of hope in suffering, songs of utter despair, songs of praise, songs of defiance, songs that speak of the historical endurance of the black Jamaican, songs that are as prophetic as they are true – such is the nature of the poetry of Jamaican music.

Burning Spear in a song called 'Ethiopians Live It Out' celebrates the endurance of the Afro-Jamaican from the days of slavery unto this day:

> O chinee men come
> they couldnt live it out
> coolie men come
> they couldnt live it out
> syrians come
> they couldnt live it out
> white men come
> they couldnt live it out
> ethiopians live it out
> how we do it
> ethiopians live it out[45]

Not only is this song a song that speaks of historical endurance, it is also a song of strength. For if the black Jamaican has survived slavery and genocide, then surely he shall live to see 'the wicked bow down and flee'.[46] It is a fact that, of all the ethnic groups in Jamaica, it was only the black Jamaican who could physically endure the brutality of the plantation system. When Burning Spear makes a comparison between the strength and endurance of the Chinese, the Indians, the Syrians and the whites on the one hand, and the black Jamaican on the other, there is also the innuendo that the latter group will outlive the former ones – because the Afro-Jamaican majority is at the bottom of the social hierarchy. Bob Marley's 'Soh Jah Seh', which may be described as a 'secular hymn', also expresses this strength and endurance and the determination to continue the historical struggle in the midst of so much desolation and sufferation. It is also a song of faith:

> soh jah seh
> not one of my seed
> shall sit on the street and beg bread[47]

Marley calls on the sufferers to 'I-nite oneself' and stop the fussing and fighting amongst each other. He then reaffirms the implacable will to continue to fight the fight of life, the struggle to survive:

> and down here in the ghetto
> and down here we suffer
> but I an I a hang on in there
> but I an I, I naw leggo[48]

It is man's faith in Jah that gives man the strength to carry on, for Jah is man's shield and buckler, Jah is man's inner strength. Again Gregory Isaacs' 'Sweeter the Victory', another 'secular hymn', laments the plight of the sufferer and tells of his historical yearning for freedom: 'Lord my people wanna be free/ just like the blind would like to see'.[49] This is also a prayer asking for guidance and for faith 'that we will see a better day'.[50] But this song should not be dismissed as religious escapism, for this prayer for faith and guidance

> give us faith to face another day
> guide us in and out along the way
> that we will see a better day[51]

is really an inward search for the inner strength to endure –
'the whip, fantastic fines, Judge Dread and Judge Four Hundred
Years, the rule of eunuchs, fops, thieves and ignoramuses who
break the law themselves, the brutish stupidity of a demoralised
police force making love to their guns'[52] – because deep down
in his heart of hearts, he knows that:

> the hotter the battle
> the sweeter the victory[53]

That the language of the poetry of Jamaican music is Rastafarian
or biblical language cannot simply be put down to the colonizer
and his Satanic missionaries. The fact is that the historical
experience of the black Jamaican is an experience of the most
acute human suffering, desolation and despair in the cruel world
that is the colonial world, which brings about an inner-felt need
for inner peace, an inner strength, for 'spiritual well being'[54]
– in short, the historical experience of the Afro-Jamaican is a
deeply spiritual experience, a religious experience in the widest
sense of the word. The quest for spiritual well-being, this
impelling need to be free of the inner pain, the inner tension,
the oscillation between the psychic states of despair and rebellion does not necessarily oppose the quest for liberation. The
historical phenomenon called Rastafarianism which is saturating
the consciousness of the oppressed Jamaican – which represents

a particular stage in the development of the consciousness of the oppressed – is in fact laying the spiritual and the cultural foundations from which to launch a struggle for liberation. Moreover, as Gordon Rohlehr has stated in his excellent 'Afterthoughts', throughout the history of black Jamaica, 'culture has had a religious basis' and that is why in Jamaica today, 'it is difficult to separate religious music from the music of open rebellion'.[55]

There is a strong note of defiance running through the poetry of Jamaican music, and this defiance as we have seen has its roots in the historical experience. So Bob Marley and the Wailers wail:

> everytime I hear the crack of a whip
> my blood runs cold
> I remember on the slave ships
> how they brutalised our very souls
> today they say we are free
> only to be chained in poverty[56]

Marley tells the oppressor: 'slavedriver/ the table is turned/ catch a fire/ you gonna get burned'.[57] In the 1960s, the era of ska and rock steady music, era of the rudie rebellion, the rudie in court tells Judge Dread that 'rudies dont fear no boy/ rudies dont fear . . . / rougher than rough/ tougher than tough', in fact, dreader than the dreaded Judge Dread.[58] In the 1970s the rudie has been transformed through the cultural dynamism of Rastafarianism into 'natty dread' but the tone of defiance is still present: 'natty dread will never run away'.[59]

In 'Only for a Time', the lyricist tells the oppressor

> no matter what you try to do
> you will never live to rule over me
> what will you do when we rule over you[60]

Similarly, Burning Spear sings this song of defiance with so much dread and defiance in his voice that when we hear it we too are strengthened, we too are defiant:

> is lucky thing I never get
> swell headed
> and started to run run run
> I will never run away
> do you hear![61]

The greater the level of repression, the more defiant and the more resolute the sufferers become and the more violent is their rebellion.

One of the many songs banned during the repressive rule of Hugh Shearer and the Jamaican Labour Party was the much celebrated 'Beat Down Babylon', which immediately caught the imagination of sufferers in Jamaica and the brutalized black youth in Britain, for it was a song which sounded out their defiance and gave fire to their rebellious fervour:

> I an' I goin beat down babylon
> I an' I goin beat down babylon
> I an' I mus whip them wicked men

O what a wicked situation
I an' I starvin for salvation
this might cause a revolution
and a dangerous pollution.[62]

In fact, throughout the last decade or so the lyricist has been telling the sufferer to 'get up and fight for your rights/ my brother/ get up and fight for your rights/ my sister'.[63] Today it is 'judgement' and 'the fulfilment of prophecy', the coming Armageddon, the coming revolution that the people's poets are singing about. They speak of Marcus Garvey's words coming to pass; they say 'swallow-field shall be the battlefield'; they say prophecy a fulfil; 'judgement has come and mercy has gone'; and

. . . di blood goin flood
an di blood goin run
blood uptown and blood downtown
blood roun' town
blood in di woods
and di blood in the country . . . [64]

declares Jah Youth, for Marcus Garvey prophecy fulfil: 'cant get no food to eat/ cant get no money to spend'.[65] We get the feeling from these songs that the oppressed Jamaican has decided that it is only a matter of time before armed struggle shall be launched and that they are prepared for it.

Over the last decade, the main preoccupation of the lyricist has been the burning social, political and economic issues of the day. In commenting on these issues, the lyricist makes a vital contribution towards the oral documentation of the history of Jamaica and to the Jamaican oral tradition. Consciously setting out to transform the consciousness of the sufferer, to politicise him culturally through music, song and poetry, the lyricist contributes to the continuing struggle of the oppressed.

Notes

1 Heptones, The, 'Suffering So', from the LP *Book of Rule* (Harry J Music, 1974).
2 Rohlehr, F. G., 'Afterthoughts', in *BIM* (vol. 14, no. 56, Barbados).
3 Johnson, L. K., 'Bass Culture', in *Dread Beat and Blood* (London: Bogle-L'Ouverture, 1975).
4 Big Youth, 'It Dread in A Babylon' (45 RPM, Augustus Buchanan Label, 1974).
5 Author's taped interview with The Heptones.
6 Johnson, L. K., op. cit.
7 Johnson, L. K., ibid.
8 Johnson, L. K., ibid.
9 Toots and the Maytals, 'Time Tough' (45 RPM, Jaguar J1100, 1974).
10 Ibid.
11 Ibid.
12 Ibid.
13 Fanon, Frantz, *The Wretched of the Earth* (London: Penguin, 1970), p. 44.
14 Ibid., p. 4.
15 Ibid., p. 45.
16 Big Youth, the LP *Screaming Target* (TRIS 61, 1973).
17 Big Youth, 'The Killer', ibid.
18 Rohlehr, F. G., op. cit.
19 Ibid.
20 Marley, Bob and the Wailers, 'Talkin' Blues', from the LP *Natty Dread* (ILPS 9281, Island Music, 1975).

21 I Roy, 'Screw Face', from the LP *Presenting I Roy* (TRLS 63, 1973).

22 Bob Marley, op. cit.

23 Ibid.

24 Ibid.

25 Ford, Laxton, 'Love is a Song' (45 RPM. Wildflower Label, Kingston, Jamaica, 324 A, 1974).

26 Clayton, Sam, 'Narration', from the LP *Grounation* (NTI 301, Ashanti Label, 1973).

27 Name of artist and title of LP not known, 'Jah Love' (P/D LP/ YU, 1975).

28 Salkey, Andrew, *Jamaica, a long historical poem* (London: Hutchinson, 1973), p. 39.

29 Ibid., p. 40.

30 Burning Spear, from the LP *Marcus Garvey* (Fox Records, Jamaica, 1975).

31 Abyssinians, The, 'Declaration of Rights' (45 RPM, Coxsone Records, 7CD 7744 A).

32 Jah Ted, 'Rasta Cry' (45 RPM, Living Music Label, Jamaica, 1974).

33 Name of artist and title of song not known.

34 Name of artist not known, 'How Long'.

35 Royals, The, 'Promise Land' (45 RPM, Jamaica, 1974).

36 Name of artist not known, 'Back to Ethiopia' (45 RPM, 1974).

37 Name of artist not known, 'Time Is Getting Harder' (45 RPM, 6649 A, 1973).

38 Hart, Richard, 'Formation of a Caribbean Working Class', parts 1–3, in *The Black Liberator* 2.2 (1975).

39 Munroe, Dr Trevor, *The Politics of Constitutional Decolonization: Jamaica, 1944–62* (Jamaica: ISER, UWI, 1972).

40 Ruglass, Joseph, '400 Years', from the LP *Grounation*, op. cit.

41 Rodney, Dr Walter, *Groundings with My Brothers* (London: Bogle-L'Ouverture, 1969), p. 66.

42 Ibid.

43 Burning Spear, 'Journey', from the LP *The Burning Spears* (Coxsone Records, Jamaica).

44 Ibid.

45 Burning Spear, 'Ethiopians Live It Out', op. cit.
46 Ethiopians, The, 'Build Back Jericho' (45 RPM, C151 A, Jericho Label, Jamaica).
47 Marley, Bob, and the Wailers, 'Soh Jah Seh', op. cit.
48 Ibid.
49 Isaacs, Gregory, 'Sweeter the Victory' (Sounds of Music Label, 1974).
50 Ibid.
51 Ibid.
52 Anonymous, 'White Fridays in Trinidad', in *Savacou* 3/4 (December 1970–March 1971).
53 Isaacs, Gregory, op. cit.
54 Prescod, Colin, 'The People's Cause in the Caribbean', in *Race & Class* 17.1 (1975).
55 Rohlehr, F. G., op. cit.
56 Wailers, The, 'Slave Driver', from the LP *Catch a Fire* (ILPS 9241A, London, 1973).
57 Ibid.
58 Morgan, Derrick, 'Tougher Than Tough' (45 RPM, Pyramid Label, 1967).
59 Mighty Diamonds, The, 'Right Time' (45 RPM, Lox 4A, London).
60 Royals, The, 'Only Fore a Time' (45 RPM, Coxsone Ital Label, SAN001A).
61 Burning Spear, 'Swell Headed' (45 RPM, CS, 00087, Jamrec Music, 1974, Jamaica).
62 Byles, Junior, 'Beat Down Babylon' (45 RPM, Justice League Label, Jamaica).
63 Abyssinians, The, op. cit.
64 Big Youth, 'Marcus Garvey Dread', from the LP *Dread Locks Dread* (KLP 9001, London, 1975).
65 Burning Spear, 'Marcus Garvey Word' (45 RPM, Fox Label, Jamaica).

Race & Class **XVII 4, 1976**

The Reggae Rebellion (1976)

To say that 'reggae' *is* modern popular Jamaican music is to say nothing; and yet it is to say everything, for this music is the very expression of the historical experience of the Jamaican working class, unemployed and peasants. Modern popular Jamaican music constitutes, lyrically and musically, an *intimation* and *imitation* of both the individual and the collective experience of everyday life. It is *of* and *for* the Jamaican masses. It is rooted in the conditions of Jamaican society.

Reggae songs are songs about rising prices and food short-ages; poverty, hunger and homelessness; unemployment, crime, political violence and 'the gun court'; repression, rebellion and revolution, as this month's British tour by a leading reggae group, Bob Marley and the Wailers, will again confirm. In the song 'Battering Down Sentence', ex-Wailer Bunny Livingston gives expression to the day-to-day experience of the unemployed youth who inhabit the ghettoes and shanty towns of West Kingston – many of whom live by the gun:

> I find myself growing up in an environment
> where finding food is just as hard as paying the rent
> in treading these roads of trial and tribulation

I've seen where some have died of desperation (to
   keep on)
battering down sentence
fighting against conviction.

The lyricism of modern popular Jamaican music is, therefore,
a social lyricism.

The largest of the English-speaking Caribbean islands and
a former British slave colony, Jamaica is now a part of the
American neo-colonialist Caribbean. With an area of just
over 4,200 square miles, Jamaica has an estimated population
of about two million. It also has all of the characteristics of
underdeveloped economies. These characteristics are: a
dualist structure (i.e., a sharp dichotomy between a 'traditional' rural sector and a 'modern' urban sector), a high rate
of internal migration and (up to the end of the last decade)
emigration, a high rate of unemployment (about 30 per cent),
a high rate of crime and violence, a high rate of illiteracy,
grossly inadequate living conditions among the masses, a weak
economic infrastructure, institutionalized corruption, intra-
party violence, and so on. After a long history of working-class
rebellion and militancy, Jamaica achieved political independence for the middle classes in 1962 under the Jamaican Labour
Party (JLP), the party of the local capitalist class and landed
interests – the other main political party being the People's
National Party (PNP), the party of the professional middle
class.

The period 1962 to 1972 was a decade of JLP rule. It was
also during this decade that reggae, along with rock steady, an

earlier form, emerged. This was a decade of growing unemployment, rising prices, food shortages, political corruption,
outbreaks of violence, strikes, shoot-outs and joint police and
military operations against the unemployed and the working
class. It was a decade of massive migration from the depressed
rural areas, based on subsistence farming, to the urban areas
– Kingston and St Andrews for the most part.

These internal migrants, the majority of whom were in their
late teens, unable to find shelter, erected makeshift shacks, using
for building materials just about anything they could lay their
hands on – from sheets of rusted zinc to old barrels. Most of
them were unable to find work; many of them turned to various
forms of crime, including party political gangsterism. The
decade of JLP rule was a decade of disillusionment, desperation,
repression and rebellion. The whole style of rebellion was
captured and depicted in the rudie songs of the sixties. The
young Wailers, then folk heroes of the unemployed youth rebels,
sang:

> Jailhouse keeps empty
> rudies get healthy
> baton sticks get shorter
> rudie gets taller
> them fighting against the yout'
> now that's wrong
> yout' a good good rudie

Mr Foundation replied with a tune called 'All Rudies in Jail',
bringing off a sort of lyrical dialectic:

Jailhouse them plenty
an' rudies getting scanty
baton sticks get taller
an' rudie getting shorter
they're fighting amongst themselves now
that's wrong
there's never been a good rudie.

In February 1972 the JLP was voted out of office by an over-whelming majority and the PNP, under the leadership of Manley the younger (Michael), had their first taste of power in an 'independent' Jamaica. But there are already signs that their rule may be coming to an end. The JLP had succeeded in mortgaging the country bit by bit to international capital. The PNP, immediately on entering office, proceeded to consolidate the interest of the middle classes even more – especially the professional middle class – through state power, under the slogan of 'democratic socialism'. Nonetheless, after four turbulent years, the PNP government now faces an organized armed challenge to its rule from the right wing, allegedly financed by the CIA. The song 'Rat Race', from the current Bob Marley and the Wailers album, *Rasta Vibrations*, is a direct comment on the existing political situation:

Don't involve Rasta in your say
Rasta don't work for no CIA
Rat race, rat race, rat race
When you think it's peace and safety
A sudden destruction
Collective security for surety.

The *sounds* of reggae, as Big Youth, one of Jamaica's most popular reggae artists, puts it succinctly in 'All Nations Bow', are 'sounds of reality'. They are the sounds of screeching tyres, bottles breaking, wailing sirens, gunfire, people screaming and shouting, children crying. They are the sounds of the apocalyptic thunder and earthquake; of chaos and curfews. The sounds of reggae are the sounds of a society in the process of transformation, a society undergoing profound political and historical change. Hence the dynamism of reggae. Moreover, these sounds are the sounds of the city, an unmistakably 'folk-urban' sound.

The characteristic features of the Jamaican experience are *suffering*, and an *endurance* sustained by a *faith* of 'black ivory and steel', as the Burning Spear put it. This experience is expressed in the form of sentiments (political, religious, racial and cultural) which are invariably expressed in a religious symbolism. The symbols are those of the apocalypse; of 'Blood and Fire' (Sir Niney); 'Brimstone and Fire' (Joe Higgs); 'Sodom and Gomorrah' (Yabby-U and the Prophets); 'Babylon Queendom' (Peter Tosh); they are the symbols of the final 'judgement', of 'Babylon Falling' (the Heptones).

What is significant about Bob Marley and the Wailers – and they are not alone in this, as the music of Cedric Brooks and the Light of Saba, Third World and the albums *Negril* and *Torch of Freedom* testify – is that they have tried to produce a kind of sound that transcends its socio-historical conditioning, its social context. Unfortunately, this attempt has been influenced by the demands of the market and has given way to contrivance and a vulgar eclecticism, mingling reggae, rock and soul. So that all of a sudden reggae, or rather the music of Bob Marley and the Wailers and, of late, Toots and the Maytals, became the vogue among rock and pop stars and white middle-class trendies. The tickets for the London stint of this month's Wailers' tour were sold out very early on.

Bob Marley and the Wailers, however, have undoubtedly set the stage for the gradual rise of reggae. They are the ambassadors of reggae. What happens from here on remains to be seen.

New Society, 10 June 1976

The Year of Reggae (1976)

'Can you feel the rhythm/ moving up, moving up?/ This ya reggae music/ moving up, moving up'. Delroy Washington's words from his debut album, *I Sus*, one of the rich output of reggae albums this year, provide us with a most succinct summary of what must surely be the most eventful year in the development of reggae music so far.

For if in 1975 we saw the music 'take off' with Bob Marley and the Wailers being launched into international stardom, then this year we saw the music in full flight; but, as events during the last six months have shown, not without problems.

1976 has seen more promotional tours and major concerts by reggae artists, more newspaper and radio adverts for reggae, more articles devoted to reggae – especially in the rock press – more variety and more controversy surrounding the music than in any other year.

And if we ask the question, why?, the simple answer is that more money has probably been invested in reggae music this year than in any other year. And the fact that it is mainly two 'rock' record companies, Island and Virgin, who are at the forefront of this new level of financial commitment to, and involvement in, reggae music is not as ironic as might first appear; for it is rock companies like these who have the capital and the machinery and the knowledge of the market to promote/ exploit reggae on the level we have witnessed this year.

The rise of investment in the music has generated a heightened level of activity within the reggae industry, affecting not only the market situation but also the types of response to and innovations within the music.

'Rockers' rhythms rose to momentous heights this year and Jo Jo Hoo Kim of the Channel One Studio must be one of the most prolific and successful producers of the year. The Channel One band The Revolutionaries, whose main spark has been drummer man Sly Dunbar, the hottest drummer in Jamaica right now, have produced hit after hit, including the unforgettable 'MPLA'. Hoo Kim's list of success includes The Mighty Diamonds' *Right Time*, Dillinger's *CB 200* album and scores of singles including Earth and Fire's 'Time to Come'.

It has also been another creative and fruitful year for the energetic producer Lee Perry, the Upsetter, a leading exponent of another style of 'rockers', with achievements like Junior Murvin's ever-popular 'Police and Thieves', Max Romeo's single and album *War in A Babylon*, and what is undoubtedly the greatest achievement in dub music yet, Perry's own super *Super Ape*. The only other memorable dub album of 1976 is *Raas Claat Dub*, a spill-over of 1975 rhythms into 1976.

'Dis yah music yah/ a strickly roots music yaah/ strickly rockers music wi a deal wid/ all over di world yu see it'. So says Johnny Clarke from the title track of his most stylistically accomplished album yet, *Rockers Time Now*, a part of the 'Virgin Rockers' output.

Virgin Records, who have certainly benefitted from Island's experience, made history this year by showing us how a rock company becomes a rock and reggae company almost overnight, with almost a dozen albums in something like eight months, including The Mighty Diamonds' *Right Time* and The Gladiators' *Trenchtown Mix-up*, the cream of their crop.

Virgin have spent a lot of money on promotion and spent it wisely with their cheap promotional album, *The Front Line*, making the Top 20 album charts, and moderately successful promotional tours by U-Roy and the Diamonds. By the end of the summer, Virgin Rockers were selling as well as, and in some cases even better than, Virgin's rock.

With the Virgin promotional machinery behind him and rockers' rhythms to jive-talk on, U-Roy, the veteran deejay dub-lyricist, has achieved a level of popular response in Britain this year with 'Dread in A Babylon' and 'Natty Rebel' which no other deejay dub-lyricist has matched.

Dillinger, during the year, also added considerably to his reputation as one of the foremost exponents of dub-lyricism, with tunes like 'Freshly' and his *CB 200* album, and Jah Woosh and Tapper Zukie had modest successes, while Big Youth's two albums, *Natty Carnival Dread* and *Hit the Road Jack*, show Jah Youth's versatility, his decline as a dub-lyricist and his rise as a singer.

On another level, we have had this year three very important 'underground' reggae albums of another style, namely rasta reggae, Jamaican music at its most basic and fundamental roots level. And if the level of popular response to these three albums in the black communities of this country is anything to go by, then Pablo Moses' *Revolutionary Dream*, Fred Locks' *Black Star Liners* and The Abyssinians' *Satta Massagana* must rank among the most important reggae albums of 1976.

Fred Locks' *Black Star Liners*, perhaps the most fundamental of the three, with its rich array of rhythms, its potent and penetrating social criticisms, is a beautiful reflection of the social reality of Jamaica, a real achievement in the artistic representation of popular consciousness.

What is especially interesting about this album, which is also shared by the other two, is an apparent tension between realism and mysticism. The realist and mystical elements in *Black Star Liners* combine to produce a unity reflecting both the social conditions in which reggae is rooted as well as the type of popular consciousness which corresponds to these conditions.

Revolutionary Dream is as interesting, from the point of view of its combination of styles, as well as the tensions it presents in Pablo Moses' version of popular Rastafarian views, beliefs and sentiments; tensions between the social and political reality of Jamaica and the utopian quest, which is a genuine desire to be free.

Like *Revolutionary Dream*, The Abyssinians' *Satta Massagana* was produced by Geoffrey Chung and shares some of the same stylistic combinations. The Abyssinians, with their cool, enchanting harmonies, majestic melodies, regal style and divine inspiration, present us with a truly moving expression of the historical experience of the Jamaican masses. And though their themes are varied – repatriation, unity and love, greatness of God, fighting for your rights – they combine to form a unitary conception of history, albeit in the form of myth.

Within the genre of rasta reggae must be included the outstanding singles of 1976: Junior Ross & The Spears' 'Babylon Fall' which, with its invigorating beat and trenchant rhythms and popular sentiments, is one of the most popular dancing tunes of the year; while Ras Allah's 'Bosrah' was impressive in its contrasting realist and biblical imagery, its slow and sombre beat and its regal horn.

For British reggae, 1976 represents a new stage in its continued evolution and development, with albums from two relative newcomers, Delroy Washington and the group Aswad, an album from the Cimarons and the most popular British reggae single of the year, Matumbi's 'After Tonight'.

Aswad's album of the same title, though a significant step in British reggae, is still largely imitating the Wailers' roots-rock sound. Likewise, Delroy Washington's *I Sus* has much in common with the international style of Marley's music. The influence of Bob Marley and the Wailers is most striking in the main nucleus of the backing group and in Delroy in particular. *I Sus* has a kind of impersonal quality about it which hints at the alienated experience of Britain's black youth.

While the achievements and successes of rockers, rasta reggae and British reggae cannot in any way be underestimated, 1976 has undoubtedly been the year of international reggae and its various hybrids of pop, rock, soul, funk and blues. These achievements are of considerable importance, for it is within this style of reggae that the innovations are coming – innovations which are largely influenced and determined by the exigencies of capital – it is here that the trends are being set; it's here that reggae is really big business.

To begin with, Island and Virgin Records have between them brought out three important and highly individual albums by the three original Wailers, Bob, Peter and Bunny, and although each album has the unmistakable imprint of their respective authors, they all have that inimitable Wailers' sound.

That Bob Marley's *Positive Vibrations* did not achieve the level of positive response anticipated is not without significance. It seems that the marked leaning towards Jamaican roots did not have the elements in it to please many who had been expecting yet another landmark in the fusion of roots and rock. At any rate, what has become apparent is the fact that Island have not been able to maintain the momentum generated around *Natty Dread*.

With the weeks of wheeling and dealing which preceded Peter Tosh's *Legalise It*, the eventual appearance of the album was something of an anti-climax. *Legalise It* is by far the least impressive of the three Wailers' albums; it is over-produced, over-mixed and over-commercialized, not coming up to anything near what an artist of Tosh's obvious talent and experience is capable of achieving.

Bunny Wailer's *Blackheart Man* was, perhaps, all that Tosh's album could have been. It is a cleverly conceived and well-presented album which shows us exactly what Bunny is capable of doing as singer, composer, arranger, producer and musician, given the right resources and promotion, with a density of imagery in his songs, matched by a corresponding density of rhythms and a rich array of melodies all combining to produce an effect of enchantment.

The Heptones, as their album *Night Food* shows, have been

sweetened with added elements of rock and pop, but not softened. Third World have now made a name for themselves with their American tour and their first album, *Third World*. They are an uptown reggae band who have produced a worthwhile album with an international flavour and a real variety of styles.

If Toots sounds so much like the immortal Otis Redding in showing us that *Reggae's Got Soul*, it is because they both share a common tradition of black church music. Likewise, Ras Michael & The Sons of Negus, on their album *Rastafari*, working within the same sacred tradition, combine the ritualistic nyah drums with electric reggae and blues rhythms, Rasta rhetoric, Rasta style and church-like songs. Their album represents a real innovation with religious music being given the full secular treatment.

It is somewhat ironic that the most outstanding international reggae album of the year, both in terms of its artistic qualities and its entertainment value, did not enjoy the level of popular response it deserved. Perhaps the fact that the music on Joe Higgs' *Life of Contradiction* sounds a little dated and the fact that Vulcan Records hardly spent any money on promotion are, in part, an explanation.

Life of Contradiction has commercial appeal but, unlike *Legalise It*, *Reggae's Got Soul*, *Night Food* or *Third World*, not ostensibly so. It has resonances of international popular music and is firmly grounded in the blues tradition.

Higgs' combination of personal and public statement, working at times within the pop idiom, at times within his own personal and poetic language; his mastery of the art of singing (for he doesn't have a great voice); and the coming together of the Afro-American and Jamaican blues traditions in his music makes *Life of Contradiction* a major classic of international reggae.

On another level, the most significant events for reggae music during 1976 were the four major reggae concerts of the year – Toots and the Maytals; Ras Michael & The Sons of Negus/ Cimarons; Bob Marley and the Wailers; and U-Roy/Mighty Diamonds/Delroy Washington – integral parts in the process of internationalizing reggae. But will 1977 at last see reggae accepted on its own terms?

Melody Maker, 25 December 1976

Marley at the Polls (1977)

Bob Marley and the Wailers' recent single, 'Smile Jamaica', is probably the most puzzling song that the master of enigma has ever done.

Seen in the context of the recent elections in Jamaica, and Bob's association with the People's National Party (PNP) campaign – which almost led to his death – 'Smile Jamaica' is almost the closest that Bob has come to outright propaganda.

To make the appeal and response as wide as possible, there are two stylistically distinct versions. Side One is typical Wailers: soulful, with a hard punchy beat that is slow and deliberate, using horns but without the cutting guitar rhythms so characteristic of reggae. But Side Two is rockers all the way, with a faster tempo, a hard, stomping beat, chopping guitar rhythms, wah-wah, but without the horns.

In this plea for national unity, Bob implores the listener to smile because he's in Jamaica; be of good cheer, he says, because everything is merry and bright.

But the song leaves us with a number of unanswered questions: who is the 'we' referred to in the line 'We're gonna help our people'? Certainly it is not Bob Marley and the Wailers, and certainly it is not the now defeated Jamaican Labour Party (JLP). That leaves us with the PNP.

Could 'Smile Jamaica' be a concealed call to vote PNP? By identifying with Michael Manley and his party in its stand against the right-wing and reactionary JLP, Marley has unwittingly put in question all that he stood for, especially when he sings lines like 'Rhythm-wise/ Dub-wise/ And otherwise/ Can't criticise/ Oh smile/ In Jamaica'.

Is this the rebel from Trenchtown who said to the Jamaican establishment with so much defiance, 'It takes this revolution to cause a solution' and 'Them belly full but we hungry'?

Is this the same universal rebel who is now saying 'Can't criticise/ Oh smile/ In Jamaica'? What about the African Dream and the African redemption? Has the Rasta rebel now become a 'responsible citizen'?

—

Prince Jazzbo's *Natty Passing Thru* (Black Wax WXLPO) and Dillinger's *Bionic Dread* (Black Swan ILPS 9455) – new albums by two of Jamaica's most popular deejays or 'toasters' – are excellent examples of that popular form of roots reggae deejays' dub-lyricism.

As a distinctive, lyrical genre of reggae music, dub-lyricism has a history that goes back over a decade to the fast rhythmic chants and grunts popularized by Prince Buster and others during the era of ska, and the early talking tunes like Buster's classic 'Ten Commandments'.

Dub-lyricism has passed through various stages of evolution, along with Jamaican music as a whole, to emerge as the most authentic and popular form of Jamaican oral poetry.

Rooted in the Jamaican sound system culture and the popular

language of the people, dub-lyricism reflects both modern and traditional elements, being an integral aspect of the modern Jamaican urban culture as well as an important part of a wider Jamaican oral tradition.

Rhythm and rhyme, a rough bass line and a keen sense of timing, popular street talk, rasta talk, righteous say, these are the ingredients of the art of the deejay/dub-lyricist.

A word/musicmaker, the dub-lyricist is poet and preacher, prophet and teacher; he is a propagandist, a culturalist, a social lyricist; and, moreover, an entertainer: a sweet soul-talker, a real jive-talker, a steady rhythm-rider.

Jazzbo's album is as unmistakeable a Lee Perry product as Dillinger's is a Hoo Kim one. Musically, these two albums represent two stylistic variations of rockers' rhythms.

In Perry's session band the bass guitar takes the lead and the emphasis is on the beat. In Hoo Kim's Channel One studio band, its emphasis here is on the rhythm, with the drum taking the lead. Thus *Natty Passing Thru* is the heavier of the two albums but lyrically the weaker.

Although we probably hear Prince Jazzbo at his best on this album, at times his voice is mixed into the music, becomes part of it, adding colour and embellishment instead of the music providing the background for his lyricism.

This is particularly evident in varying degrees on 'Story Come to Bump', 'Natty Passin Thru Rome', 'Bloody Dunza', 'Life is Gonna Easy' and 'Ital Corner'.

And, yet, these cuts, together with 'Prophet Live' and 'Dreadlocks Corner', are the most powerful numbers on the album, enhanced by the libidinous and dread pulsations of Boris

Gardiner's bass guitar and Lee Perry the Upsetter's acute sense of rhythm and engineering skill.

Like the Upsetter's *Super Ape*, *Natty Passing Thru* is yet another remarkable achievement. It captures, through its beat, rhythm, deejay lyricism and sound effects, the vital pulse and energy of the Jamaican sound system culture.

In terms of lyricism, Jazzbo never really has a great deal to say, but what he has to say is well said, or rather, intoned.

Dramatic effect and style seem to play a greater part in his lyricism than consistency of meaning and making sense.

He lacks the lyrical agility of U-Roy, reggae's fastest-talking deejay, or the flow of Dillinger, but chants as well as Big Youth or anyone else.

On most of the numbers on *Natty Passing Thru*, the emphasis seems to be more on deejaying than on lyricism. The role of the sound system deejay is to act as a musical pace-setter (and sometimes peace-keeper), spurring and urging his audience of dancers on, lending an added impetus to the music with his rhythmic statements and melodic phrases.

Thus, 'Weepin' and Wailin'', 'Live Good Today', 'Life is Gonna Easy', 'Hold My Hand' and 'Story Come To Bump' are musical exhortations which find Jazzbo at his most fluent.

We also get a taste of the characteristic Jazzbo humour in 'Weepin' and Wailin'', where he says 'It shall be weepin' and wailin' an' gnashing of teeth/ An' who doan have noh teeth the gum shall feel it . . .'.

The title track is one of the heaviest on the album, with its awesome and threatening beat, regal horns and sharp, chucky-style guitar rhythms.

Prince Jazzbo's popularity lies in his ability to make you skank to the rhythm and rock to the beat, with his slow speech, his distinctive style of intonation, his Black Power stance and his rhetorical statements, which are at times rich in symbolism. *Natty Passing Thru* will no doubt add to his popularity.

—

Dillinger, on the other hand, has emerged as the real inheritor of Big Youth's former title as the foremost exponent of the art of dub-lyricism. Though he's influenced by Big Youth and U-Roy, 'the originator', Dillinger has brought a fresh dimension and a highly individual approach to the art of dub-lyricism.

He is completely at ease with the hard stomping beat and drum-dominated rockers' rhythms, and achieves a remarkable consistency of meaning and fluency in his lyricism – remarkable, for the deejay's art is improvisatory.

Bionic Dread does not always come up to the standards of the excellent *CB 200*, Dillinger's first album, but is nevertheless extremely entertaining.

Dillinger's musical poetry celebrates the lifestyles of the unemployed and sections of the working class in Kingston and, in particular, the natty rebel.

Thus the title track, 'Bionic Dread', together with 'King of the Road', 'Invisible Dread' and 'Natty B.Sc.', are poems praising the strength and brain power of natty dread.

Bionic Dread, then, is another fine album from one of the giants of dub-lyricism.

Melody Maker, 5 February 1977

Bob Marley and the Reggae International (1977)

REVIEW: *Exodus* (ISLP 9498, Island)

It is now four years since Bob Marley – the only reggae artist with superstar status – entered the stage of international popular music along with the Wailers. *Catch a Fire*, the album with which they made their historic entry, with its far-reaching innovations at the levels of production, marketing and, most important of all, in the music itself, heralded nothing less than a revolution in Jamaican music. It is not at all surprising, therefore, that for the average non-West Indian listener, the word 'reggae' is conterminous with Bob Marley and the Wailers. With their obvious talent and creativity, the group has managed to create a sound that transcends the local, national limitations of popular Jamaican music, taking it into the mainstream of the popular music of Europe and North America. Given the particularity of reggae and its rootedness in Jamaican history, society and culture, this is quite a remarkable achievement.

Such a giant step has not been taken without concessions and compromises, contradictions and ambiguities. But these do not detract from the importance of the enormous success of Bob Marley and the Wailers in breaking down the rock barrier and penetrating the international rock music market. This success has in fact generated a whole new style of reggae music,

Race Today

VOICE OF THE BLACK COMMUNITY IN BRITAIN   JUNE/JULY 1977   25p

GRUNWICK GATES
THE ENTRY TO UNIONISATION

CARIBBEAN POLITICAL PRISONERS

The cover of *Race Today*, June/July 1977.

which I call *international reggae*, as it reflects a process of internationalization.

The recent European tour of the group, which culminated at the Rainbow Theatre on Saturday 4 June, where thousands of enthralled fans, black and white alike, were taken once again through the 'Trenchtown experience', and their new album, *Exodus*, shows quite powerfully that Bob Marley and the Wailers are still the leading exponents of *international reggae*. Marley himself has become *the ambassador of reggae*, a role which he has played with confidence and competence and, as his biography and career show quite clearly, a role for which he was well rehearsed. He has been exposed to and influenced by the diverse musical forms indigenous to his native Jamaica as well as other musical forms of internationally popular music, in particular black American (rhythm and blues, soul and funk). Moreover, his travels through Europe and the USA have brought him into further contact with the metropolitan sounds of modern popular music culture.

Since the revolution of *Catch a Fire*, the next five albums, including *Exodus*, have been successive steps in consolidating the revolution. The music on *Exodus* is characteristic Wailers' sound. It is a taut, terse sound wherein Jamaican roots are creatively combined with elements from the metropolitan sounds of Europe and North America. With the exception of the title track, which is a fusion of rockers' beat and funky rhythms, there are no new innovations in the music but, as is the case with *Equal Rights*, another international reggae album by ex-Wailer Peter Tosh, there are new combinations of old ones. And, as was the case with *Rastaman Vibration*, Bob Marley

and the Wailers' last album, there is a strengthening, a solidi-
fication and accentuation of the input of Jamaican roots in the
rhythm section, the nucleus of the music. Aston Barrett's bass
is as bouncy as ever and a little more jazzy and accentuated.
Carlton Barrett has developed and updated his highly individual
style of drumming, incorporating elements from the military
style into his rockers' repertoire. Tyrone Downie has, since
joining the group, added gyrating, sweetening, soaring touches
to the music. The new sensational lead guitarist, Julian Marvin,
adds a new toughness to the hard rock element in the Wailers'
music as the song 'The Heathen' exemplifies. The use of brass,
which was first heard on *Natty Dread*, the rock critics' favourite
Wailers album, is here continued on three songs. The backing
vocals of the I-Threes, who have never been real substitutes
for Peter Tosh and Bunny Wailer, blend well with Marley's
vocal. On the whole, the new combinations of beat, rhythm
and melody on *Exodus* achieve a comfortable balance between
roots, rock and hints of funk.

Thematically, *Exodus* was born out of the drama which
preceded Bob Marley's 'Smile Jamaica' concert in support of
Michael Manley's PNP during the last Jamaican general election. 'Smile Jamaica', Marley's current hit single at the time,
was a call for national unity, imploring the gun-shocked
Jamaican populace, referred to in the song as 'soulful people',
to 'smile' as they are in Jamaica, a 'soulful town' with people
having fun. This was during the period of heavy manners! In
spite of the heavy manners, an assassination attempt was made
on Marley's life which he only narrowly escaped. Hence the
first song, 'Natural Mystic', on the first side of the album.

Marley here interprets his violent experience in terms of some preordained, natural mystical order of events. As a professed Rastafarian he no doubt sees the 'miracle' of his escape from the jaws of death as the work of a divine mystical force, namely Rastafari. Furthermore, there was a quote on the sleeve of the last album to Joseph, whom 'the archers have sorely grieved . . . and shot at him and hated him'. Marley is Joseph, according to Twelve Tribe principles.*

There were a lot of conflicting rumours as to who was responsible for the assassination attempt and the reasons behind it. One rumour was that it was the work of the JLP opposition party fearing the impact of the 'Smile Jamaica' concert on the outcome of the election results. Another rumour was that it was the work of the PNP trying to win support and sympathy by discrediting the opposition. A third rumour was that it was linked to Marley's alleged involvement in the ganja trade. There were other rumours. Hence the songs 'So Much Things to Say', 'Guiltiness' and 'The Heathen'. The first of these three songs, 'So Much Things to Say', is a verbal castigation of those rumour-mongers. Here he declares that Rasta does not come to fight flesh and blood, 'but spiritual wickedness in high and low places'. 'Guiltiness' is similarly a verbal castigation of those responsible for the assassination attempt and Marley cries woe to them. 'The Heathen', with its awesome beat, soaring rock guitar, stabbing piano rhythms and prophetic and defiant stance, is as much an expression of retributive justice as it is an

* Rastas who subscribe to the Twelve Tribes of Israel's version of Rastafari take on biblical names according to the month in which they were born.

soaring rock guitar, stabbing piano rhythms, prophetic and defiant stance, is as much an expression of retributive justice as it is an expression of sheer jubilation at his escape. Here Marley is Shadrack, Mescheck and Abednigo, who were cast into the fiery furnace but did not get burn. He is the unscathed Daniel who was cast into the lion's den; he is him who 'fights and run away', living to 'fight another day'. Having drawn comparisons between his own fate and that of Marcus Garvey and Jesus Christ in 'So Much Things To Say', in the song 'Exodus' he describes himself as 'another brother Moses from across the sea'. So that it becomes apparent that whilst 'Exodus' may be 'the movement Jamaica', then the assassination attempt has, as it were, shocked him back to his previous perception. 'Smile Jamaica' was quite clearly propagandist. Now Marley is 'leaving babylon', going to his father's land.

The songs on Side Two of the album are somewhat different from the private/public themes which dominate Side One. Here the emphasis is more on the entertainment aspect of the music. 'Jamming', like 'Lively Up Yourself,' 'Roots Rock Reggae', etc., is an open invitation to the listener to participate in the music of Bob Marley and the Wailers who are a 'living sacrifice' and who are 'jamming right straight from yard'. It is a jazzy sing-a-long song with a hint of rag-

Image from LKJ's *Race Today* article
'Bob Marley and the Reggae International'.

expression of sheer jubilation at his escape. Here Marley is Shadrack, Meshach and Abednego, who were cast into the fiery furnace but did not get burnt. He is the unscathed Daniel who was cast into the lions' den; he is him who 'fights and run away', living to 'fight another day'. Marley draws comparisons between his own fate and that of Marcus Garvey and Jesus Christ in 'So Much Things to Say'.

The song 'Smile Jamaica', as I pointed out in a *Melody Maker* article of 5 February, contradicted the previous anti-establishment stance of songs like 'Them Belly Full', 'Revolution', 'Burnin and Lootin' and many others. Once again, what was expressed in that song now contradicts what is being said in *Exodus*. For if Jamaica is such a 'soulful town' with such 'soulful people' all 'having fun', why the 'Exodus', the movement of Jah people, of whom Bob Marley is one? It would seem that if Marley's perception of Jamaica as 'babylon' had been blurred in 'Smile Jamaica', then the assassination attempt has, as it were, shocked him back to his previous position. 'Smile Jamaica' was quite clearly propagandist. Now Marley is 'leaving babylon', going to his father's land.

The songs on Side Two of the album are somewhat different from the private/public themes which dominate Side One. Here the emphasis is more on the entertainment aspect of the music. 'Jamming', like 'Lively Up Yourself', 'Roots Rock Reggae' etc., is an open invitation to the listener to participate in the music of Bob Marley and the Wailers, who are a 'living sacrifice' and who are 'jamming right straight from yard'. This is followed by two very different love songs: 'Waiting in Vain' and 'Turn Your Lights Down Low'. The former song is an invigorating rockers' hopper with a jazzy, bouncy bass line, a gyrating organ grind that pumps the rhythm along and some very pretty guitar picking. The latter song, 'Turn Your Lights Down Low', is pure soul; it is a soulful ballad in the same vein as 'Johnny Was', but different in theme. 'Three Little Birds', with its rhythm and blues and ska resonances, is a song of reassurance. The message here is not to worry, 'cause everything's gonna be alright'. The bass line here echoes strongly of the Skatalites' 'Beardman Ska' and, like 'Waiting in Vain', has a dated sound that is nonetheless refreshing to the ear. The final song on the album, 'One Love', is an updated version of an old Wailing Wailers' song from the ska era of the 1960s which, as the title suggests, is a lyrical expression of the Rastafarian motto calling for unity, love and oneness amongst the oppressed black Jamaicans. The new version of the song is a little slower in tempo, but equally entertaining.

Since his entry on the international stage Bob Marley has made six highly individual albums whilst maintaining a certain degree of continuity in his art. Together with the Wailers, he has had a great impact and has also made an invaluable contribution to popular music internationally, and to the reggae international. What direction the music of Bob Marley and the Wailers will take in the future remains to be seen. One thing is certain: that *Exodus* is a fine album. People all over the world are 'jamming' to the music of Bob Marley and the Wailers and, like them, we too 'hope the jamming last'.

Race Today, June/July 1977

'Blackbeard' in Profile:
Laying the Foundations (1981–2)

Reggae music in Britain has come a long way since the mid-sixties. Then, a handful of first-generation musicians made tentative attempts to copy the Jamaican sound, itself at a nascent stage of its development. The music has now moved to a more self-assertive stage of 'lovers rock' which has a large young black following. It is a distinctly British genre of the Jamaican form.

Lovers rock, dominated by female singers, is romantic reggae. Invariably, it combines the main conventions of laid-back and up-tempo rhythms with soft vocals and heart-throb lyrics, to produce a form of British pop reggae.

The process through which we arrived at the stage of lovers rock constitutes the relatively short history of struggle to establish a viable reggae tradition in Britain.

A major contribution to the development of the tradition came from Dennis 'Blackbeard' Bovell, a twenty-eight-year-old Barbadian-born musician, composer, arranger, vocalist, recording engineer and producer.

The first thing one notices about Bovell's contribution is its range. No other reggae artist has had such a wide range of involvement in almost every area of the creation and production of reggae in Britain.

Matumbi

Firstly, he is a founder member of Matumbi which, for nearly a decade, was regarded as one of Britain's top reggae bands. Bovell's considerable range of talents and knowledge of other musical forms were brought to bear on the group's development and impact on the reggae tradition. Matumbi was one of the first British-based reggae bands to capture the Jamaican roots sound. They combined this with a black American style of vocal harmonies and a mixture of love and protest lyrics which produced an overall sound imbued with a British feel.

The fact that they were one of the few reggae bands around to play 'yard style' music made Matumbi one of the only bands able to back visiting solo performers like Ken Boothe, Johnny Clarke, Pat Kelly, I Roy and others. Bovell co-wrote the music for, played on and produced the band's first hit single, 'After Tonight'. This song, and their other early hit single, 'The Man In Me', a reggae rendition of the Bob Dylan original, were the prototypes of what was later to become lovers rock. Matumbi's success gave other emerging reggae bands the confidence to create out of a British feel, while having regard for the traditional requirements of form. The band went on to win a recording contract with EMI Records. In 1980, they achieved a chart success with their Glenn Miller style arrangement of an original song, 'Point of View', illustrating the versatility of reggae and its ability to incorporate other styles.

LKJ and Dennis 'Blackbeard' Bovell on tour in Berlin, January 1990. Its photographer, John Kpiaye, was the guitarist in the Dennis Bovell Dub Band and, with Dennis Bovell, was one of the major producers/ developers of lovers rock.

The Producer

Dennis Bovell has made his most important contributions as recording engineer, arranger and producer. He was the first recording engineer in Britain to capture the real Jamaican sound on tape. This has made him the most sought-after engineer in reggae circles. Bovell's engineering skill, in my view, was the single most important factor in the transformation of British reggae. Working from Berry Street, DIP and Gooseberry studios, Bovell recorded the leading reggae artists here in Britain. He was responsible for recording the main body of home-grown reggae. He recorded for most of the small independent reggae 'producers' – like Lloyd Coxsone, Clem Bushay, Dennis Harris, Castro Brown, Patrick Cann and others.

In many cases, the producers and artists who worked with Bovell knew little about the recording process. This meant that he often had to double up as arranger/producer. He is largely responsible for the production work on the earlier lovers rock music from artists like Brown Sugar, Fifteen, Sixteen and Seventeen, Louisa Mark, Janet Kay, Marie Pierre and many more. In fact, his production of Louisa Mark's 'Caught You in a Lie' established the lovers rock style. And he recorded and arranged the first lovers rock tune to make the British top ten, Janet Kay's 'Silly Games', a classic of the genre.

Outside the lovers rock groove, Bovell produced for Jimmy Lindsay, Rico Rodriguez, Errol Dunkley, I Roy, myself and others. It was Bovell who at a talent competition in Birmingham in 1974 discovered the band Steel Pulse. They went on to become one of Britain's top reggae bands. He was a judge in the competition and the first prize was a recording session with him. He recorded the band's earlier material, including the celebrated 'Handsworth Revolution', later released on their debut album for Island Records. He has a recording studio, Studio 80, in south London.

Engineering Skills

In the creation and production of reggae music in Jamaica, the recording engineer occupies a status similar to that of the musician, singer and dub-lyricist. This is largely due to the emergence of 'dub' or drum and bass music. Here, the recording engineer, through skilful manipulation of the controls, the use of echo, reverb, phasing and other sound effects in the mixing of the rhythm tracks, is able to lend the music an added rhythmic and illusory effect, making it particularly suited to dancing. Bovell has been able to bring dub music into the mainstream of the British reggae tradition, not only with his dub mixes for the version side of singles and twelve-inch forty-fives, but also through celebrated dub albums like *Leggo! A-Fe-Wi-Dis*, *Ah Who Seh? Goh De!*, *Scientific*, *Higher Ranking Dubb* and others.

Disc Jockey in Prison

Bovell's dub-making skills are linked to another chapter in his varied career – his involvement as a sound system disc jockey. He was able to make his own exclusive versions of popular rhythms on the sound system circuit. This added advantage helped to establish Sufferer's Hi Fi as one of the top sound systems around during the early seventies. They played at the Metro youth club in Notting Hill and, later, other popular venues like the Carib Club in Cricklewood. During a session at the Carib Club in 1974, the police stormed the club on the pretext that they were looking for someone. They were driven out by the revellers who later barricaded themselves inside. The police returned with reinforcements and attacked the revellers. Many were arrested that night and charged with various offences. The following day, on hearing that the police were looking for Sufferer's deejay, Bovell presented himself at Golders Green police station. He was arrested and charged with incitement to riot and affray. Nine of the twelve defendants were acquitted. Bovell was one of three defendants on whom the jury could not agree. A retrial was ordered. He was found guilty and sentenced to three years' imprisonment. He served six months in Wormwood Scrubs and was later freed after a successful appeal against conviction.

Dennis Bovell's involvement in music extends beyond the reggae tradition. He has created and produced all kinds of popular music, from punk rock to funk, working with groups like The Pop Group, The Slits, Angelic Upstarts, Garland Jeffreys, Viola Wills, the Thompson Twins and others. Recently, he composed, recorded and produced most of the music in Franco Rosso's movie *Babylon*.

From the Roots

He was born in May 1953 in Rose Hill, St Peter, Barbados. His parents joined the army of Caribbean labour which came to Britain in the fifties and early sixties; his father went to work for London Transport as a bus driver and his mother joined the nursing profession. The young Bovell was left in the care of his maternal grandparents. His grandparents were devout Seventh Day Adventists and Bovell was subjected to a sheltered life with them. Though bright enough to win a free place in the local government school, he was not particularly interested in the learning process. He was more inclined towards cricket, going to the beach and music. His inclination towards music was a family characteristic. Bovell explains: 'My father is a musician; he plays the piano and was a student at the Royal College of Music. He met my mother when my grandfather was teaching him music. He went and liked off the man daughter. My grandfather is a great musician and an elder in the church. My mother and my sisters all read music. I don't. I prefer to feel it and play it. My uncles had a vocal quartet from the church called the Walker Brothers, and they'd be on the radio on Saturday nights and sometimes on Sundays. Another of my uncles had a band called Barbara and the Originates. He introduced guitar music into the church, a very controversial thing at the time in a Seventh Day Adventist church . . .'

Bovell's first exposure to music came from the church and his immediate family circle. The only exposure to secular music was provided by a neighbour's radiogram: 'In our area, we had a man on our corner named Lutha who had a very powerful radiogram. He would supply the whole neighbourhood with sounds from Friday night right back to Sunday morning, with tunes by the Mighty Sparrow and other calypsonians, the Drifters, Ray Charles and more.' Bovell was nine years old when his fifteen-year-old uncle taught him to play the guitar. He had discovered the young Bovell messing around with his guitar. He taught him to play 'When The Saints Go Marching In', and so Bovell's involvement with music began.

Battersea in '65

By the time he arrived in Britain in 1965 to join his parents in Battersea, south London, Bovell had obtained a rudimentary knowledge of the guitar. His arrival in Britain marked an important turning point in his musical development. He now found himself, for the first time in his life, in a completely secular environment. His father held fortnightly blues at their Battersea home, and also possessed a vast collection of records which varied from 'organ recital music to African music to pop and American music'. Bovell persuaded his mother to buy him a guitar, and he set about the business of developing his musical talents. The prevailing social atmosphere was marked by a striking creativity in popular music internationally.

Like most second-generation blacks joining the British school system at secondary school age, Bovell was placed in the lowest of the four streams at Spencer Park school. After a year, he was promoted to the B stream and came into contact with white pupils. He joined his first group, a school band of whites called Roadworks Ahead, playing English pop. He soon joined another band consisting of black sixth-formers playing soul music. Bovell recalls: 'The first gig I did with them, they put me to stand on the piano. I was the smallest fellow there and I was playing bass. So, at the age of thirteen, I was in two bands at the same time. On the one hand I was playing pop music with thirteen-year-old white fellows and I was playing soul with these older black guys.' This duality of involvement, with both black and white musicians, has been a constant feature of Bovell's career. He went on to play in a number of bands, playing a variety of mainly black American music, deepening his knowledge of music and developing his musicianship.

Bovell's interest in reggae came later. He was fifteen when his friend's younger brother, who was well steeped in the music, succeeded in initiating him. Bovell recalls: 'He was younger than us and he used to go places like the Roaring Twenties, Ram Jam, Flamingo and all the clubs. He was telling us to get with it, but we were more into American music.'

Bovell became a reggae fan and started hanging out with a sound system called Rocket 69. At the same time, he discovered a recording studio at school. He took over the studio and began his apprenticeship as a recording engineer: 'I used to tape records and cut out the instrumental section and remake the whole tune. That's where I began to learn about engineering. I did it first with "Young Gifted and Black" in an instrumental version, and got some teachers to play trombones on it. Jim Daddy sound system was playing at a blues dance one night in Balham, and I went and sold him my version for £3, a lot of found guilty and sentenced to three years imprisonment. He served six months in Wormwood Scrubs and was later freed after a successful appeal against conviction.

Dennis Bovell's involvement in music extends beyond the reggae tradition.

Town on the south coast of Barbados. His parents joined the army of Caribbean labour which came to Britain in the fifties and early sixties; his father went to work for London Transport as a bus driver and his mother joined the nursing profession.

going to the beach and music. His inclination towards music was a family characteristic. Bovell explains: "My father is a musician; he plays the piano and was a student at the Royal College of Music. He met my mother when my grandfather was teaching him music,

continued on page 14

He has created and produced all kinds of popular music, from punk rock to funk, working with groups like The Pop

Cutting from *Race Today Review*, December 1981/January 1982.

money in them days. I also sold him a version of "Guantanamera" on wax. We use to call these exclusive cuts wax in them days. I once dressed Marie Pierre up as a boy and took her into school and recorded a tune with her. I was recording things at school and I'd take them to R. G. Jones* and cut acetates so that I could put on a record in my house and say I made that. Later I started giving them to the sound systems.'

Bovell's stock of musical experiences and his social background prepared him to make the important contributions he has made to the reggae tradition in Britain over the last decade.

Earlier this year, Phonogram released Dennis Bovell's first solo album, *Brain Damage*. It consists of eight songs and eight dubs which reflect a wide knowledge of popular forms and influences, his diverse skills as a musician (he plays drums, bass, guitar, keyboard and percussion on most of the tracks) and his recording and mixing skills. The songs vary from roots reggae to lovers rock, from rhythm'n'blues to soca, disco and rock. It is the most daring and eclectic album ever produced by a reggae artist.

Race Today Review, December 1981/January 1982

---

* R. G. Jones is a pioneering sound engineering company based in south London and local to Bovell.

Exodus: The Poetry of Exile (2007)

I should not have been surprised when Bob Marley's *Exodus* was voted Album of the Twentieth Century by *Time* magazine. After all, it was the record that propelled Marley, a Jamaican reggae artist, from global stardom to superstar status. Whilst many of his fans would beg to differ with *Time*'s choice, *Exodus* has some of Marley's most memorable tunes and certainly, lyrically, is one of his most uplifting.

Marley often began his songs with a statement of his topic followed by elaboration, conclusion and restatement in the normal chorus–verse–chorus or verse–chorus–verse structure. Proverbs, aphorisms and sayings of everyday Jamaican speech, together with biblical quotations, provide his metaphors and allusions. Marley's lyrics cannot be read without being heard; his rendition of his songs, the way he uses his voice, are clues to meaning. His method of composition is oral and improvisatory.

Exodus was recorded in London after Marley survived a politically motivated assassination attempt. The lyrics of the songs on the album can be read in that context. Even though some of the songs were composed before the shooting, it is my contention that, if we exclude the two love songs, the other eight can be read as a sequence that constitute an organic whole, a movement from darkness to light. Two songs connected to the attempt on Marley's life, 'Running Away' and 'Ambush in the Night', appear on the albums *Kaya* and *Survival* respectively, released after *Exodus*. However, the choice of 'Natural Mystic', 'Guiltiness', 'Three Little Birds' and 'One Love' only becomes significant in the light of the assassination attempt. It is in Marley's Rastafarian faith, his implacable belief in a 'natural mystic', that we locate the thematic thread in songs about faith, betrayal, persecution, defiance, resistance, recuperation, love and hope.

The album opens with the brooding melancholy of 'Natural Mystic', a meditation on life's contradictions and the intractability of their resolution. The mood is of despondency in the face of a cycle of suffering: 'Many more will have to suffer/ many more will have to die'. The fatalism of these lines is tempered by faith. The persona of the song declares that his statement of gloom cannot be explained – 'don't ask me why' – but immediately gives an explanation: 'there's a natural mystic blowing through the air'.

This simple statement of belief when confronted with the perplexities of life's trials and tribulations is followed by 'So Much Things to Say', the first song on the album that speaks directly to the assassination attempt and speculation about its cause. It is a powerful riposte to the rumour-mongers who had cast aspersions on Marley's character, one which finds him in a lyrically combative and self-assertive mood. His theme here is betrayal and persecution. The names of Jamaican national heroes Marcus Garvey and Paul Bogle as well as Jesus Christ

– all iconic figures of betrayal and persecution – are invoked. He implores the youth to remember 'who you are and where you stand in the struggle', and declares that his fight is 'against spiritual wickedness in high and low places'. Towards the end of the song he employs mockery as a tool of derision against his detractors.

'Guiltiness', written before the assassination attempt, reads like a comment on the crime. A bitter song of vengeance, it fits neatly in the sequence of songs as a visceral indictment of 'the big fish' who 'would do anything to materialise their every wish'. Marley takes on a prophetic voice as he cries 'woe to the downpresser' whose lot 'will be the bread of sorrow'.

'The Heathen' is a good example of the economy of Marley's lyricism and his deft use of biblical metaphor and allusion for rhetorical effect. With its portentous bass line, 'The Heathen' is a powerful yet simple statement of defiance and reaffirmation. Inspired by the attempt on Marley's life, it is a call to arms: 'rise up fallen fighters/ rise and take your stance again/ tis he who fights and run away/ live to fight another day'. Here the personal need for a boost in morale becomes a collective stance of defiance addressed to 'fallen fighters'. But it is the repetition of the one-line chorus 'de heathen back dey pon de wall' that gives the song its hypnotic sense of dread.

'Exodus' and 'Jamming', the other two songs that relate to the assassination attempt, are both celebratory. 'Exodus' signals a shift in mood from the sombre musing of the earlier songs to a more upbeat mood. Here Marley delights in the rightness of his cause, the righteousness of his vision of redemption, underpinned by the Garveyite project of repatriation. He celebrates the Rastafarian movement to which he belongs, a movement of like-minded souls who have 'trod through great tribulation' and 'seen Jah light'. 'Exodus' is ultimately a song of faith and yet it speaks to the sense of alienation that comes with the postmodern experience of mass migration and global diasporas.

'Jamming' communicates the sheer exhilaration Marley must have felt having escaped death and the demons that came in the wake of his traumatic experience as he embarked on a new stage of his career. Notwithstanding the obvious sexual connotation, 'Jamming' is employed here as a metaphor of togetherness and unity ('Jah-Jah children must unite'). The song celebrates life and is a statement of reaffirmation. With confidence Marley declares 'no bullets can stop us now/ we won't beg nor we won't bow/ neither can be bought or sold'. That confidence is an expression of faith born of experience.

'Waiting in Vain' and 'Turn Your Lights Down Low' allow for a romantic interlude. These two songs of seduction can also be read as recuperative, avoiding a breach in the sequence. 'Waiting in Vain' (an all-time favourite of mine), with its invigorating bass line, is a plea for love reminiscent of The Impressions' 'Minstrel and Queen', rock-steady versioned as 'Queen Majesty' by The Techniques. However, the supplicant in Marley's song is no mere humble minstrel. Marley's rhetoric of seduction is finely balanced between coyness and confidence, between uncertainty and resolve. The chorus line 'I don't wanna wait in vain for your love' is both plea and veiled threat. The humility of 'I know that I'm way down your line' is contrasted by 'I know how to do my thing' and 'it's my love that you running from'. 'Turn Your Lights Down Low' pales in comparison with 'Waiting in Vain', both lyrically and musically. This bedroom ballad of rekindled love lacks conviction. The repeated line of desire 'I want to give you some good, good loving' would perhaps be more convincing had it been one of intent: 'I'm *gonna* give you some good, good loving'.

'Three Little Birds' and 'One Love' reconnect and complete the sequence. 'Three Little Birds' is a song of hope; a catchy chorus that is at once infectious. Its simple message of reassurance: 'don't worry about a thing/ cause every little thing gonna be alright' immediately touches a universal chord. The imagery of three little birds is endearing. 'One Love', an old Wailers' song inspired by Curtis Mayfield, again finds Marley in an exuberant mood. This song of praise, rejoicing and giving thanks, a plea for brotherly and sisterly love and a restatement of faith is an apt ending. By the time we get to 'One Love', we have been through a range of moods and emotions that have journeyed us from despair to hope in a movement from darkness to light.

Marley's 'lyrical genius', as Jamaican author Kwame Dawes calls it, lies in his ability to translate the personal into the political, the private into the public, the particular into the universal, with a seeming simplicity that guarantees accessibility. The lyrics of the songs from *Exodus* are ample evidence of this.

The Independent, 1 June 2007

African Consciousness in Reggae Music: Some Examples (2013)

When in Jamaica I sometimes used to listen to *Perkins on Line*, a radio talk show hosted by Wilmot Perkins. A few days before Christmas 2009 I tuned in just in time to hear someone berate a previous caller for talking nonsense about Africans. I have no idea what the previous caller had said, but the programme's host, Joan Williams, who was sitting in for Mr Perkins, defended the previous caller, saying that the Africans she had met didn't like Jamaicans, who they regarded as mere descendants of slaves. The new caller talked about Jamaica's African heritage, invoked the name of Marcus Garvey and mentioned a recent visit to Jamaica by an African head of state. Ms Williams was having none of it. She declared that she was Jamaican, not African (as if ethnicity and nationality were the same thing); that she could not say what race she belonged to as she was too 'mix-up'; and, furthermore, that Africans had sold us into slavery. And that was that. Next caller. I must say that I was a little taken aback by how tersely the caller was dealt with by Ms Williams.

Around the same time, just before Christmas, my sister gave me a Scotia Bank calendar for 2010, with a nice picture on the cover of a handsome, blonde-haired, blue-eyed white boy and a pretty black girl with their arms around each other. The calendar was beautifully presented with lovely photographs which attempted to visually portray Jamaica's national motto, 'out of many one people'. The English, Irish, German, Jew, Portuguese, Taino, African, Syrian, Lebanese, Indian, Chinese and Spanish were all represented. But the Welsh and Scot were not. After leafing through the calendar, the thought crossed my mind that if I was an outsider who knew nothing of Jamaica, I would not have guessed that the country is over 90 per cent black.

Andrea Levy's novel *The Long Song*, set in Jamaica during the period before and after the abolition of slavery, chronicles the life of 'July', a mixed-race girl born into slavery. When a new master arrives on the plantation, July is anxious to distance herself from her African ancestry in order to impress him. She tells him, 'You must not think me a nigger, for me is mulatto'.

Rigorously researched, *The Long Song* credibly depicts a period of turbulence in Jamaica's troubled history and its impact on plantation life. Although Levy's book is fiction, it neverthe-less offers historical context to the *Perkins on Line* conversation and the Scotia Bank calendar for 2010. Ms Williams clearly has a point about being racially mixed; and the Scotia Bank calendar more or less accurately represents the multiracial nature of Jamaican society. But both point to a persistent ambivalence about race in Jamaica which Andrea Levy's novel dissects.

In spite of warnings about the risk of skin cancer, skin bleaching is practised in Jamaica by a minority of men and women. The notorious Jamaican dancehall artist Vybz Kartel defended bleaching his own skin by quoting the line from Haile

Selassie's anti-racist speech to the League of Nations about the insignificance of the colour of one's skin or eyes, later recorded by Bob Marley as the song 'War'.

Notwithstanding useful sociological concepts like pluralism, notions of compartmentalization, creolization and hybridity, the fact is that race is an important dimension of Jamaican society and culture. It could be argued that our national motto is but a fig leaf masking unpalatable truths – what Jamaican academic Rex Nettleford would probably dub 'obscenities' – about the nature of social relations in Jamaica. It seems to me that official society is in denial about the politics of race in Jamaica, a denial that Jamaican poet and critic Mervyn Morris would probably describe as 'almost pathological'. Jamaicans may have made progress in coming to terms with the multifaceted nature of our historical heritage, but we still have a long way to go in the decolonization of the mind. And yet Jamaican reggae music is replete with expressions of African consciousness.

What do I mean by African consciousness? Simply, an awareness of connectedness to the continent of Africa by its diaspora as ancestral homeland and identification with Africa. British–Jamaican cultural theorist Stuart Hall identifies two approaches to African consciousness: 'cultural nationalist' and 'pan-African imaginary'. The emphasis on the first being identity and the other, solidarity. He opts for the latter because it is that approach, he asserts, which has kept the consciousness or what he calls the 'connections' alive. I would argue that both the 'cultural national' and the 'pan-African imaginary' find expression in reggae music.

There is ample historical and anthropological evidence that

the slaves who were taken to the New World from Africa brought Africa with them, that African traditions were interwoven into the fabric of their cultural lives. In his book *The Development of Creole Society in Jamaica, 1770–1820*, Edward Kamau Brathwaite shows us that the orientation of the folk culture of Jamaican slaves was decidedly African. He offers as evidence customs related to the life cycle, sexual and domestic unions, death, funerals and burial, religious ideas and practice, dress, dance and music. Moreover, the maroons, runaway slaves, had established autonomous communities where African traditions and cultural practices thrived.

Jamaican novelist and sociologist Erna Brodber rightly asserts in her book *The Continent of Black Consciousness* that slavery negated the tribal consciousness of the transported slaves and produced an African consciousness instead. The African slaves in the New World were moulded into one people, sharing many things in common, including identity. Slavery 'made them into Africans'. Brodber goes on to argue that this African consciousness provided the basis for the emergence of black political thought and action which culminated in the emergence of black nationalist movements in the twentieth century.

Peter Tosh's song 'African' provides a succinct expression of African consciousness. If 'black man' is gender-neutral, Tosh's definition of African is inclusive and all-embracing. 'Don't care where you come from/ as long as you're a black man/ you're an African' declares Tosh. It matters not what parish of Jamaica you are from, what part of the Caribbean you are from, what shade of black you are, what church you are affiliated to, what country you are from. If you're black, you're African.

In May 2013 during the celebration of the fiftieth anniversary of the African Union in Addis Ababa, at a panel on Pan-Africanism and the African Renaissance, Jamaican Prime Minister Portia Simpson-Miller said that Jamaica and the Caribbean community are 'proud of our African heritage'. It was Peter Tosh's song 'African' that was played as former Jamaican Prime Minister P. J. Patterson and Mrs Simpson-Miller joined the panel.

Even before the emergence of reggae in the late 1960s, there were some expressions of African consciousness in Jamaican popular music. The work of folklorist Olive Lewin provides evidence that there are a number of Jamaican folk songs in which Africa is remembered; songs which mention Congo and Guinea, for example. Noted jazz musician and musicologist Marjorie Whylie is an expert on African-derived drum rhythms like kumina, etu, bhurru, gerrey, gombey and nago, which are still played in Jamaica. During the era of ska, the visionary trombonist Don Drummond named one of his instrumental compositions 'Addis Ababa' after the Ethiopian capital and another 'The Reburial' in reference to the re-interment in Jamaica of Marcus Garvey, the greatest and most effective political advocate of black/African consciousness. Prince Buster, in his famous talking tune 'Judge Dread', declares that he has come from Ethiopia to preside over the trial of rude boys in Jamaica charged with robbing and shooting black people. Buster's black nationalist sentiment can be heard in several of his recordings including 'Black Head Chinaman', where he castigates singer Derrick Morgan for leaving his stable to go and record for a Jamaican Chinese producer. During the short rock steady period between ska and reggae 1966–8, we begin to get songs like Desmond Dekker's 'Pretty Africa' expressing the sentiments of Garvey's 'Back to Africa' movement and the Rastafarian demand for repatriation. In the song Dekker describes Africa as 'the land of our fathers . . . where we belong'. The growth of the Rastafarian movement and the alienation felt by the poor and marginalized youth of urban Jamaica ensured that the theme of repatriation would become a consistently restated one in many reggae recordings. 'Send I back to Ethiopia land/ it is our fathers' land/ Selah' sing the aptly named Ethiopians in one of their early recordings. In another song from the rock steady period, Bob Andy declares 'I've Got to Go Back Home'. Jamaica couldn't be home 'cause I can't get clothes to wear/ can't get no food to eat/ I can't find a job to get bread/ . . . nothing like a future here'. The persona of the song threatens to commit suicide if he cannot leave.

This sense of alienation/unbelonging and hopelessness rooted in the failure of the abolition of slavery to radically transform the lives of the former slaves and disillusionment with the material conditions of postcolonial existence for the poor and marginalized urban youth finds expression in many reggae songs. Over a decade after Jamaican independence, during the turbulent 1970s, Rastafarian singer Fred Locks still finds inspiration in the ill-fated Black Star Liner shipping company which Marcus Garvey's Universal Negro Improvement Association (UNIA) had established to transport New World blacks to Africa. 'Seven miles of Black Star Liners coming in the harbour' announces Fred Locks. For him this is a vision of the fulfilment of Garvey's prophecy of freedom, a vision that persists amongst some Rastafarians. 'It's repatriation/ black liberation' chants Fred Locks.

Marcus Garvey's currency had declined by the time of his death in 1940. As Colin Grant tells us in his book *Negro With a Hat*:

> It wasn't until [...] when crises hit the black world with the rise of the militant Black Power Movement in the USA in the 1960s, and the emergence of black leaders in Africa and the Caribbean seeking to forge new national identities, that people started to think again of Garvey.

Burning Spear's 'Old Marcus Garvey' was released around the same period as Fred Locks' 'Black Star Liners' in the early to mid-1970s. By then, Garvey was not only one of Jamaica's national heroes, he was back in currency. But whilst Fred Locks reaffirms the Garveyite vision of African redemption, Burning Spear laments its betrayal. All of Jamaica's male national heroes are being talked about, sings Burning Spear, but 'no one remembers old Marcus Garvey' is the song's paradoxical refrain. Nanny of the Maroons, Jamaica's only national heroine, is not mentioned in the song.

Some expressions of African consciousness in reggae take the form of statements of pride in African ancestry like Johnny Clarke's 'African Roots', for example, where he sings 'We've been taken away from Africa/ more than 500 years/ but one thing they couldn't take/ was the roots out of my mind/ African roots/ Just call me African roots'.

At the heart of African consciousness in reggae music is

the historical experience of slavery, its legacy of brutality, exploitation, marginalization, hopelessness and centuries of colonial indoctrination of black inferiority. A common theme of many expressions of African consciousness in reggae music is that of remembering. 'Do you remember the days of slavery?' asks Burning Spear rhetorically in his song 'Slavery Days'. In the song 'Africa' from their 1976 album *Right Time*, the Mighty Diamonds not only declare that Africa, their ancestral land, is calling them home, slavery is memorialized: 'I remember those chains/ how my people was in slavery time and time ago'. Bob Marley sings, 'I remember on the slave ship how they brutalize our very soul'. Marley's invocation of the memory of slavery in 'Slave Driver' is about retributive justice: 'slave driver/ the table is turned/ catch-a-fire you gonna get burn'. Fire is still a potent metaphor of retribution in Rasta discourse. Like Marley's 'Slave Driver', songs like Peter Tosh's 'Four Hundred Years', Burning Spear's 'Old Marcus Garvey' and Bob Andy's 'I've Got to Go Back Home' are not just expressions of African consciousness, they also critique post-colonial Jamaica.

Sometimes expressions of African consciousness in reggae take the form of naming. For example, groups give themselves names like the Abyssinians, the Congos, the Ethiopians and the Burning Spears. Solo artists give themselves names like Queen Ifrica, Sizzla Kalonji and Mutabaruka. Cedric Brooks names two of his instrumental compositions 'Tales of Mozambique' and 'Nigerian Reggae'. Some songs lament the loss of name, loss of identity. In 'Give I Fe I Name', Pablo Moses demands of the colonizer the return of his original African name. Chinese are called 'Chin and Chung', 'McIntosh' is from Scotland and Indians are called 'Raja and Gavaskar', Moses informs us. Moreover, he is sure that 'Smith' is not an African name. He tells of his embarrassment on reaching Ethiopia having to tell his idren his name is 'Morris'. However, having rejected the colonizer's name, the singer opts for Spanish and Jewish names: Pablo and Moses. Similarly, during the era of ska Lord Brynner, in the topically titled 'Congo War', treats the theme of loss of name with irony.

Africa becomes iconic and takes on a utopian dimension in some reggae songs. The group Third World, for example, mythologize Africa in their song 'Tribal War' as a place where there was an absence of tribal conflict. The Abyssinians in 'Satta Massagana' describe Africa as 'a land far far away/ where there's no night/ there's only day'. The lyrics of Bunny Wailer's 'Dreamland' can be interpreted as a utopian, romanticized vision of Africa.

When anti-colonial and anti-apartheid struggles were being waged in Africa during the 1970s and 1980s, some expressions of African consciousness were couched in the language of Pan-Africanism. These were basically statements of solidarity like the Abyssinians' 'South African Enlistment', for example. 'If Africa noh free, black man can't free', declared the Twinkle Brothers in the song 'Free Africa'. 'Africa must be free/ by the year 1983' sang the youthful Hugh Mundell. There was Tapper Zukie's celebratory 'MPLA', alluding to the victory of the revolutionary forces in Angola during the anti-colonial war against the Portuguese, with its banal chorus 'MPLA/ natty going on a holiday'. Bob Marley's 'Zimbabwe' celebrates the triumph of the liberation struggle in that country and calls for unity of purpose, a call he repeats in 'Africa Unite'.

These are just a few examples of the many varied expressions of African consciousness in reggae music. There was a marked decline in these expressions during the 1980s, which coincided with the decline of roots reggae and the ascendancy of dance-hall deejay ragamuffin music. In Jamaica out went the PNP and democratic socialism and in came the JLP, IMF structural adjustment policies, with slackness and gun talk in the dancehall. By the early 1990s roots reggae began a tentative revival and by the end of the twentieth century dancehall music had begun to reflect once again African consciousness through artists like Garnett Silk, Sizzla, Capleton, Morgan Heritage and others. This revival was itself a reflection of a new wave of Rasta revival amongst the youth of Jamaica with the rise of the bobo shanti dreads, followers of King Emmanuel.

The re-diasporization of New World blacks in Europe, as Stuart Hall calls it, saw the establishment of a Caribbean diaspora in Britain. My generation developed not only a West Indian or Caribbean consciousness; we also developed an African consciousness. In racialized Britain, with the legacy of slavery which resulted in post-Second World War migration and which still impinges on our lives, a continuity of consciousness was inevitable. In the same way that the slaves had brought Africa with them to the New World, black people brought Africa with them from the Caribbean to Britain. The Black Power Movement of the late 1960s and early 1970s was a political expression of African consciousness in the UK as well as a black working-class movement.

For second- and third-generation young blacks in Britain, reggae music was an important factor in the formation of new identities of un/belonging. Reggae music, through sound systems, provided a nexus for a culture of resistance to racial oppression. So expressions of African consciousness in the Jamaican reggae we socialized around were an important influence. It also facilitated the growth of Rastafari in Britain.

British reggae, too, reflected a continuity of African consciousness through bands like Aswad, Matumbi, Misty in Roots, Steel Pulse, deejay Macca B and others. The success of Bob Marley and his elevation on the world stage as a superstar had inspired a new generation of British roots reggae exponents. Although lovers rock, that particularly British genre of romantic reggae, continues to hold its own, by the end of the twentieth century, roots reggae in the UK had begun to decline and with it expressions of African consciousness in the music of young black Britons. The technologically driven music of young blacks at the start of the new millennium seems to reflect more the realities of urban life and the dominant consumerist ethos of our time. This American-influenced ethos is also to be found in the music coming out of Jamaica. However, expressions of African consciousness still continue in reggae and dancehall music in Jamaica today, five hundred years after Africans were first brought to Jamaica.

To summarize, then, African consciousness is rooted in the Atlantic slave trade, the historical experience of slavery and its legacy. A cultural dimension of this consciousness is its expression in reggae music. These are often expressions of despair and affirmation, defiance and illusion, resistance and hope.

The Jamaican diaspora in the UK facilitated a continuity of expression which influenced formations of Black British identities. Whilst expressions of African consciousness declined in Jamaican popular music during the 1980s, it endures in the twenty-first century in Jamaica, but has declined in Britain. This decline reflects the demise of reggae as the dominant music of today's Black British youth.

LKJ lecture, July 2013

The People Speak (2015)

Introduction to
So Much Things to Say by Roger Steffens

In an essay I wrote on the lyrics from Bob Marley's *Exodus*, voted Album of the Twentieth Century by *Time* magazine, I said of his lyrical genius that it was based on his 'ability to translate the personal into the political, the private into the public, the particular into the universal'.* Genius, it can be argued, is not merely an exceptional personal attribute; it is historical in the sense that it becomes manifest when there is a conjunction of the biographical and the historical. The second half of the 1970s, the period when Bob Marley began to reap the rewards of his long apprenticeship as a musician, was a time of turbulence not only in Jamaica but around the globe. The Cold War was at its most intense; proxy wars were being waged between East and West in developing-world countries; anti-colonial wars were still being fought in Africa; there were anti-imperialist struggles taking place in South America. Jamaica was on the brink of all-out civil war as the opposition, aided and abetted by the CIA, sought to wrest power from Michael Manley's democratic socialist government. Bob Marley almost

---

* In Williams, Richard, ed., *Exodus: Bob Marley & The Wailers: Exile 1977* (London: Weidenfeld & Nicolson, 2007).

lost his life during that conflict. His music is resonant of that period; it reflects the zeitgeist. At the apotheosis of his career he had become a kind of Che Guevara of popular culture.

I have the dubious distinction of writing a critique of Marley's rise to fame at a pivotal time in his career. As a fan of the Wailers triumvirate of Bob Marley, Peter Tosh and Bunny Wailer, I was deeply disappointed when they went their separate ways. Then, on top of that, Marley was being hailed in the rock music press as the new 'king of rock' following the release of his first solo album, *Natty Dread*. As far as I was concerned that was a travesty – and I was not alone in harbouring such sentiments. Bob Marley was, after all, a top-ranking Jamaican reggae artist who belonged to the world of black music and was being appropriated by the white rock world. In the article I wrote titled 'Roots and Rock: The Marley Enigma', published in *Race Today* in October 1975, I not only criticized the way Marley was being marketed, I laid the blame at the doorstep of Chis Blackwell, founder of Island Records.[*] Back then I was a twenty-three-year-old sociology undergraduate and I had just published my second book of poems, *Dread Beat and Blood*. Three years later I was signed to Island Records by Blackwell and, a year after that, by Marley to Tuff Gong. With the benefit of hindsight, I can say that my analysis of the marketing strategy was more or less correct, even though the sentiments were misplaced.

When it became clear that Bob Marley would not recover

---

[*] Republished in Cateforis, Theo, ed., *The Rock History Reader* (New York and Abingdon: Routledge, 2007, 2nd edn. 2013).

from the cancer he was battling, the newly elected Jamaican government, led by Edward Seaga, awarded him the Order of Merit, the nation's highest civilian award. It was in recognition not only of Marley's enormous popularity in Jamaica but also of the kudos he had brought to the nation by his achievements abroad. No other Jamaican has done more to boost the brand name Jamaica. As reggae music's greatest ambassador, Marley made an enormous contribution to its globalization and its impact on popular culture around the world. Since his demise he has grown in stature from superstar to legend to iconic status, a remarkable achievement for someone from such a humble background. The astute and at times obscene marketing of Marley as a brand name cannot detract from the fact that no other recording artist in the late twentieth century, in any genre, has had the global reach and influence that Marley has continuing into this millennium.

The Rastafarian soul rebel, armed with his distinctive voice, a guitar, a great backing band and fine backing vocals, was a man on a mission to challenge the 'isms and schisms' of principalities and powers as he fought against 'spiritual wickedness in high and low places'. His legacy of catchy danceable songs of defiance, resistance, rebellion, love and hope continues to reverberate around the world; his lyrical and melodic genius guarantees the contemporaneity of his music. What kind of a man and musician was Robert Nesta Marley? Many books have been written about him including a Marley reader for the academy. He has appeared in fiction too. What makes Roger Steffens' *So Much Things to Say: The Oral History of Bob Marley* unique is that the author does not present a portrait of the artist through his own lens but instead presents us with a collage of impressions seen through the eyes of others. For many years Steffens travelled the world telling Marley's story with his illustrated 'Life of Bob Marley' lecture. Here he allows those who knew Marley to give their versions. Roger Steffens, writer, broadcaster and photographer, a respected scholar of reggae and renowned archivist specializing in Bob Marley recordings and ephemera, has put together seventy-five interviews with people close to Marley who speak candidly about what they witnessed of the singer's life and times. The respondents range from people who knew Marley intimately to those who crossed paths with him including family, friends, musicians, record company personnel, journalists, photographers and filmmakers. The evidential nature of this book, with at times conflicting narratives, guarantees a riveting read. Some of the testimonies confirm what was already known, some offer different versions, some contest myths about Marley; others say more about the witness than the man.

There are some startling revelations and contentious claims. We hear from Clement 'Sir Coxsone' Dodd about the young Marley's time at Studio One; the reputed Mafia-connected Danny Sims on his dealings with Marley and Johnny Nash; Bunny Wailer on his friend's composition technique; Beverley Kelso, an original Wailer, on the relationship between Rita Marley and Bob; Joe Higgs on his schooling of the original Wailers and Marley's character; Dermot Hussey, Jamaican broadcaster and musicologist, on the interview about the break-up of the Wailers that Marley wanted destroyed. There are interviews with all of the original Wailers. Other respondents include Cedella Booker, Marley's mother; Cindy Breakspeare, former beauty queen and mother of Damian 'Junior Gong' Marley; Alan 'Skill' Cole, Marley's close friend; Third World's Cat Coore; and Rastafarian guru Mortimo Planno.

Steffens sometimes makes editorial interventions, introducing a speaker or providing context for what is being said. He rarely opines, allowing his witnesses to tell their stories in their own words, structured chronologically from Marley's childhood to his demise. The overall impression we get of Marley is that of a man of some complexity: taciturn and jovial by turns, worldly and spiritual, a sleeping lion capable of violent rage, a peacemaker, a ladies' man and a man of prodigious generosity. The most striking observation that emerges from several witnesses is how serious Marley was about his art, his single-mindedness and his consummate professionalism. Marley's story is a poignant one of humble origins, privation, struggle, survival, trials and tribulations, triumph and tragedy.

Introduction to *So Much Things to Say: The Oral History of Bob Marley* by Roger Steffens (New York: W. W. Norton, 2017), written 2015

The Upsetter (2021)

Introduction to
People Funny Boy by David Katz

British reggae pioneer Dennis Bovell, one of the 'Cricklewood Twelve', once told me about the circumstances that led to him being arrested and charged with incitement to riot in 1974. He was playing Sufferer's sound system in a sound clash against Lord Koos and Count Nick's at a venue called Burtons.* Lee 'Scratch' Perry was in attendance, supplying him with dub plates. The police entered the venue and tried to make an arrest just as one of the selecters began playing Junior Byles' 'Beat Down Babylon', produced by Perry. Fighting broke out between the revellers and the police. According to Bovell, Perry declared, 'I am the Upsetter,' turned up his collar and made a speedy exit.

I once described Lee 'Scratch' Perry, the Upsetter, as the Salvador Dalí of reggae. I wasn't thinking so much about their art, but more about the audacity of their public image. In my youth I was a big fan of Perry's music, especially his instrumental productions. Having met him on a few occasions over the years, beginning in 1977, hearing several anecdotes from people who had encountered him, and seeing him briefly in performance,

---

* Also known as the Carib Club, which was above Burton's, the men's clothes shop.

I have been left with the impression that he is a man with an impish sense of humour and Anansi-like attributes. Eventually an octogenarian, the phenomenal Jamaican music-maker and performer lived a rollercoaster life of epic proportions. Renowned for his creative wizardry in the world of reggae music, Perry had already become a legend by the age of fifty. What makes his story so extraordinary is the fact that he has never been proficient on any musical instrument, and yet the cream of his prolific output of recordings belongs to the reggae canon. His innate gift for music, rooted in his Jamaican rural background where he was grounded in Afro-Jamaican folk culture, first found expression in his talent as a dancer. Musicians, vocalists and producers alike have all spoken about the magical power of Perry's creativity and his sonic genius in the recording studio. He had a talented pool of session musicians to draw from. Moreover, he soon found access to the growing market for reggae music in Britain.

Perry served his apprenticeship under the tutelage of pioneering record producer Clement (Sir Coxsone) Dodd, learning every aspect of the music business, and became his right-hand man before branching out on his own. One of his early songs, 'People Funny Boy', signalled the arrival of the reggae beat in the late 1960s and Perry's rise to fame as song-writer, arranger, producer, recording engineer and entrepreneur. Not blessed with a great singing voice, it was as a producer that Perry soon established a reputation as the man with the Midas touch. What set him apart from his competitors were his unique creativity, his idiosyncratic approach to music-making and his peculiar sonic sensibility.

It was during the late 1960s and early 1970s that Perry established his reputation as a hit-maker, with tunes like Susan Cadogan's 'Hurt So Good' and The Upsetters' 'Return of Django'; he also worked with Bob Marley on some of the Wailers' classic tunes. He reached the apotheosis of his creativity during the Black Ark years when, with the convenience of his own studio, he was able to give free rein to his creative imagination, producing his own unique sound, enhancing his credentials as the undisputed master of the sonic art of dub with the classic album, *Super Ape*. With success came enormous pressures. The Black Ark Studio became a magnet, not only for singers and players of instruments, but also undesirables, leading to its eventual demise by fire. It was all too much for the Upsetter, who at the time appeared to have undergone some kind of nervous breakdown and assumed the new persona of Pipecock Jackson. His utterances were sometimes outrageous; his behaviour bizarre.

Perry's newly acquired reputation as a madman enhanced his notoriety, magnified his mystique. The last two decades of the twentieth century were a remarkably productive time for him in the studio and on the road. It was during this period that Perry realized his ambition as a solo artist and performer. With Britain as his new base, he was able to make forays into Europe and further afield. Moreover, he embraced opportunities for engagement with the new musical forms of the digital age. By the end of the last millennium, he had settled in Switzerland, continuing his musical journey.

People Funny Boy, David Katz's critically acclaimed biography of Perry, a work of keen scholarship, is truly a labour of love.

Meticulously researched, it maps Perry's journey from his Jamaican peasant roots to his cult status as reggae guru on the global stage. In the telling of Perry's story, Katz's main focus is on his career in music, but we also learn something about his personal life. It is a book not just for fans of Lee 'Scratch' Perry, but also reggae scholars in general, as it illuminates the history of reggae and its impact on other popular musical genres. This new edition allows the author to deal with a few inaccuracies and omissions in the first edition whilst bringing us up to date with the first two decades of the twenty-first century. The Lee 'Scratch' Perry of his later years was the old warrior of yesterday who, having conquered his demons and slain the dragons, continued to chart his own course. May his sounds continue to vibrate on.

Introduction to *People Funny Boy: The Genius of Lee 'Scratch' Perry* by David Katz (London: White Rabbit, 2021; original edition Edinburgh: Payback Press, 2020), written 8 September 2021

2.
'STORY' –
LITERATURE

The Swamp Dwellers
by Wole Soyinka (1975)

Review of the play directed by Howard Johnson
at the Keskidee Centre, 16–30 August 1975

The creative literature of post-independence Africa is, perhaps
more than anything else, an introspective literature. From the
poet to the essayist, from the novelist to the dramatist, the main
preoccupation has been that of self-examination. Colonialism
has left behind, in Africa, many wounds which are yet to heal;
wounds that have festered into neo-colonialism. And it is these
wounds which have been subjected to the prognosis of the
creative writers of Africa, not as social or political surgeons,
but quite simply as concerned artists.

In this introspective literature, tradition versus modernization has emerged as one of the central areas of focus. Achebe's
Things Fall Apart, a classic of contemporary African literature,
lamented 'the breaking down of tribal traditions and the weak-
ening of the moral values of the old system'. Similarly, Soyinka's
play *The Swamp Dwellers*, Keskidee's most recent production,
also addresses itself to the theme of modernization versus
tradition among others. However, unlike Achebe's novel which
laments the breaking up of tradition, Soyinka's play is ques-
tioning tradition. Achebe's novel belongs more to what may be
described as the anti-colonialist stage of African literature

whilst Soyinka's play belongs more to the post-independence stage.

The play is a village drama which tells the story of a son, Igwezu (played by a very competent Imruh Caesar), who, along with his twin brother, went off to the city in search of his fortune only to return in debt, disillusioned, disappointed and bitter. Igwezu's return to the village is the occasion of the drama. In this low-keyed polemic against a redundant trad-itionalism, inertia, ignorance, corruption, deception and greed are identified by Soyinka as maladies of contemporary village life in Nigeria. Makuri (a very convincing Lari Williams) and Alu (played by Benita Enwonwu), Igwezu's aged parents, personify the inertia and ignorance. The Kadiye, the village priest, typifies the corruption, deception and greed. It is the Kadiye to whom all gifts are presented to appease the Serpent of the Swamps, the deity which controls the destiny of the swamps.

Igwezu, the young rebel, whose only hope was the harvest of his farm, returns to find his hope withered and faded. He is bitter. He is inspired by a blind beggar – who begs not food but only to be allowed to work the soil with his hands – to verbally slay the Kadiye to whom many gifts were given to appease the Serpent of the Swamps in order that the farm prosper in his absence.

IGWEZU: . . . ever since I began to till the soil, did I not give the soil his due? Did I not bring the first of the lentils to the shrine, and pour oil upon the altar?
KADIYE: Regularly.

The cover of *Race Today* magazine, September 1975.

IGWEZU: And when the Kadiye blessed my marriage, and tied the heaven-made knot, did he not promise a long life? Did he not promise children? Did he not promise happiness?
KADIYE: (does not reply)
IGWEZU: Why are you so fat, Kadiye? . . . You lie upon the land, Kadiye, and choke it in the folds of a serpent.

After the verbal slaying of the Kadiye, the Beggar calls Igwezu 'slayer of serpents', which is perhaps Soyinka's most blatant indictment of the bogus man of god. Igwezu decides to leave for the city immediately. He tells the Beggar, who has pledged himself as his bondsman, to stay and tend the farm. Perhaps the key to the whole play lies in Igwezu's reply to the Beggar's question: 'You are not going now, master?' Igwezu replies, 'I must not be here when the people call for blood'. At the end of the play, the Beggar is left standing alone on the stage. He has the last word: 'I shall be here to give account', he says, as the curtain falls.

Although it is the outdated village tradition that is Soyinka's main target in *The Swamp Dwellers*, modernization as represented by city life is perhaps also being questioned. In fact, *The Swamp Dwellers* is a deceptively simple play which seems to be saying a lot of things at the same time. It is at times humorous, at times taut with suspense. It is good drama and Howard Johnson has read this work intelligently and has directed it thus.

Race Today, **September 1975**

Caribbean Chronicles (1977)

The Iguana's Tail: Crick Crack Stories from the Caribbean by Sir Philip Sherlock

REVIEW

Crick Crack stories, like Anansi stories, not only illustrate the richness of Caribbean folklore and culture, they also reflect the resilience of the African cultural heritage which exists in the Caribbean, side by side with that of Europe. They are animal stories which were brought to the Caribbean by African slave labour and which have increased in popularity among both children and adults over the centuries. *The Iguana's Tail* is a selection of six of these delightful stories by Philip Sherlock, distinguished West Indian scholar and folklorist, which takes us into 'a world where animals speak and think and laugh like human beings'. It is simply and relevantly illustrated by Gioia Fiammenghi. The stories are, for the most part, explanatory in nature: they tell us why the Donkey hee-haws and the Mosquito buzzes; why the Pelican is such a good fisherman and how Tortoise came by his cracked and jagged shell; and, like many folk-tales the world over, each story usually has a moral.

Philip Sherlock tells the stories with charm and imagination. There is drought on the land and a small group of forest-dwellers – Green Parrot, Little Capuchin Monkey, Hacka Tiger,

Chimpanzee, Brown Owl, Armadillo and not forgetting Firefly – set out in search of more fertile ground for their new home. At the end of each day's journey or during an afternoon's respite, the animals gather together and each animal takes its turn to tell a Crick Crack story. 'Crick, crack', exclaims the storyteller at the beginning of each story; 'Break my back', reply the animals, and the teller goes into his story. At the end of the story he will say, 'Wire bend', and the listeners will say, 'Story end'. The stories entertain the animals and help to keep up their sagging spirits during the long and arduous trek. And there is a continuous line of suspense throughout the journey, and throughout the book, as Hacka Tiger draws closer to Iguana, awaiting his chance to pounce upon her and sink his sharp teeth into her succulent flesh.

Philip Sherlock has here made a significant contribution to Caribbean folklore by rendering these oral tales into literary form without any significant loss in the transition. In doing so, he has made them available to a much wider audience, an important section of which are those children born in Britain of Caribbean parents, cut off from the cultural roots of their parents and yet often living in a Caribbean sub-cultural environment. For these children, books like *The Iguana's Tail* go a long, long way towards filling an enormously wide gap.

Sir Philip Sherlock, *The Iguana's Tail: Crick Crack Stories from the Caribbean*, illustrated by Gioia Flammenghi (London: André Deutsch, 1977, ISBN 0233966870).
Times Literary Supplement, 25 March 1977

Echo by Orlando Wong [the former name of Oku Onuora] (1977)

A new and powerful voice in Jamaican poetry right now is that of twenty-five-year-old Orlando Wong. Imprisoned in 1971 for his part in an armed robbery, Orlando was freed in September, largely as a result of public recognition of his poetic talents. His first volume of poetry, *Echo*, belongs to that of a new generation of Jamaican poets, whose poetic sensibilities have been fired by the concrete social realities of urban life in Jamaica, as it is experienced by the unemployed; it also reflects the rising consciousness of sections of the working class and unemployed and, in the case of Orlando, prisoners in Jamaica.

The backdrop of Orlando's poetry is that of political violence, economic crises, food shortages, subhuman housing conditions for the masses, illiteracy, widespread crime and violence, curfews, states of emergency, widespread permanent unemployment and 'democratic socialism' financed by international capitalism. In the absence of a welfare state, life for the unemployed is lived purely at the level of survival. Here the law of the jungle is easily invoked. As Big Youth would say, 'only the fittest of the fittest survive'. And so it is that:

> de ooman dung de Street
> 13-year-ole son ded
> wid a shotgun
> inna him han
> ('Sketches')

So it is that 'The sounds of sirens/ CRACK/ the stillness of the night/ And another youth drops dead' (from 'Unite'). So it is that, 'de washy lookin pickney dem/ a play inna place worse dan hag pen' with 'de look a hunga inna dem eye' and 'every youth . . . / a bawl bout poverty/ an police brutality' and 'ole heapa mad people! . . . a roam de street/ an de olda head dem/ pon side walk a beg/ an de . . . youth/ inna de prison dem' (from 'Bwoy').

Like the reggae lyricist and the calypsonian – the first popular poets of the Caribbean masses – Orlando writes about his immediate society and his class, in their language, their rhythms and from their point of view; and he succeeds. He succeeds in creating striking sketches of life in the ghettoes and shanties of West Kingston:

> wall slogans
> scrawled
> in dred
> burnt out houses
> tell tales
> of terrible nights
> guns
> spitting lead

        people sprawled
        dead
        mirrored in blood –
        shot eyes.
        ('Reflection')

Orlando writes about 'dread times' when 'earth a blaze' and 'man a rage' when 'Pressure Drop':

        eart tun red
        curfew
        man screw
        gun blaze
        knife flash
        man run hot . . .
        ('Pressure Drop')

He writes about the ghetto youth from personal experience:

        fi di ghetto youth
        it kinda cute
        all day I trod earth
        a look fi work
        ('Echo')

and, in so doing, speaks for many like himself, for whom crime is the only means of survival.

The rising political consciousness that informs and underlies the poems in *Echo* is a combination of black and revolutionary consciousness, as the poems 'Change', 'Beat Vu Drums', 'Decolonisation Yesterday/Today/Tomorrow' and others reflect. Here we find some thematic and stylistic similarities with the black American soul-poetry of the 1960s and early 1970s, exemplified by the work of people like Sonia Sanchez and Don L. Lee:

> soul
> ful
> fingersnappin
> handclappin
> laughin
> blackchild
> ('Change Yes Change')

or

> blak body
> movin
> teasin
> rousin pride
> ('Poem')

Apart from these stylistic similarities with black American poetry, Orlando works mostly within the Caribbean oral tradition. He often employs the rhythms of street and yard talk; dread talk and the word-music of dub-poetry. Indeed, Orlando's poetry – oral poetry for the most part – has much in common with that of reggae dub-lyricists like Big Youth, Prince Pampado, Dillinger, Dr Alimantado and others:

it hot
hot hot
man jus a bus shat
it red
red red
dem shot John Tom ded.
('Sketches')

Orlando's attitude to his art is expressed in the first poem in the book, called 'I Want to Write A Poem'. His conscious aim is 'to write/ a poem/ that'll wake/ the senses' and 'kindle/ a burnin desire in man/ to destroy exploitation'. And yet, it is Orlando's claim that he is 'no poet' but just 'a voice'. The irony here is only apparent, for in order to achieve the aim set out in 'I Want to Write A Poem', Orlando can only be 'a voice' that 'echo the people's/ thought/ laughter/ cry/ sigh' (from 'No Poet'). The immediacy of his themes, his use of popular language, his crafts and skill of words and rhythm, all these elements assure Orlando some degree of success.

Published by Sangster's (Jamaica); should be available from most black bookshops.
Race Today, **September 1977**

Language as Power (1986)

Decolonising the Mind
by Ngũgĩ wa Thiong'o

REVIEW

Ngũgĩ wa Thiong'o's new book *Decolonising the Mind* begins rather unconventionally with a statement by the author giving public notice of his intention to stop writing in English. 'From now on', he declares, 'it is Gikuyu and Kiswahali all the way'. The rest of the book is an explanation of how and why he arrived at that decision.

Ngũgĩ wa Thiong'o not only has the distinction of being one of Kenya's and Africa's foremost writers. Through his work as a cultural and political activist, he has also earned the reputation of being an irrepressible champion of a truly national patriotic people's culture in his native Kenya. His unrelenting opposition to 'cultural imperialism' in Kenya has resulted in his imprisonment and subsequent exile. But as previous books and now *Decolonising the Mind* so powerfully demonstrate, his resolve has been strengthened rather than weakened by repression.

In *Decolonising the Mind* Ngũgĩ wa Thiong'o argues with great clarity, cogency and eloquence for an African literature which is true to the African experience, a literature which accurately reflects Africa's history and culture. Language, he argues, is the key to achieving this goal, or it is at least a prerequisite. His point of departure is colonialism and neo-colonial cultural practices in Africa which, he argues, go hand in glove with the economic and political exploitation of Africa by foreign interests. 'Economic and political control of a people can never be complete without cultural control', says Ngũgĩ, and the latter is largely facilitated through the imposition of the language of the colonizer.

Then we get to the heart of the matter. It is absurd, argues Ngũgĩ, to describe the body of literature written by African writers (including his own work) in English, French and Portuguese as 'African literature'. What African literary practice has in the main produced so far is 'another hybrid tradition' which can only be termed 'Afro-European', contends Ngũgĩ. But what about those writers who have incorporated aspects of African culture into their work by drawing from African orature, for example? Ngũgĩ's reply is that they are simply appropriating African cultures to enrich European ones.

Ngũgĩ rejects the idea of 'the fatalistic logic of the unassail-able position' of French, English and Portuguese in African literature. 'What is the difference', he asks, 'between a polit-ician who says Africa cannot do without imperialism and the writer who says Africa cannot do without European languages?'

In arguing for the ascendancy of African languages in African literature, Ngũgĩ is not rejecting the literature of other cultures. Neither is he simply advancing a chauvinistic position. His vision for the future of African literary practice is best summar-ized by the following quotation from *Decolonising the Mind*:

Race Today

BRITAIN'S LEADING BLACK JOURNAL   DECEMBER 1986   70p

THE BLACKS IN BLUE

interviews
with black
police
officers

POLITICS & ECONOMICS
IN THE
EASTERN CARIBBEAN

Wole Soyinka
Nobel Prize Winner
on Southern Africa

Cover of *Race Today*, December 1986.

When the African writer will naturally turn to African languages for his creative imagination, the African novel will truly come into its own, incorporating into itself all features developed in different parts of Africa from the different cultures of the African peoples as well as the best progressive features of the novel or fiction developed in Asia, Latin America, Europe, America, the World.

Moreover, Ngũgĩ does not see writing in African languages as an end in itself:

Writing in our languages . . . will not itself bring about the renaissance in African cultures if that literature does not carry the content of our people's anti-imperialist struggles to liberate their productive forces from foreign control.

Ultimately then, the writer's choice of languages is a political act which depends on whom he or she is writing for. Ngũgĩ wa Thiong'o has chosen the workers and peasants of Kenya. We look forward to reading him in translation in the future.

Ngũgĩ wa Thiong'o, *Decolonising the Mind: The politics of language in African literature* (James Currey/Heinemann, 1986). **Race Today, December 1986**

Searching for Answers:
Caryl Phillips in Conversation (1987)

By far the most outstanding writer that second-generation blacks in Britain, born of West Indian parents, have so far produced is the novelist and dramatist Caryl Phillips. Born in St Kitts in 1958, he came to Britain only weeks old. He grew up in Leeds and Birmingham in 'predominantly white working-class areas, which featured skylines broken up by twenty-four blocks of flats'. Educated in 'mainly white-dominated middle-class schools', he graduated from Queen's College, Oxford in 1979 with a degree in English literature. He has written several plays for radio, stage and television including *Strange Fruit* (1981), *Where There Is Darkness* (1982) and *The Shelter* (1984), all published by Amber Lane Press. In 1985 Caryl Phillips' first novel, *The Final Passage*, published by Faber and Faber, won the Malcolm X Award; his second and latest, *A State of Independence*, was published last year. His first collection of essays, *The European Tribe*, will be published shortly. Below he talks to Linton Kwesi Johnson about the forces which led him to literature and the experiences which have helped to shape the characters of his fiction.

LINTON KWESI JOHNSON: Coming to Britain only months old, your experience of St Kitts was nil until you started going back for vacation.

CARYL PHILLIPS: Funnily enough, up until 1979 when I left university, St Kitts was in my mind as somewhere where my parents were from. I think the crisis, the desperation to discover the Caribbean was forged in me whilst I was at university, because the '76 riots happened then and there were the disturbances in '77. In fact, during those three years, there was a lot of social ferment. I remember watching a film by Menelik Shabazz in the common room. It was a documentary he had on in '78. I forget the title, but it was a film about my experience and the environment in which I was watching it was this common room in this rarefied and super-traditional college atmosphere. It caused, as the three years progressed, a tugging at my heartstrings, a desire to discover how on earth I'd landed in this place. The papers I was reading, the debate I was interested in, had nothing to do with the academic climate any more. There was more and more an urgency about my generation finding a voice. I decided that when I left college I wanted to write, but as a tandem to that I'd have to go to the Caribbean and begin to piece my identity that way.

LKJ: But what led you to literature?

CP: Well, I don't know, because I didn't really have any interest in literature over and above an academic one. I was good at literature at school. I was good at literature at university. In fact, I didn't go to university to study literature, I went to do neurophysiology and psychology. But I switched

Horace Ove

Searching
for Answers

Caryl Phillips in Conversation with Linton Kwesi Johnson

Cutting from LKJ's interview with Caryl Phillips,
Race Today Review, 1987

after a year, because I found the work boring. And then again there was the kind of crisis of being away from black people, because the black people at Oxford were largely Black Americans or Africans. There were very few people from the Caribbean. There were very few people who were Black British. There was no sense of a community, and I suppose the strength of identity that the Africans had about where they were from, the strength of identity that the Black Americans had again served to accentuate the fragility of my own grasp of what it means to be a black person in Britain at this time. I began to try and find out the answers in books. Not the books I was supposed to do on the syllabus. And I found a kind of dearth of material around me, I didn't find the answers. So, I suppose the combination of my reading literature and not finding the answers in the books that I needed led me to decide that I wanted to write.

The first play I wrote was *Strange Fruit*. It is about two [black] youngsters in Britain, one of whom had gone back to the Caribbean, to his grandfather's funeral, and discovered a whole lot of things about himself and his family and his past, which threw into relief what was happening in Britain. I think that that play in a sense was a microcosm of my own dilemma.

LKJ: If I remember rightly, one of the brothers in *Strange Fruit* went to the Caribbean and came back to England very disturbed, very angry.

CP: I felt that some of the things which that guy discovered in the Caribbean changed his attitude to what was happening here. He felt that, in a sense, he'd been nurtured with ideas and dreams, fed information that wasn't the whole story and wasn't fully relevant to dealing with here. However, at the very end of the play, there is a sort of touching moment where he does pack his bag and leave and decide that he has to piece together his own appreciation of what it means to be in Britain. But he goes over and kisses his mother, who's asleep, and he leaves a photograph – I mean, it's not a complete rejection. His return [from the Caribbean] meant that there would be a new beginning, a new kind of independent assessment. And in a sense that mirrored my development.

LKJ: What about *Where There Is Darkness*, what were you trying to say in that play? Albert, the main character, comes over as a fellow who is bitter about life in general.

CP: Well, Albert, perhaps more than most characters, perhaps more than any character I've ever written, is based upon a brief time I spent doing some research. I got to know a couple of guys from the Commission for Racial Equality who, unfortunately, reminded me of Albert. They had become race relations professionals who were actually functionaries of the state. They were trying to be the moral keepers of the black community. And their whole personal life was completely and utterly at odds with their professional life, because their behaviour personally and their behaviour morally bore no resemblance to the professional facade. And it was out of observing one guy, in particular, in that race relations industry, that I began to build up a picture of a man who could have come over here as a railway worker or as a transport worker of some sort, worked his way up – via the various changes, political changes and promotions and so on that had been afforded to black people in the sixties and seventies and was basically, to be crude about it, still the same hustler that arrived off the boat in the sixties but just had a suit. I don't believe that Alberts don't exist, I think they do exist. I don't think that the quality of self-disgust which is manifested in the thing should be underestimated, because I think there are a lot of people in the black community who do have very ambivalent feelings about not only their actions, but about themselves. I mean, they're not sure any more who they are.

LKJ: Albert, though, sort of comes over as a kind of tragic character because, in the end, all this bile . . .

CP: . . . is self-consuming.

LKJ: Well, it does sort of destroy him in the end.

CP: Yeah, I think so, because the Alberts of this world, to me they're to be pitied more than they're to be kind of grappled with as a serious problem. They're to be pitied because eventually they will self-explode. They certainly have no political base in the black community, and they certainly have no moral base. They are tragic, I suppose, because they are a waste, a waste in every sense.

LKJ: Now, let's go to your other play, *The Shelter*. Can you just briefly describe it?

CP: Yeah, *The Shelter*'s a play in two acts, which picks up one of the more controversial elements, I suppose you could say, of *Where There Is Darkness*, which is the relationship between the black man and a white woman, him and his wife. I'd always been sort of fascinated by the whole notion of inter-racial marriage in this country and the taboo which is fostered around it, and I wanted to write a play which was about that, in a sense, and which perhaps drew on some of the historical reasons for the fear and the loathing which the relationship often provokes in people. The first half, the first act of the play, is set in the mid-eighteenth century on a desert island, where a black man and a white woman . . .

LKJ: Is it a kind of a Prospero–Caliban?

CP: Yeah, a similar sort of thing, exactly. They happen to have been washed up on this shore. We discover that they were on a ship that was on its way to probably Sierra Leone at the time. And they talk and it's about him trying to build a shelter for them, 'cos they have to spend the night there. The second act is set in a pub off Ladbroke Grove in the fifties and it's a black guy, same actor and actress, who as they talk we discover that she's pregnant with his child, but he's only been in the country a couple of years and he can't possibly stay any longer and he wants to go back now. He's had enough. And it's about their relationship right at the start of what became, if you like, a resurgence of the taboo of that relationship again with immigration. The motivating force for the second piece is that I was reading about the 1958 riots in Notting Hill and, apparently, one of the incidents which sparked off the riots was a black man in a pub with a white woman who – the pair of them – were subjected to abuse and the black man either pushed or punched somebody. That wasn't the only incident, but that was apparently one of the contributory incidents. And then that gave me a setting for the second act of the play.

LKJ: Let's leave your plays alone for the time being and go

on to your award-winning novel, *The Final Passage*. The title suggests the final stage of a long journey from Africa to Britain via the Caribbean. Did you set out to write a novel about Caribbean migration to Britain, and the experiences of early migrants, or were you just simply trying to tell an individual story, the story of a young black woman's quest for love, for meaning, for some sense of stability in her life? And in that sense the novel is not so much about migration, but more a story of about deep personal alienation.

CP: Yeah, well that's what it is. When I set out to write it, I set out to write a novel about the migratory experience. But what I find happens with my work is that it's often propelled by, if you like, social or historical themes and then the characters take over. And once the characters have taken over, which is what they should do, because it should be about people and human emotions, once they took over, say, on the first or second draft stage, then I was no longer sure about whether it was a novel about migration or whether it was a novel about the migratory struggle. That became irrelevant in a sense. So I do feel that it is the story of one woman's deep, deep alienation in a society.

LKJ: Michael (Leila's husband) comes over as a very cold, callous person who seems to have been hardened by his own biographical experiences. Were you sketching a typical or an atypical character there?

CP: No, I don't think he's typical at all. This is one of the things which people have asked continually. I mean, is the West Indian male like this? Well, the West Indian male isn't like that in the main. Michael is a guy, as you said, who is hemmed in by his own particular biographical experience. He's condemned within the framework of the book quite strongly. I mean, his very best friend threatens to beat him up. Yet often I've found critical feedback on the book has ignored the fact that his best friend is a hellishly responsible man who, when his girlfriend becomes pregnant, not only marries her, you know, he moves into the shop with her and begins his business, settles down, goes to church with his wife. So there are two sides. I mean, Michael may be the sort of dominant character in terms of space and time in the novel, but he's certainly not morally.

LKJ: In a sense, he seems to share Leila's dilemma, this quest for meaning and fulfilment in life.

CP: Well, I think that's what drags them both together in the end, because they're both ambitious and they're both impatient. And often what may appear to be opposites, in the sense that Leila's very quiet and Michael's very boisterous – when we first meet him he's sitting there pissed outside of some bar – there's enough about them, which, you know, like poles attract, opposite poles attract each other sometimes, and there is that element of fate about the relationship. But you see time and time again people who you think, 'Jesus, these people should not be together because they're different.' They get together and after a couple of years the whole thing mashes up. But people do find that in each other. The other half of their personality which isn't perhaps developed. The noisy half or the quiet half.

LKJ: Michael comes over as a similar sort of character to Albert in *Where There Is Darkness*.

CP: Yeah – you see, I wrote *Where There Is Darkness* about three years before I wrote *The Final Passage*, and looking back now, I can see in both *Strange Fruit* and *Where There Is Darkness* seeds of what would eventually emerge in *The Final Passage*. In a way, Leila (the mother in *The Final Passage*) could be the mother in *Strange Fruit* – because she already has one son, she's pregnant and she has no husband. In the play we don't know what happened to the husband, except that we know he's not around. We find out eventually. So, in a sense, she could be a projection forward to that Leila character in *The Final Passage*, and Albert could be seen as a very early and crude depiction of what might have happened to Michael.

LKJ: The scenario that you sketch of 1950s Britain came over very convincingly. Did you do some research?

CP: Yeah, I did, because a couple of years ago I was working for a TV company with a photographer called Vanley Burke in Handsworth, and we were hoping to put together a little programme for Central TV about fifties Britain, of which he has a lot of photographs he took when he came from Jamaica. I spent a lot of time looking at old documentary footage in various BBC libraries and so on and so forth, and that fed the gaps in my mind when it came to depicting that period.

LKJ: One thing I've noticed about *The Final Passage* is that there's an awful lot of narrative compared to dialogue.

CP: Yeah, well, it was – I think it was also partly an attempt to prove to myself that I'd made good use of my research, if you see what I mean, because I did go to St Kitts a lot. I mean, I do go a hell of a lot now, but certainly in those first couple of years when I couldn't afford to go, I still made it my business to find a way to go and to sit and to think, look and to describe and to make copious notes on the flora and the fauna and all of that, so that when I did come to write this novel, I would be able to describe the places as though I'd had a first-hand knowledge of it rather than a research knowledge. And similarly, with the fifties thing, I'd watched so much film and I used to make my notes as the film was going through.

LKJ: Let's talk about your latest novel, *A State of Independence*. It tells the story of Bertram, a bright student who left the Caribbean to study here in Britain, but didn't make a go of it. After some years he returns to his native island with hopes of establishing a business, but finds that everything has changed, including his old school friend, Jackson, now a leading politician.

CP: Well again, Bertram came out of my experience of seeing guys coming back to the Caribbean, usually with a wife and maybe a couple of kids, to see if they can live there. I mean, it's something which I've noticed in the last few years. Because a lot of West Indian guys in this country are now reaching the stage where their kids are grown up. If they have a job they're beginning to work their way into the structure of the society. They have a terraced house somewhere that's now empty, just them and their wife. And they're beginning to think, well, maybe now's the time. We came for five years, we've been here twenty-five, the kids are grown up, they have this country. We should perhaps think about a return. And I've sat with guys in Antigua and in Barbados and in St Kitts particularly who are going through a crisis. They've got, say, a few more days left before they go back and they don't know yet whether or not to sell their house and to make this the break. And that's what *A State of Independence* came out of. Grafted onto that was the other experience which I had, the good fortune, I suppose to be there in 1983 when St Kitts became independent. And I witnessed the birth of that island, if you like, as an independent, inverted commas, entity. And it was those two factors that I wanted to write a short novel about.

LKJ: Would you say that the character Jackson, the arrogant, middle-class sort of fellow, is typical of today's Caribbean politicians?

CP: Well, one of the disappointments for me, in a sense, is the political leadership afforded most of the countries in the Caribbean, with the exception of Cuba, off the top of my head. Because I do find that a whole generation of Caribbean leaders have lined their pockets and they've emptied the coffers of the country. I also think that they've done nothing to establish any kind of independent status for those countries. I mean, they've moved swiftly from one period of British colonialism to a new period of American colonialism. They've neglected to forge any kind of political links with Africa or with Asia. I just find them a disappointment, quite frankly, and the worship of America has placed the Caribbean in real danger of becoming just an extension of the Miami Florida Keys. And that to me is a tragedy. And, of course, the question of interdependence is at least a beginning. And I am generally disappointed with the leadership in the Caribbean, and Jackson, I suppose, the character of Jackson, is evidence of my disappointment.

LKJ: When I read *A State of Independence* I thought to myself, this is the first part of a possible trilogy. I mean, you're left wondering, what's happened to Bertram, you know? How does he make out?

CP: Well, there might well be another. I'm being canny, because I have thought hard about it. I really seriously thought hard about it and I'll do even more thinking. It is left, I mean the novel is left, there's no doubt – I got a review from America the other day which said as much. It's left too soon. The reviewer said it's the only novel she's read in ten years which is too short and I have to say more about Bertram, whether or not I say it more about him and his predicament and the predicament of the nation, using the same character, or whether by waiting and see some different characters in the book. I don't know yet. But you're absolutely right, the story isn't over at the end of the novel.

LKJ: What are you working on now?

CP: I have two pieces coming out quite soon, one is a film called *Playing Away* set in Britain, and a lot of it is set in Brixton. It's quite a humorous film in a way, but I didn't actually set out for it to be humorous. It's a film about a cricket team from Brixton who get invited to play a Third World Aid Week game in an English village in Suffolk. It's about two groups of people, neither of whom really has any understanding about who the other group is. It's about West Indians in this country who grow up in the concrete jungle and don't understand that the heart of Britain is nothing to do with inner cities. I mean, the power in Britain is located in those awful places, in Suffolk and Kent and Sussex. But these guys discover a different Britain. After all this time they think, you know, Britain actually has quite a beautiful facade, rural Britain. And, of course, the English team discover a whole heap when these guys turn up.

The second piece of work, a much more serious piece of work, is a book I have coming out in February called *The European Tribe*. In 1984, just after I'd finished *The Final Passage*, I travelled from Morocco to Moscow overland on my own. It took me about nine months. And I wrote a book, which is fourteen essays about different aspects of Europe. For instance, there's an essay about James Baldwin in the south of France, there's an essay about racialism in Mitterrand's France. I was in Oslo when Desmond Tutu was getting his Nobel Prize, so there's an essay about that and what happened around that. There's an essay about meeting African students and Cubans in Moscow. The final essay is called 'The European Tribe', which is quite autobiographical. I felt that there were things that I had to say about England. There were things I had to say about growing up here, and there were things I had to say about the England of right now. And I just got kind of fed up of waiting to distil it through fiction and theatre, and I thought I really want to say this and the only form I have, of my expressing this, is to actually just step out of fiction for a moment and talk direct.

Race Today Review, 1987

Speaking in Tongues (1996)

Dictionary of Caribbean English Usage, edited by Richard Allsopp

REVIEW

The poor performance of Jamaican students in the English examinations of the Caribbean Examination Council recently prompted a leading Caribbean educationalist to call for the teaching of English as a foreign language in Jamaica. This request is not so outrageous as it seems when one considers that, whilst the official language of Jamaica and other Caribbean states of the Commonwealth is English, the vast majority of Caribbean people speak a different tongue.

Richard Allsopp's pioneering *Dictionary of Caribbean English Usage* is a timely response to this paradox. It is the first attempt at a systematic inventory of Caribbean English usage on a regional basis, covering an area with a population of six million speakers, stretching from Belize to the Bahamas to Guyana.

The vocabulary of Caribbean English, he says, consists of a 'core' of English words with inputs from African, American, Indic, Amerindian, Chinese and European sources. Yet, as Allsopp puts it, 'the great value of the etymological investigations recorded is their demonstration that although the dialects of the British Isles . . . have played a predictable part in the development of Caribbean English, the linguistic and social forces originating particularly in sub-Saharan Africa have also played a striking part in that development; so striking indeed as to raise the question whether their influence has not been much greater'.

Another defining characteristic of Caribbean English usage is what Allsopp calls the 'functional shift', whereby words are 'converted at all levels . . . in part-of-speech and sense'. So that adjectives may functions as adverbs, nouns as adjectives, ideophones as verbs and vice versa.

There are lots of fascinating discoveries to be made here. The fruit they call 'ginnep' in Jamaica is called 'akee' in Barbados, St Lucia and St Vincent. But 'ackee' in Jamaica is an entirely different fruit, cooked with salted codfish. Again, the Jamaican might be surprised that the medicinal bush they call 'carasee' is known by the same name in the Bahamas, Barbados and the Cayman Islands, but that it is called 'bon-carailla' in Guyana and Trinidad, 'maiden bush' in Antigua, 'pomme coolie' in Dominica, 'popilolo' in Tobago and 'konkonmkouli' in St Lucia. The more nationalistic Jamaican may become indignant on discovering 'tampi', the Grenadian and Trinidadian word for marijuana, but no 'ganja', its Jamaican equivalent. And why has Jamaica been left out of the list where the word 'merino' or 'marina' is used for sleeveless vest?

It is delightful too to find modern terms like 'dub-poetry' in the dictionary, even if the definition for it is a simplistic one. Rastafarian words, which have spread largely through reggae music, are also included, albeit selectively.

But these niggles are few and in no way distract from Allsopp's considerable achievement. This important work will be welcomed by teachers and students, and by creators and consumers of Caribbean literature. It represents a tangible contribution to the Caribbean vision of self.

Richard Allsopp, ed., *Dictionary of Caribbean English Usage* (Oxford: Oxford University Press, 1996), 697pp, £50.

The Guardian, 19 April 1996

Writing Reggae: Poetry, Politics and Popular Culture (2010)

'We shall never explode Prospero's old myth
until we christen language afresh'

(GEORGE LAMMING, *THE PLEASURES OF EXILE*)[1]

'Recall and recollect Black speech'

(BONGO JERRY, 'MABRAK')[2]

At the dawn of the new millennium, with my fiftieth birthday looming, looking back on my life with feelings of nostalgia, I consoled myself by taking stock of my modest achievements as a reggae artist and kept melancholy at bay. By then I had sustained a successful career as a reggae artist on the international stage for nearly twenty-five years; my record sales to date were in seven digits; I had performed all over the world, sometimes playing to audiences of over twenty thousand or more at music festivals; some of my recordings were already seen as a part of the global reggae 'canon'. I began with the word and was already a published poet in 1977 when I began to make records. The music was not only a vehicle to take my verse to a wider audience but was organic to it, was born of it. Notwithstanding my conceit, I realize that my success in the world of popular music has more to do with the power of reggae music than the power of my verse.

133

And yet, at the dawn of the new millennium, I had earned a reputation as a poet at home and abroad, had published four books of poetry, was a part of the alternative poetry scene in Britain and Europe; my work was being taught in schools and universities, translated into Italian and German, and I was beginning to receive some critical attention. All of this I achieved on my own terms from a position of cultural autonomy. I had not sought validation from the arbiters of British poetic taste. I came to poetry through politics. In the context of the anti-colonial, anti-racist, anti-fascist and class struggles that were being waged, it was easy for a young aspiring poet like me to eschew the luxury of an aesthetic based on the notion of 'art for art's sake'. In the beginning, writing verse was for me a political act and poetry a cultural weapon in the black liberation struggle. I sought validity from the black community.

So in January 2001, when I was approached by Ellah Allfrey, then an editor at Penguin, with an invitation to compile a selection of my poems for publication in the Modern Classics list, I was at once surprised and suspicious. Yes, I had jointly published a collection, *Tings an Times*, with Bloodaxe, a mainstream publisher with an inclusivist agenda and a keen eye on the market share. My other three books were published by small independent radical and black publishing houses, Towards Racial Justice, Bogle-L'Ouverture and Race Today. So when the offer came from Penguin I wondered if it was some kind of plot to undermine my street cred. Ellah Allfrey assured me that her invitation was based on the best of motives and *Mi Revalueshanary Fren* was published in 2002 in the Modern Classics list.[3]

Needless to say, the response from the guardians of the canon of British poetry was predictable. 'Some readers may find the ushering of Linton Kwesi Johnson into the circle of immortals a little premature', mused JC in the *Times Literary Supplement*.[4] On BBC Radio Four's *World Tonight*, critic Sean O'Brien went a bit further:

> One problem is the prevalence of what might be called the expressivist fallacy, which assumes that the only function of an artist is to convey feeling. Art is something made with craft skills. It's not direct from brain to tongue. Feelings deserve to be expressed, but their expression doesn't guarantee any kind of literary success or seriousness.

Poetry editor Michael Schmidt, commenting on the same programme, was more forthright if less pretentious. He said:

> Nowadays, when you set out to promote a book, you have to promote it on news-worthiness. And so you say – this poet killed the Prime Minister, this poet swam the Channel, and you don't say this is really a great first collection, or this is really a good poet. Because great doesn't mean anything; good doesn't mean anything. What means something is news-worthiness and Linton Kwesi Johnson is newsworthy.[5]

Schmidt must have no doubt had in mind the *Daily Telegraph*'s 18 March 2002 front-page story under the headline 'Reggae radical joins Betjeman', which sounded the alarm that the fortifications had been breached.

It is not my intention to use this lecture to reply to critics and commentators. What I intend to do is to talk about the influences which have shaped my verse, the roots of my poetics, so to speak.

My Jamaican Childhood

I was born in August 1952 in the rural town of Chapelton in the parish of Clarendon, Jamaica. My parents both came from a peasant background and belonged to a generation who could no longer survive on the land. My father did odd jobs before becoming a baker. My mother did domestic work and sewed to supplement her meagre earnings. My father was illiterate and my mother's sporadic schooling ended when she was fourteen years old. My parents separated when I was seven. They both went their own way to Kingston in search of better opportunities, and my older sister Eva and I were sent to live with our maternal grandmother, Miss Emmy. My grandmother was a subsistence farmer and a widow. She lived in a village called Sandy River at the foot of the Bull Head Mountain, not far from James Hill, the birthplace of Claude McKay, the pioneering poet and novelist. Many years after leaving Jamaica I was able to relive aspects of my Jamaican childhood reading McKay's *My Green Hills of Jamaica*.[6]

My grandmother was illiterate but steeped in Jamaica's rich oral culture. Apart from schoolbooks and the mobile library that passed through Sandy River on rare occasions, the only book in my grandmother's house was the Bible, King James Version. My grandmother was a member of the Staceyville

Baptist church and I was required to read to her from time to time. She was particularly fond of the Psalms, Proverbs and the Songs of Solomon. I grew to like the language of those books of the Old Testament and regular reading of them was my first immersion in written verse. I say written verse, but the Bible is in fact part of Jamaica's oral tradition. It is not uncommon to find illiterate Jamaicans who can quote passages from the Bible. Everyday speech in Jamaica often has Biblical references. In fact, the lyricism of Jamaican reggae and dance-hall music is full of Biblical language and allusions. Bob Marley's 'Small Axe', for example, begins:

> Why boasteth thyself O evil man
> Playing smart but not being clever
> You're working iniquity to achieve vanity
> If a soh a soh
> But the goodness of Jah-Jah I-dureth for I-ver[7]

Psalm 52 begins 'Why boastest thou thyself in mischief, O mighty man? the goodness of God endureth continually./ Thy tongue deviseth mischiefs; like a sharp razor, working deceitfully'.[8]

Reggae deejay Big Youth's 'I Pray Thee' is similarly a rendition of Psalm number 2, drum and bass style:

> I pray thee
> Why do the heathen rage and the people imagine a
>   vain thing?
> The Kings of the earth set themselves

And the rulers take counsel together
Against the Lord God Jah Rastafarai and against his
    anointed, saying
'Come let us break their bands asunder
And cast away the cords from us'[9]

Another reggae deejay, the late Prince Far I, also has a version of Psalm 2 on an album consisting entirely of reggae renditions of psalms, drum and bass style.[10] The Guyanese literary critic Gordon Rohlehr, commenting on the religious basis of Jamaican folk-urban culture in the early 1970s, asserted: 'It is difficult today to separate religious music from the music of open rebellion'.[11] As the recordings of contemporary Jamaican dancehall artists like Buju Banton, Anthony B, Capelton and others illustrate, Rohlehr's observation holds as true today as it did over thirty years ago.

I began attending Chapelton All Age School when I was six years old, staying there for about a year before moving to Sandy River, where I attended Staceyville All Age School up to the age of eleven before leaving for London. We were taught nonsense rhymes and other nursery rhymes and poetry parrot-fashion. Some of those rhymes left an impression on my mind, such as:

Labour for learning before you grow old
For learning is better than silver and gold
Silver and gold will vanish away
But a good education will never decay

and:

> Good, better, best
> Never let it rest
> Until your good is better
> And your better best.

All I can remember of the poems are two lines about the wind: 'O wind a blowing all day long/ O wind that sings so loud a song'. I also remember an image from the poem of the wind lifting a lady's skirt. What did leave a lasting impression was the oral culture into which I was socialized from birth: folk songs, work songs, sacred songs, Anansi and duppy stories, riddles, skipping rhymes, word games, ring games and proverbs.

Sandy River, my mother's place of birth, was almost untouched by modernity. There were no asphalted streets, piped water, electricity or public transport. People walked for miles or rode donkeys. The social life of the village revolved around the Baptist church or the two grocery/rum shops. In the absence of radio and television, children created their own entertainment, and sometimes we would be entertained by adults, especially grandparents, on moonlit nights and at wakes. My grandmother was an accomplished teller of Anansi stories that made you laugh and duppy stories that gave you nightmares and made you even more afraid of the pitch black night. Sometimes my grandmother would entertain my sister and me with riddles that delighted and stimulated the imagination. 'John Brown dead and bury long time but him body never rotten. What is that?' my grandmother would ask. When my sister and I finally gave up after a number of wrong guesses, she would answer, 'Noh glass bottle, glass can't rotten!' Or she would ask: 'Look under mi skin, yu si mi hair; look under mi hair, yu si mi seed; look under me seed, yu si mi wood. What is that?' Wood in Jamaican Creole is also a word for penis and seed is testicle. However, I would not dare let my grandmother know what I was thinking and would reply, 'Mi no know.' My grandmother's answer would be, 'Noh corn!' When you remove the skin from the corn, you see the hair, when you remove the hair, there is the seed, and once you remove the seed the husk or the 'wood' is what remains.

There were times when I was misbehaving, or 'a faam fool' as my grandmother would put it, and she would give me a coded warning, in the form of a proverb, to cease. She would say in a serious tone, 'Fire deh a muss-muss tail him tink a cool breeze' (there's fire at the mouse's tail but it thinks it's a cool breeze blowing). I knew at once that if I did not stop whatever I was doing, the consequence would be serious. Or she would say, 'Chicken merry hawk deh near' (the chicken is merry but the hawk is near), another coded warning. We children knew about the wide-winged hawk that would hover, then suddenly swoop down and steal a recently hatched chick pecking in the yard. Children played a chase game based on this hunter-and-hunted scenario, which involved the use of call and response. Whoever was 'it' would be the hawk/crier and the others would be the chicks/chorus. The chicks would stand in line, one behind the other, with the hawk facing them.

The hawk would pretend to be a human calling the chicks for feeding, pointing to this chick or that one, improvising description based on physical attributes or dress. The hawk speaks first and the chicks reply:

HAWK: chick chick chick
CHICKS: mi noh waan no cawn
HAWK: chick chick chick
CHICKS: mi noh waan no cawn
HAWK: yu si da long neck wan deh
CHICKS: mek im tan
HAWK: yu si da red head wan deh
CHICKS: mek im tan
HAWK: yu si da sore foot wan deh
CHICKS: mek im tan
HAWK: yu si da dry head wan deh
CHICKS: mek im tan

Then the hawk would say, 'Peehaw di hawk is coming!' at which point the chicks would scatter in all directions. The hawk would give chase and whichever chick was caught would become 'it' and the game would start all over again.

Many ring games and word games involve the use of call and response. In 1983 I had the pleasure of joining the honourable Louise Bennett, aka Miss Lou, actress, educator, folklorist and mother of Jamaican dialect poetry, on stage during one of her rare London concerts at the Lyric Theatre in Hammersmith. We performed a word game called 'Mawnin Buddy' together. There are several variations of this game:

Mawnin buddy/ mi noh buddy fi yu

Den a who den?/ Missah tennah

Which tennah?/ Tennah saw

Which saw?/ Sakah Bya

Which Bya?/ Bya flash

Which flash?/ Flash cord

Which cord?/ Cord Bennett

Which Bennett?/ Mistah Bennett

Is a man who go roun di toun

Who play di fiddle fi di lickle gal Rosie Bentical

Fimi like a fimi gyal

Woae cow/ Noh buck

Woae haas/ Noh bite

A whey mi have a whey mi gi mi gyal[12]

The call and response structure is common to many Jamaican folk songs, especially digging songs. One digging song that rural Jamaicans of my generation know is 'One Shut Mi Gat' ('The Only Shirt I Have' or 'My Only Shirt'):

One shut mi gat

Ratta cut it

Some place it cut

Mumma dawn it

Some place it dawn

Fire bun it

Some place it bun

Teacha lick mi

Teacha lick mi an mi kin right ovah

Teacha lick mi an mi kin right ovah
Teacha lick mi an mi kin right ovah.

In the late 1970s the deejay Jah Lloyd, aka Jah Lion, recorded a reggae version of this song where the hapless rural persona of the song is urbanized and becomes poor I natty dread from Trench Town. One of the interesting things about Jamaican popular music is the fact that the lyricists are constantly drawing from the folk tradition, updating it and keeping it alive. The late Jamaican poet Michael (Mikey) Smith was adept at bringing elements of Jamaican oral culture into his poetry.

I once talked to a class of predominantly black children at St Jude's Junior School in my neighbourhood in south London. I was giving them an example of a skipping rhyme I remembered from my childhood in Jamaica. So I began, 'Maskitta one,' and to my surprise all the girls joined in with, 'Maskitta two/ maskitta jump inna hat calalou' (calalou is Jamaican greens, like spinach). Was this an example of Louise Bennett's 'colonisation in reverse?', I asked myself.[13] When I was a boy in Jamaica, skipping was mostly a girls' pastime, but there were always boys who joined in. I was one of them. My favourite skipping rhythm was:

One two three
Aunty Luelu
Four five six
Aunty Luelu
Seven eight nine
Aunty Luelu

Ten Aunty Luelu
Ten Aunty Luelu
Ten Aunty Luelu

Another element of Jamaica's folk culture that I experienced as a boy was music of the fife and drum. On public holidays like Emancipation Day, Christmas and Easter, there would be festivities in the village square: maypole dancing, merry-go-round and fife and drum music. There were also times when I could stand in the village square and hear strains of pocomania drums of the Revivalist church. I also remember hearing a mento band playing at a wedding reception. Like many boys in Sandy River, during the holiday festivities I would make my own bamboo fife using a hot piece of nail-like metal to bore the holes. I also used to make my own drum using a discarded butter or milk can with a piece of old cloth tied on for the skin. I would rub mud and green bush on the skin to chord the drum to get the right pitch. Another boy would make a bamboo guitar and three or four of us would get together with our rude instruments and get into the groove.

So, by the time I left Jamaica in 1963, aged eleven years, I was immersed in and had absorbed significant aspects of Jamaica's culture. I brought my Jamaican roots to Britain with me and they took to British soil. When I began to write verse and make music, it was this grounding in the cultural creativity of the Jamaican peasantry, my cultural heritage, that provided me with an artistic orientation. It is what I began with.

Finding Myself in Britain

The Britain that I grew up in during the 1960s and early 1970s bears little resemblance to Tony Blair's so-called 'cool Britannia' of multiculturalism, now apparently in crisis. Even a decade after the Notting Hill and Nottingham race riots of 1958–9, Britain was still a decidedly racially hostile place for non-whites. Racial abuse was commonplace, racial discrimination rife, racist and fascist attacks rampant. There was not an institution of the state not riddled with racial prejudice, none more so than the police and the judiciary, who together ensured the criminal-ization of a significant section of my generation of black youth. Members of the Flying Squad, it was said, were rewarded with a tie with an ace of spades logo on it after they had put a certain number of blacks behind bars. Black children were routinely sent to schools for the educationally sub-normal – ESN schools. Teachers had low expectations of black students, which in turn gave some of us low expectations of ourselves. The colour bar was alive and well.

It is in this context that the Caribbean cultural heritage that we brought to Britain, which our parents had begun to institu-tionalize, was crucial in forging an autonomous cultural identity. Building on the foundation laid by our parents, the black youth of my generation developed a subculture of resistance to racial oppression. The nexus of this subculture was ska, rocksteady and reggae, the rebel music of the youth of post-colonial Jamaica, influenced by the liberation philosophy of the black conscious-ness movement and the ideology of Rastafari. The reggae music coming from Jamaica spoke to our condition in Britain. When Burning Spear asked in a song, 'Do you remember the days of slavery?';[14] when Junior Byles declared, 'I an I goin beat down babylon';[15] when Bob Marley asked, 'Where is the love to be found/ in disya concrete jungle';[16] and when Peter Tosh asserted, 'You can't blame the youth',[17] there were resonances in these songs for Britain's black youth. Reggae music from Jamaica not only spoke to our condition here, it was the umbilical cord that kept us connected to our roots, reinvigorating our language with the street talk of Kingston's rude boys and the dread talk of Rastafari. With its Rastafarian influence, reggae was a source of spiritual nourishment. We also embraced African-American r&b and soul music, especially those that spoke to our experience, like James Brown's 'Say It Loud, I'm Black and I'm Proud', Sly Johnson's 'Is It Because I'm Black', Curtis Mayfield and The Impressions' 'People Get Ready', The Temptations' 'Power to the People' and Marvin Gaye's 'What's Going On'. But reggae was *our* music.

I bought my first record when I was about fifteen years old. In those days the music coming out of Jamaica was rocksteady. Within a year it had changed to reggae. A couple of school friends and I started up a little sound system at our youth club in Brixton. I was already a keen student of the music when I became a sociology undergraduate at Goldsmiths College. I wrote my dissertation on the sociology of reggae lyricism. I wrote two essays on Jamaican popular music: 'Jamaican Rebel Music'[18] and 'The Politics of the Lyrics of Reggae Music',[19] published in the mid-1970s. In 1982 I researched, wrote and presented a ten-part series on the history of reggae for BBC Radio One.

LKJ's student ID, Goldsmiths College 1973–6.

The African-American poet Amiri Baraka (formerly LeRoi Jones) has talked about the centrality of the blues to his conception of poetry, to his poetics. Baraka says,

> I got my understanding of words . . . from the use of words and music . . . If you listen to the blues, particularly *talking blues*, even in urban blues, you'll hear people like Larry Darnell, people like that, where actually their whole blues is speaking. They don't do a lot of singing except on the choruses . . . The music was just a vehicle for the words.[20]

Baraka goes on to say that the verse was poetry, and understanding that was fundamental to his approach to poetry. He cites Langston Hughes as the first poet of the blues. Baraka says that combining jazz with poetry was, therefore, a natural thing for him to do. He adds, 'the idea of being able to speak freely over music has always connected in my mind with poetry'. When, as a teenager, I heard early talking tunes from Jamaica by people like Sir Lord Comic, Lee 'Scratch' Perry and Prince Buster, I made the same connection.

Prince Buster was the master of these talking tunes. Buster's rap would sometimes take the form of a dialogue, introducing a theatrical element into the music; at other times he would use monologue. 'The Ten Commandments' is a straight narrative over a ska backing, where Buster adapts the laws of the Old Testament for a secular purpose from a decidedly male chauvinist perspective:

This is the ten commandments of man
Given to woman
Through the inspiration of I
Prince Buster
One:
Thou shall have no other man but me.[21]

'Ghost Dance' (aka 'Tribute to the Toughest') takes the form of a letter, addressed to the narrator's departed friend, somewhere in the underworld, named Boneyard:

Dear Keithus my friend
Good day
Hoping you're keeping the best of health
How is the music down there
In boneyard?[22]

The third example is Prince Buster's best-known talking tune, 'Judge Dread'. The immediate post-independence period in Jamaica saw the emergence of a generation of disillusioned and rebellious youth and a rise in lawlessness. The rudie/rude boy became a topic of many rocksteady recordings. One of the most popular was Derrick Morgan's 'Tougher than Tough', which celebrates the rudie. Morgan sings:

Rudies don't fear no boy
Rudies don't fear
Rougher than rough
Tougher than tough

Strong like lion
We are iron[23]

Prince Buster's 'Judge Dread' is a reply to Derrick Morgan's 'Tougher than Tough' – a corrective. Judge Dread, otherwise known as Judge Hundred Years, has come 'from Ethiopia to try all you rude boys for shooting black people':

Order, Now my court is in session.
Will you please stand.
First, allow me to introduce myself
My name is Judge Hundred Years
Some people call me Judge Dread
Now I am from Ethiopia
To try all you rude boys
For shooting black people
In my court only me talk
Cause I'm vex
I am the rude boy today[24]

Prince Buster's reply to 'Tougher than Tough' was an instalment in an ongoing lyrical war with Derrick Morgan, which began with Buster's 'Black Head Chinaman' and Morgan's riposte, 'Blazing Fire'. Both 'Black Head Chinaman' and 'Judge Dread' reflect Prince Buster's black nationalism. In 'Judge Dread', the fact that he has come from Ethiopia, the birthplace of Haile Selassie, the Rasta God, and the cradle of black civilization, adds moral authority and weight to Judge Hundred Years' credentials. Buster's black nationalism prefigures the black consciousness ethos that was to become a hallmark of roots reggae.

The Emergence of Dub Poetry

That was 1967. By the early seventies a new lyrical genre had emerged called toasting or deejay music, known today as dance-hall or ragga. This new style of verbalization evolved from the rhythmic utterances of the disc jockey over the microphone, spurring on the revellers in the dancehall. The spontaneous improvisations of the deejay toaster were transferred from the dancehall to the recording studio. From the early jive-talk of people like Sir Lord Comic with his 'I was walking down Orange Street/ Trying to get some life in my feet/ Cause I got music in my teeth' emerged a distinctive lyrical genre.[25] The advent of multi-track recording and the introduction of sound effects like echo and reverb facilitated the emergence of a particular style, a sub-genre of reggae if you like, called dub. Dub is the recording engineers' art of deconstruction, where a reggae composition is stripped down to its drum and bass skeletal structure and reconfigurated, recreated, with fragments of other instruments, enhancing the danceability of the music. This recreated minimalist rhythmic structure provided the perfect background for the deejay/toaster to hone his lyrical skills. Some examples of the lyricism of the deejay/toaster are Prince Jazzbo's 'Prophet Live', Yellowman's 'Gun Man' and Peter King's 'Me Neat Me Sweet'.[26]

For me this was a most exciting development in reggae which constituted a new form of oral poetry, something akin to the

griot tradition in Africa which I variously called 'dub-lyricism'
and 'dub-poetry'. I also used the term dub-poetry to describe
some of the poetry of Oku Onuora when I reviewed his book
Echo, published under his former name Orlando Wong, in *Race
Today* in 1977.[27] That is how the term came into currency in
the 1980s for the new movement of orality in Jamaican poetry;
and Oku Onuora was responsible for that. In a footnote to my
article 'Jamaican Rebel Music' I describe the art of the reggae
deejay like this:

> The 'dub-lyricist' is the deejay turned poet. He intones his
> lyrics rather than sings them. Dub-lyricism is a new form of
> (oral) music-poetry, wherein the lyricist overdubs rhythmic
> phrases on the rhythm background of a popular song.
> Dub-lyricists include poets like Big Youth, I Roy, U-Roy,
> Dillinger, Shorty, Prince Jazzbo and others.[28]

Poetry and Politics

I have said before that I came to poetry through politics. As
a teenager in the late sixties I was swept along in the tidal
wave of black consciousness that came in the wake of the civil
rights movement in the USA. I joined the British Black Panther
Movement and discovered black literature. Discovering books
written by black authors about black people was a revelation
to me, because nothing in my schooling in the UK had given
me the slightest hint that such a body of writing existed. I
am a slow reader but I read as avidly as I could: history,

politics, philosophy and creative writing. I didn't understand a lot of what I read but one book in particular left a deep and lasting impression on me: *The Souls of Black Folk* by W. E. B. Du Bois.[29] One sentence that registered on my consciousness was when he wrote about the problem of the twentieth century being about the problem of the colour line. Du Bois wrote movingly about the 'shadow of the veil' that blighted black life in the USA. What I found amazing about this was that Du Bois was making those observations at the dawning of the twentieth century. Moreover, although Du Bois had written about the experiences of African-Americans in the immediate post-emancipation period, I could relate what I read to my own experience. *The Souls of Black Folk* changed my life. It awakened something within me and I felt an urgent need to express myself, to articulate my thoughts and feelings about the black experience in Britain. That is how my engagement with poetry began.

One of the first books of poems I read was a thin volume of African-American poetry simply titled *Black Poetry*.[30] The twenty-five poets featured included Arna Bontemps, Gwendolyn Brooks, Countee Cullen, Langston Hughes, LeRoi Jones (aka Amiri Baraka), Claude McKay, Sonia Sanchez, Don L. Lee and Margaret Walker. I was immediately struck by the range of style, form, language and themes: from the sonnets of McKay and Countee Cullen, the lyrical elegance of Jean Toomer, Dudley Randall's wit, Brooks' powerful call to action, Jones' unusual diction and Lee's hip street language. *Black Poetry* whetted my appetite for poetry and set me on a journey of discovery. In the Black Panther Movement I got a chance to

LKJ at Lou Rose's tailor's shop in Brixton in
south London, circa 1969–70. LKJ worked
there as a teenager.

hear the recordings of The Last Poets who, like Lee, used the everyday language of black Americans as the vehicle of their poetic discourse, accompanied by drums.

Then I found out about New Beacon Books, Britain's first black publishing house and bookshop. I had no idea at the time that New Beacon was the source of most of the black literature I had found in the Panthers. The bookshop was located in the front room of its founders, John La Rose and Sarah White, in Finsbury Park. My first visit to the shop lasted an entire afternoon, most of which was spent talking to John La Rose, one of the most remarkable people I have ever met. Through him I got to meet Andrew Salkey, the Jamaican poet, novelist and broadcaster. They both became my mentors and introduced me to a whole range of literature, including poetry by Aimé Césaire, Kamau Brathwaite, Okot p'Bitek, Christopher Okigbo, Tchicaya U Tam'si, Derek Walcott, Martin Carter and Bongo Jerry, as well as literary journals from the Caribbean like *BIM* and *Savacou*.

In 1966 Brathwaite, La Rose and Salkey founded the Caribbean Artists Movement (CAM), a unique coming together of Caribbean writers, visual and performing artists and intellectuals whose impact continues to reverberate in Britain and the Caribbean. I caught the tail-end of the movement in the early seventies. I consider myself a beneficiary of CAM's legacy; I am what the cooling embers of the movement spawned. In the preface to her book on the Caribbean Artists Movement, Anne Walmsley writes of the organization's aims and objectives:

They sought to discover their own aesthetic and to chart new directions for their arts and culture; to become acquainted with their history; to rehabilitate their Amerindian inheritance and to reinstate their African roots; to re-establish links with the 'folk' through incorporating the peoples' language and musical rhythms in Caribbean literature; to reassert their own tradition in the face of a dominant tradition.[31]

I recall attending CAM events at the Keskidee Centre in north London; meeting or just seeing people like writers Wilson Harris, George Lamming, Sam Selvon, painters Errol Lloyd, Aubrey Williams and sculptor Ronald Moody. It was around that time that I met Eric and Jessica Huntley, whose small black publishing house, Bogle-L'Ouverture, later published my second book of poems, *Dread Beat and Blood*, when no one else would. Through the literary journals *BIM* and *Savacou* I was able to get a sense of what was being written in the English-speaking Caribbean and the critical response. *Savacou* was the journal of CAM and I would look forward to getting a copy from New Beacon. *Savacou* 3/4, a special issue of new writing, much of which reflected the new black consciousness of the time, had a tremendous impact on me. Two poems by Bongo Jerry, 'Sooner or Later' and 'Mabrak', captured my imagination, perhaps because I'd heard Andrew Salkey recite them before I saw them in print. This is the start of 'Sooner or Later':

> Sooner or later.
> But mus'.

The dam going to bus' and every man will break
  out
and who will stop them?[32]

Savacou 3/4 was not well received in some quarters. The poet
Eric Roach from Trinidad and Tobago wrote an article attacking
the contents for its emphasis on blackness, singling out Bongo
Jerry's poems. Gordon Rohlehr's spirited reply to Roach in two
articles/essays, 'West Indian Poetry: Some Problems of
Assessment' and 'Afterthoughts',[33] both published in *BIM*, have
endeared me to his literary criticism. A year or two later came
Salkey's anthology of Caribbean poetry, *Breaklight*,[34] where I
read for the first time a poem by Louise Bennett called
'Colonisation in Reverse'. Other poems from that book which
stuck in my mind were 'The Song of the Banana Man' by Evan
Jones and Martin Carter's 'Poems of Shape and Motion', Tony
McNeil's 'Ode to Brother Joe', Dennis Scott's 'Uncle Time'
and Mervyn Morris' 'The Early Rebels'.

By 1972 the Black Panther Movement had become the
Black Workers Movement, signalling a shift to a politics in
pursuit of racial equality and social justice. Within a matter
of months, it disintegrated. Bereft of any organizational framework through which I could make a meaningful contribution
to revolutionary change, I became more focused on cultural
activities. My Black Panther experience had given me a solid
political grounding. We had studied Eric Williams' *Capitalism
and Slavery*, W. E. B. Du Bois' *Black Reconstruction in America*,
C. L. R. James' *The Black Jacobins*, E. P. Thompson's *The
Making of the English Working Class*, Frantz Fanon's *The*

Wretched of the Earth[35] and bits of Marx, Lenin and Mao. I was now in a better position to locate myself in the world. Finding out about CAM could not have happened at a more crucial stage of my quest for self-discovery. Then I came across a recording by Count Ossie and the Mystic Revelation of Rastafari called *Grounation*, a three-album set of Rasta drumming, singing, poetry and oratory on black history. *Grounation* blew my mind. I began to adopt the external trappings of the Rasta youth; stopped eating pork and tried unsuccessfully to grow dreadlocks. I embraced Rastafari but refused to call myself a Rasta because I could not accept the divinity of Emperor Haile Selassie. Neither could I reconcile myself to the notion of repatriation as a viable or even desirable political project. I had already rejected Christianity and Islam because of their complicity in the enslavement and colonization of black people. But there was something about the spirituality of Rastafari, its anti-colonial stance and its alternative world view, that I found alluring.

I teamed up with a group of drummers I had been at school with who were learning the art of nyabinghi drumming. They called themselves Rasta Love and I would improvise and chant my verse accompanied by them. I learned to play a bit of percussion too. The Jamaican painter and playwright Dam X (aka Stephen Hall) also joined the group. I wrote *Voices of the Living and the Dead* for voices, drums and dancers and it was staged at the Keskidee Centre in 1973, directed by the Jamaican poet and novelist Lindsay Barrett. Lindsay gave me a Ghanaian box drum which became my instrument in Rasta Love. It was from then that I began to try and find my voice for myself as a poet. Prior to that I had been writing in English, imitating whoever I happened to be reading at the time without proper absorption. Then I started to experiment with language, rhythm and form using Jamaican Creole. Having no grounding in poetry, I started with a clean slate, improvising, inventing and learning my craft as I went along. For a while I felt that my lack of formal training in the art of writing verse was a disadvantage. I was disabused of that notion by Sam Selvon, who insisted the opposite was true. Selvon told me that starting with a clean slate allowed for the possibility of originality; and he cautioned against listening to too much talk about 'proper poetry'. I told Andrew Salkey that what I was trying to do in my way was related to 'the tension between Jamaican Creole and Jamaican English and between those and English'. I think he understood what I was trying to say.

In the end I opted mostly for the language I was most comfortable with and confident in, my first language, Jamaican Creole or what Kamau Brathwaite calls 'nation language'. I made other choices too. I wanted to write poetry that was accessible to those whose experiences I was writing about, namely the black community; I wanted to write verse that was relevant, that people could relate to their everyday experience; I wanted to write oral poetry that could hold the interest of the reader as well as the listener. I heard music in language and I wanted to write word-music, verse anchored by the one-drop beat of reggae with metre measured by the bass line or a drum pattern; I wanted to write lines that sound like a bass line or a drum pattern.

Having made these choices, I embarked on my long apprenticeship in search of this elusive thing called poetry.

*

End of the original lecture
I am reliably informed that I will no longer have to bear the burden of being the only living poet on Penguin's Modern Classics list, a dubious status I acquired since the passing of Czesław Miłosz in 2004. Instead, I will be joining mere mortals like Carol Ann Duffy and Roger McGough on the more 'appropriate' Selected Poems list. I am, after all, a middle-aged Black British Caribbean poet of the 'little tradition'. Let the guardians of the 'great tradition' stand at ease.

Notes

1 Lamming, George, *The Pleasures of Exile* (London: Michael Joseph, 1960), pp. 118–19.
2 Bongo Jerry, 'Mabrak' in *Savacou* 3/4 (December 1970/March 1971), p. 15.
3 *Tings an Times* (Northumberland: Bloodaxe, 1991); *Voices of the Living and the Dead* (London: Towards Racial Justice, 1974); *Dread Beat and Blood* (London: Bogle-L'Ouverture, 1975); *Inglan is a Bitch* (London: Race Today Publications, 1980); *Mi Revalueshanary Fren* (London: Penguin, 2002).
4 JC, 'NB' in *Times Literary Supplement* (15 March 2002), p. 16.
5 BBC Radio Four, *The World Tonight* (18 March 2002).
6 McKay, Claude, *My Green Hills of Jamaica and Five Jamaican Short Stories*, ed. Mervyn Morris (Kingston, Jamaica: Heinemann Educational Books, 1979).
7 Wailers, The, 'Small Axe' on album *Burnin* (Island; ILPS9256), side 2 track 1.

8 Bible, Psalm 52 verse 1.

9 Big Youth, 'I Pray Thee' 7" 45 single (Negusa Nagast).

10 Prince Far I, 'Psalm Two' on album *Psalms For I* (Carib Gems; CGLP1002), side A track 1.

11 Rohlehr, Gordon, 'Afterthoughts' in *BIM* Vol. 14 no. 56 (Jan–June 1973), p. 230.

12 Bennett, Louise, 'Mawnin Buddy' from the LP *Yes M'Dear* (Island; ILPS9740), side 2 track 5B part 3.

13 Bennett, Louise, 'Colonisation in Reverse', *Selected Poems*, ed. Mervyn Morris (Kingston, Jamaica: Sangster's Book Stores, 1982), pp. 106-7.

14 Burning Spear, 'Slavery Days' from the LP *Marcus Garvey* (Micron Music; MM7021A), side 1 track 1.

15 Byles, Junior, 'Beat Down Babylon' from the LP *Beat Down Babylon* (Trojan; TRL52B), side 2 track 1.

16 Marley, Bob, 'Concrete Jungle' from the LP *Catch a Fire* (Island; ILPP9241), side 1 track 1.

17 Tosh, Peter, 'Can't Blame the Youth', 7" 45 single (Intel-Diplo; PT2259A).

18 Johnson, Linton Kwesi, 'Jamaican Rebel Music' in *Race & Class* (Spring 1976).

19 Johnson, Linton Kwesi, 'The Politics of the Lyrics of Reggae Music' in *The Black Liberator* (1977).

20 Baraka, Amiri, 'Talk at the Free Jazz Weekend at Penn State' in *Mixed Blood* no. 1 (2004), pp. 8–9.

21 Prince Buster, 'Ten Commandments' from the LP *Fabulous Greatest Hits* (Prince Buster; MS.1 TGI 0075), side B track 4.

22 Prince Buster, 'Ghost Dance' from *Fabulous Greatest Hits*, side B track 3.

23 Morgan, Derrick, 'Tougher than Tough' from the LP *Pressure Drop: Volume Three* (Mango; MBOX 25 3), side E track 8.

24 Prince Buster, 'Judge Dread' from *Fabulous Greatest Hits*, op. cit., side B track 1.

25 Sir Lord Comic, 'The Great Wuga' from the LP *More Intensified Volume Two – Original Ska 1963–67* (Island; IRSP3), side B track 4.

26 Listen to: Prince Jazzbo, 'Prophet Live' from the LP *Natty Passing Thru* (Black Wax Label; WAXLP 1), side A track 5; Yellowman, 'Gun Man' from the LP *Them a Mad Over Me* (J & L Records; JJo6o), side A track 3; Peter King, 'Me Neat Me Sweet' from the LP *Great British MCs* (Fashion Records; FADLPoo1), side A track 4.

27 Johnson, Linton Kwesi, 'Reviews: The New Caribbean Poets' in *Race Today* 9.7 (November/December 1977), pp. 164–6.

28 Johnson, Linton Kwesi, 'Jamaican Rebel Music', op. cit., p. 398.

29 Du Bois, W. E. B., *The Souls of Black Folk* (orig. pub. Chicago: A. C. McClurg, 1903).

30 Randall, Dudley, ed., *Black Poetry: A Supplement to Anthologies which Exclude Black Poets* (Detroit, Michigan: Broadside Press, 1969).

31 Walmsley, Anne, *The Caribbean Artists Movement, 1966–1972: A Literary and Cultural History* (London: New Beacon Books, 1992), p. xvii.

32 Bongo Jerry, 'Sooner or Later' in *Savacou* 3/4 (December 1970/March 1971), p. 12.

33 Rohlehr, Gordon, 'West Indian Poetry, Some Problems of Assessment' in *BIM* 14. 4 (1972); and 'Afterthoughts', op. cit.

34 Salkey, Andrew, ed., *Breaklight* (London: Hamish Hamilton, 1971).

35 Williams, Eric, *Capitalism and Slavery* (1944, repr. Chapel Hill: University of North Carolina Press, 1994); Du Bois, W. E. B., *Black Reconstruction in America* (1935, repr. New York: Free Press, 1998); James, C. L. R., *The Black Jacobins: Toussaint L'Ouverture and the San Domingo Revolution* (1963, repr. New York: Vintage); Thompson, E. P., *The Making of the English Working Class* (London: Victor Gollancz, 1963); Fanon, Frantz, *The Wretched of the Earth* (New York: Grove Press, 1965).

Adapted from a lecture first given as the Arthur Ravenscroft Memorial Lecture at the University of Leeds, 2005.

Jamaica Journal, **December 2010**

I & I: The Natural Mystics
by Colin Grant (2011)

Colin Grant is an engaging writer whose two books to date exhibit a rare talent for storytelling in an author of non-fiction. His first book, on the life and times of Marcus Garvey, a titan of the black liberation struggle and the founder of the black nationalist movement, was an impressive debut. Its inane title, *Negro With a Hat*, is the only disappointment. Meticulously researched, it is scholarly without being pedantic; a riveting and insightful book. We are offered not only a portrait of Garvey the man, but also a sense of the milieu that spawned him and the historical drama in which he was a main protagonist. Grant's portrayal of Garvey is sympathetic without being sentimental or sycophantic. Indeed, his penchant for irony and more than a modicum of cynicism are all too evident in his narrative. So the impression we get of Garvey from Grant is that of a great visionary leader with formidable oratorical power and a talent for organizing, who laid the foundations of the black liberation movement but, like other great men and women, was not without flaws. Garvey's impact went far beyond his native Jamaica, where he became that country's first national hero. His legacy lives on across continents.

Colin Grant has now chosen to write about three other

famous sons of Jamaica, Bunny Livingston, Bob Marley and Peter Tosh, the core members of the Wailers, who brought fame to their native land through the impact of their particular style of reggae music abroad. In his new book, *I & I: The Natural Mystics*, Grant describes the Wailers as 'a trio of extraordinary poetic and powerful natural mystics', who were instrumental in transforming 'a tiny island into a musical superpower' (*I & I*, 4).

At first glance, the title of the book seems to be a merging of two song titles: 'I and I' by Bob Dylan and 'Natural Mystic' by Bob Marley. However, it soon becomes clear that this 'I and I' refers to the Rastafarian identity of the group. Of course Grant, like Kwame Dawes in his book *Natural Mysticism: Towards a New Reggae Aesthetic* (Leeds: Peepal Tree, 1999), is alluding to Bob Marley's song 'Natural Mystic', which echoes Bob Dylan's 'Blowin' in the Wind'. Marley's song is a statement of faith, a belief in the existence of a supernatural force or forces in which the answers to troubling questions like the persistence of oppression, injustice and other unfathomable perplexities of human existence can be found. For Dawes, Marley's songs 'articulate the indissoluble connections between the natural world [. . .] and the mystical' (Dawes, 19). Grant argues persuasively that Marley's cosmological orientation was something shared by all three members of the Wailers. He writes, 'The youthful Tosh was to share with Livingston and Marley the conception that life was a constant duel between good and evil abroad in the land' (Grant, *I & I*, 31). The triumvirate shared rural roots steeped in African spirituality and Christianity. Tosh, whose father was a part-time preacher, was raised by his great-aunt and uncle, who were devout Christians; Marley's maternal grandfather was a healer of the African Myal cult; and Livingston's father was a shepherd healer of the African-orientated Revivalist Christian sect.

Unlike Livingston, who was raised by both parents, Marley and Tosh grew up fatherless. Livingston and Marley were neighbours and schoolmates. All three were musically inclined from an early age, with Tosh the more musically advanced, having learned to play the piano at an early age. The key factor that brought the three youngsters together was migration from countryside to town, Marley with his mother, Livingston with his parents and Tosh to live with an aunt and later an uncle. They all settled in Trench Town in West Kingston, the destination of many rural migrants at the time and a hub of cultural creativity. According to Grant, 'The three boys, having recently arrived from the country, appear to have lived a feral existence at this phase of their lives' (45).

They were mentored by the late Joe Higgs, then a young singer resident in Trench Town, who teamed them up with three other young hopefuls to form a group called The Teenagers in 1962. A year later they secured a recording deal with Studio One boss Clement Dodd, and became the Wailing Wailers – later simply The Wailers – without the other three members of The Teenagers. Grant charts the vicissitudes of The Wailers' career, their lack of financial success with various local record producers, their attempts at autonomous production, the setting up of their own individual record labels as solo artists, and their eventual breakthrough, securing a contract with Island Records, then owned by Jamaican entrepreneur

Chris Blackwell. We learn of the circumstances surrounding the dissolution of The Wailers as they were poised for international success, and the role of Blackwell in that debacle. The final chapter of the book covers the tragic death of Bob Marley from cancer and the murder of Peter Tosh.

Given the paucity of facts about the early lives of the trio, Grant has pulled off a remarkable feat in the telling of their individual stories. He manages to give us some idea of their individual characters. Livingston emerges as taciturn, spiritual, judgemental, shrewd; Marley seems to be driven, focused, pragmatic; whilst Tosh comes across as confrontational, militant, witty and a little paranoid. Grant skilfully interweaves anecdote, biographical details and reportage with context in his telling of the stories of The Wailers. Although he employs some narrative devices of a novelist, the structure of his narrative is sociological. *I & I: The Natural Mystics* is as much about the milieu that produced The Wailers as it is about the group. The bulk of the book is contextualization, historical, cultural, social and political.

Grant's point of departure is the island-wide rebellion of sugar workers in Jamaica in 1938 at the Tate & Lyle factory in Frome, which set in motion the formation of a labour movement, the formation of political parties and the granting of adult suffrage in 1944, the year Peter Tosh (the eldest Wailer) was born. Grant asserts that 'Nothing was the same after Frome. The early lives of the young boys who would become the Wailers were defined by the fallout from that rebellion' (*I & I*, 7). The topics explored by Grant's roving pen include education, urbanization, religion, migration, entertainment, race, class, sexual mores and politics. Marcus Garvey's reinterment in Jamaica and his elevation to national hero is treated with barely disguised cynicism. The emergence of the Rastafarian movement and the persecution of Rastafarians is documented, so too the use of marijuana. Another topic to which Grant gives much attention is the widespread practice of obeah, suppressed and outlawed in colonial times as African witchcraft.

Grant's contextualizing is at times so detailed that it drifts to digression. His anecdote about a meeting with a self-taught sculptor is an example; so too is the account of two randy geriatric Jamaicans discussing their current sexual exploits. Thankfully there are not too many of these moments of comic relief. Occasionally, Grant adopts a moralizing tone of gener- alization, as when he claims that 'wife or girlfriend beating was a common pastime in Jamaica' (*I & I*, 76). Although he gives us some insights into the Jamaican recording industry during the first decade of The Wailers' career, we are not offered a sense of what was happening musically in Jamaica and are, for example, left wondering: what were some of the popular tunes of the decade after independence; who were some of the main rivals of The Wailers; what was the role of radio; how did the music of The Wailers reflect the time they were living through? Perhaps there could also have been more information about the Barrett brothers, whose bass and drum was crucial to The Wailers' sound.

In spite of these minor deficiencies, *I & I: The Natural Mystics* is an absorbing read that sheds new light on the famous trium- virate. Grant has given us some clues as to how a confluence of the historical and biographical can give rise to cultural creativity that reflects the prevailing zeitgeist and strikes a universal chord. In so doing, he has confirmed that he is a gifted writer with a keen intelligence and a sociological imagination.

Colin Grant, *I & I: The Natural Mystics* (London: Jonathan Cape, 2011).
Wasafiri, July 2011

3.

'DI ANFINISH REVALUESHAN'
– POLITICS

Jamaica Uncovered (2002)

Life and Debt,
a film by Stephanie Black

REVIEW

'The issue is to make globalization work for all. There will be
no good future for the rich if there is no prospect for a better
future for the poor.' That glib, cynical statement made by
International Monetary Fund (IMF) Director Horst Köhler is
brilliantly exposed for the platitude it is in Stephanie Black's
engaging documentary *Life and Debt* (Tuff Gong Films). Black's
film is incisive in its examination of how IMF and World Bank
policies, determined by the G7 countries, led by the USA,
impact on poor developing countries.

Life and Debt focuses on Jamaica as a typical example of a
small, developing country that has taken the IMF medicine.
Having made modest strides in shaking off the legacy of slavery
and colonialism, on the road towards self-reliance during the
first decade of independence, Jamaica was suddenly plunged
into deep financial crisis by the rise in the price of oil in 1973.
The late Michael Manley, the then left-wing leader of the
People's National Party, who served two terms as prime minister
in the 1970s, was rudely awoken to the realities of international
finance. 'In Washington they just looked at us and said, "No,

no, no. Your inflation last year was 18 per cent and we are not allowing you to lend your farmers [our money which we lent you] at 12 per cent. You must charge 23 per cent.'" The IMF told Manley that he could get a short-term loan under their conditions but would not entertain any discussion about long-term solutions. At first the Manley government was defiant. Manley's espousal of 'democratic socialism', his friendship with Fidel Castro and his activism in the Non-Aligned Movement did not endear him well to Washington. Jamaica's financial crisis was further deepened by CIA destabilization, which was exposed by dissident CIA agent Philip Agee. In the end the Manley government had to go back to the IMF cap in hand for a loan and Jamaica has been swallowing the IMF medicine ever since.

Jamaica's ongoing financial crises, high unemployment, lawlessness and social turmoil have to be seen against the background of IMF/World Bank policies that governments of both the left and the right have been forced to pursue for well over two decades. *Life and Debt* graphically illustrates how those policies have impacted on workers, small businesses, farmers and Jamaican society in general. We visit the local farmer whose enterprise is no longer viable because, like his neighbours, he cannot compete with the cheap imported onions and carrots from the USA. Local farmers were able to make a decent living selling their produce to the local market before the IMF insisted on the removal of tariffs on imported goods. When the farmer tried to diversify to honeydew melons for export, he was told by his prospective American client that the produce did not meet their specifications. 'We use machete to farm . . . can machete compete with machine?' asks the farmer.

The same story is told by the dairy farmer who has to pour his milk down the drain because he cannot compete with the cheap imported subsidized milk powder from the USA. We hear from the chicken farmer whose business is no longer viable because his fifty cents a pound chicken cannot compete with the twenty cents a pound chicken parts from the USA. At a Rasta camp we encounter three dreadlocked elders reasoning about the state of the Jamaican economy. One of the elders says that he never saw chicken backs in any supermarket when he visited the USA, yet they are exported to Jamaica. His bredrin explains that, from the days of slavery, the master kept the best for himself and the scraps were left for the slaves. There are also testimonies from banana farmers whose industry has been devastated by the USA-instigated WTO ruling that robs them of their secured tariff-free markets in Europe. The furniture-maker who shifted to making coffins is doing good business though.

In *Life and Debt* we see Jamaica through the eyes of the tourist. We also see the Jamaica that the tourist rarely encounters; slum-dwellers watch themselves on news footage of riots, political violence and industrial unrest. The Antiguan novelist Jamaica Kincaid's essay 'A Small Place' is aptly adopted to provide a poetic narrative. Footage of the slums of Kingston is underscored by reggae and ragga music and dub poetry, lyrical meditations on the state of the nation. 'I and I want to rule I destiny' chants Buju Banton. Anecdotes from Manley about his 'bitter, traumatic' experience with the IMF, World Bank and the Inter-America Development Bank are juxtaposed with IMF Deputy Director Stanley Fischer's diagnosis of and prescription for the Jamaican patient. Women working in unregulated, tariff-free sweatshops called free zones talk about their struggle to make ends meet on their weekly salaries of US $30.

What Stephanie Black's film shows is the spectacular failure of the IMF 'remedy'. After the structural adjustments, the cuts in public expenditure, the removal of tariffs on imports, the privatizations and devaluations, Jamaica is still plagued by financial crisis. Development plans have been abandoned as the vision of independence recedes. *Life and Debt* is a very powerful weapon in the arsenal of the global movement for a more equitable economic order.

The Guardian, 28 February 2002

We Have Not Forgotten (2011)

Prologue to *The New Cross Massacre Story: Interviews with John La Rose*

'[. . .] at the present time blacks are really very much inside British society [. . .] no longer on the periphery'

— JOHN LA ROSE, 2003

The most significant date in the history of the black experience in Britain during the second half of the twentieth century is the year 1981. It began inauspiciously in the early hours of 18 January with a racist arson attack on a sixteenth birthday party in south-east London, which resulted in the deaths of thirteen young black people and twenty-six revellers suffering serious injuries. The response of the police, aided and abetted by sections of the media, with the implicit approval of the government, was to use their power to deny justice to the survivors of the fire, the bereaved and the dead. The shock, sorrow and outrage felt by black people throughout the country found expression in concrete political action. On 2 March, some six weeks after the fire, the New Cross Massacre Action Committee, chaired by the late John La Rose, mobilized twenty thousand people for a march through the streets of London. That Black People's Day of Action was an unprecedented demonstration

of black political power. It was a wake-up call for the authorities, a watershed moment that signalled a paradigm shift in
race relations in the UK. Moreover, with the Day of Action
came a leap in Black British consciousness of the power to
bring about change.

Then, in April, came the uprisings which began with the
Brixton riots and spread to inner cities throughout the country.
After three decades of racial oppression and marginalization,
second- and third-generation young blacks made it abundantly
clear that things would have to change. We would no longer
tolerate being treated as third-class citizens – if citizens at all;
we were no longer prepared to remain on the periphery of
British society, and were willing to fight fire with fire.

In 1981 Britain was undergoing deep structural changes in
the wake of the economic crises of the 1970s. It was a turbulent
time of class conflict. Racism was rampant and racial prejudice
permeated every institution of the state. The new Conservative
government of the day, led by Margaret Thatcher, had launched
an assault on the gains won by the British working classes after
the Second World War. It was a time of racial tension, exacer-
bated by right-wing politicians like Thatcher, whose
anti-immigrant rhetoric fanned the flames of hatred and
emboldened racist and fascist organizations. By then there was
a mass movement of politicized young blacks and several autonomous organizations engaged in the struggle for racial equality
and social justice.

Racist acts of terror against blacks and Asians did not begin
with the New Cross arson attack, but coincided with Caribbean
migration to the UK in the 1950s. There were the Notting Hill

THE NEW CROSS MASSACRE STORY

Interviews with John La Rose

prologue by Linton Kwesi Johnson and epilogue by Gus John

The New Cross Massacre Story book was published in 2011 with a cover from a painting of the Black People's Day of Action 1981 by Chris Abuk.

and Nottingham riots of 1958 and 1959, where blacks fought back, and the murder, also in Notting Hill, of Antiguan worker Kelso Cochrane. After the Conservative Member of Parliament Enoch Powell made his infamous inflammatory 'rivers of blood' speech in 1968, demanding the repatriation of black Commonwealth immigrants, there was a marked increase in racist attacks and the rise of fascist organizations such as the National Front, the British Movement and Column 88. In 1971, a decade before the New Cross fire, there was a similar arson attack on a West Indian party in Forest Hill in south-east London where, luckily, no one died. The New Cross area, in particular the London borough of Lewisham, was notorious as a hotbed of National Front activism and racist arson attacks. In 1977, the Moonshot, a black youth and community centre, was fire-bombed. That year Lewisham also witnessed street battles between National Front supporters on the one hand and anti-racists from the Anti-Nazi League, supported by black youths, on the other. In 1978, the Albany Theatre in Deptford was fire-bombed in a suspected racist attack, as was the Lewisham Way Centre in 1980. The New Cross fire was, therefore, not an isolated act of barbarism, but the latest and most devastating in a history of racist terror.

There were two inquests into the New Cross fire, both of which returned open verdicts. If the first, held with indecent haste just three months after the fire, was a travesty of justice, with crucial evidence suppressed by the coroner, then the second inquest, held in 2004, was a farce, as no new evidence was produced. However, on both occasions the police failed to convince the jury that the fire was the result of 'black on black' violence. The open verdicts have not allowed closure for the bereaved and the survivors of the fire, but the Black People's Day of Action and the uprisings that followed in 1981 and again in 1985 were harbingers of change. These dramatic demonstrations of black self-empowerment left the Conservative government of the day with no alternative but to implement policies that would accelerate the emergence of a black middle class and a move towards inclusion.

The New Cross Massacre Story: Interviews with John La Rose is the only authoritative account of an important juncture in recent British history. As Chairman of the New Cross Massacre Action Committee (NCMAC), John La Rose was able to give a detailed account of the black communities' response to the fire, the formation of the NCMAC, the conduct of the police and their collaborators and the Black People's Day of Action. This publication also includes an appendix, with the 'Declaration of New Cross', the public statement made on the Black People's Day of Action; letters to the Prime Minister, the Commissioner of Police and the Speaker of the House of Commons; the Early Day Motion signed by some Labour Members of Parliament; a statement to the Press Association; the names of the thirteen young black people who died in the fire; and a public statement on the inquest and the appeal against the open verdict.

Documents and papers from the New Cross Massacre Action Committee's campaign for justice for the victims of the fire are stored in the archives of the George Padmore Institute and can be accessed by the public.

'Prologue', *The New Cross Massacre Story: Interview with John La Rose* (London: George Padmore Institute, 2011), written March 2011

Riots, Rhymes and Reason (2012)

I am often asked why I started to write poetry. The answer is that my motivation sprang from a visceral need to creatively articulate the experiences of the black youth of my generation, coming of age in a racist society. Some of my early work dealt with fratricidal violence and internecine warfare, not too dissimilar to the mindless gang warfare of today. Back in those early days when I began my apprenticeship as a poet, I also tried to voice our anger, spirit of defiance and resistance in a Jamaican poetic idiom.

Forty years ago, in 1972, I wrote a poem of resistance titled 'All Wi Doin is Defendin' in which I said 'all oppreshan can do is bring/ pashan to di heights of erupshan/ an songs af fire we will sing/ [. . .] sen fi di riot squad quick/ cause wi runnin wile/ wi bittah like bile'. A year later, in 1973, in a poem called 'Time Come', I wrote, 'fruit soon ripe fi tek wi bite/ strength soon come fi wi fling wi might/ it soon come/ look out look out look out! [. . .] it too late now I did warn yu'. Those were the prevailing sentiments of many young black people back then, because of our everyday experience of racism in general and racist police oppression in particular.

After the carnival riots of 1976 and 1977 in Notting Hill,

LKJ in Peggy's cafe in Brixton, south London.

the Bristol riots of 1980 and the uprisings of 1981 and 1985, some people began to say that my early seventies verse was prophetic. I don't know about that; what I do know is that if you were a young black person in the early 1970s living in urban Britain, you did not have to be prescient to know that sooner or later the police would ignite an explosion. I wrote two poems about the 1981 uprisings: 'Di Great Insohreckshan' and 'Mekin Histri'. I wrote 'Di Great Insohreckshan' from the perspective of those who had taken part in the Brixton riots. The tone of the poem is celebratory because I wanted to capture the mood of exhilaration felt by black people at the time.

And what a time it was! It was a time of intense class warfare. The Thatcher-led government had set in motion policies designed to claw back the gains the working class had won in the post-World War Two settlement. The labour movement was fighting back. The black working class was involved in those struggles. There were autonomous organizations like the Black Parents Movement, the Black Youth Movement, the Race Today Collective and the Bradford Black Collective struggling for racial equality, social justice and radical change. Every institution of the state was riddled with racism, and none more so than the police. The gutter press fanned the flames of racial hatred. Racist and fascist attacks against black and Asian people were rampant. The most horrific incident was the New Cross fire on 18 January 1981, the result of an arson attack on a party which resulted in the deaths of thirteen young black people, with twenty-six suffering serious injury.

The response of the black communities to that atrocity and the attempt by the police to cover up the truth and frame some of the party-goers for the fire was the mobilization of twenty thousand people by the New Cross Massacre Action Committee, chaired by John La Rose, for a march from New Cross to Hyde Park to protest the deaths of those young people and to demand justice. It was the most spectacular expression of black political power ever seen in this country; a watershed moment in our struggle for racial equality and social justice. That march, on 2 March 1981, known as the Black People's Day of Action, gave black people up and down the country a new sense of our power to resist racial oppression and to fight for change. It became clear for all to see that second- and third-generation black people – my generation – were no longer prepared to endure what our parents had. We were the rebel generation, a politicized generation, and we were fighting back. One month later, in April, the uprisings began in Brixton.

On 6 August last summer [2011] when the riots began in Tottenham, I was performing at a reggae festival in Belgium accompanied by the Dennis Bovell Dub Band. Two of the tunes we performed were 'Di Great Insohreckshan' and 'Mekin Histri'. It was quite late when we got to our hotel and all retired for the night as we had another gig on the Sunday in France. I was in bed when the phone rang. It was Dennis Bovell, a Tottenham resident. He said, 'Linton, turn on your TV, riot a gwaan a Tottenham.' I tuned into BBC World and saw Tottenham burning. The television set in the cheap hotel where we stayed in France on Sunday did not have BBC World, Sky or CNN, but Dennis received quite a few text messages and we were kept up to date with was happening. I thought everything would have calmed down by the time I arrived back in London, only to discover that the riots had intensified and had spread to towns and cities all over England.

Some of the scenes I saw on the television were unbelievable. What was most astonishing was that the police seemed power-less to act. It seemed as though they were working to rule or taking some kind of unofficial industrial action. It is not as though they were inexperienced in dealing with riots. It seemed to me at the time like a blatant dereliction of duty. I was not at all surprised that the riots began in Tottenham in the light of the cold-blooded killing of Mark Duggan by a police officer, the misinformation put out by the Independent Police Complaints Commission, and the history of conflict between the police and the black community in that part of London. Given the continuing deaths of black people at the hands of the police or in police custody, the criminalization of young black people, the disproportionate use of stop and search against black people, the charge of joint enterprise and the marginalization and demonization of sections of the working class, black and white, a riot was just waiting to happen. What did surprise me was the ubiquity of the riots.

To my mind, faced with the prospect of a twenty per cent cut in their budget, the police wanted to make a point to the government. It was as though they were saying to the Chancellor of the Exchequer and the Home Secretary, 'This is what could happen if our manpower is reduced.'

Soon after I got home from France, I received requests from national newspapers in Belgium, France, Russia and the USA for comments on the riots. I declined because I surmised that if they wanted to speak to me, it would be to portray the riots in purely racial terms. It was clear to me that the causes of the riots were racial oppression and racial injustice, as well as class oppression and social injustice. The most widespread expression of discontent that I have ever witnessed in this country has to be seen in the context of the marginalization of sections of the working class and the ideologically driven austerity measures of the Tory-led government. The police have done little or nothing to eradicate racism from the way they carry out their duties. The rank and file never accepted the findings of the 1999 Macpherson inquiry into the murder of black teenager Stephen Lawrence in 1993 in south-east London that stated they are institutionally racist. My grandson has lost count of the number of times he has been stopped and searched by the police and he's not a gang member. As far as policing and young black people are concerned, nothing has changed since I was a youth, nothing has changed since the uprisings of 1981. Never mind what Trevor Phillips says.

However, black people as a whole have made significant advances since the end of the 1980s. We are no longer as marginalized as we were in 1981. We had to resort to insurrection to integrate ourselves into British society. As the late John La Rose observed nearly a decade ago, black people are now very much inside British society; we are no longer on the periphery. Yet, after the progress of the nineties and early noughties, there is a perception amongst some black people that we have hit the glass ceiling and racial equality is no longer on the agenda of New Labour, the Tories and Liberal Democrats. In fact, the budget of the Equality and Human Rights Commission has been cut by 63 per cent. People like Professor

Gus John, for example, rightly continue to critique the educational system for failing black working-class children. Recent government statistics show that the unemployment rate for young black people is now over 55 per cent. Just as black Christians had to start their own churches many years ago, so black police officers have had to form their own staff association, as the police force is still pathologically racist.

Joseph Harker of the *Guardian* rightly observes that the dozen or so black Members of Parliament are one step removed from their communities. It was churlish of Simon Woolley from Operation Black Vote to accuse him of nostalgia. There is no evidence that our black MPs, having reached where they are now, will champion the case of racial equality or campaign against racist police practices. The onus is still on our communities.

Local Brixton speech, 24 March 2012

Thatcher and the
Inner-City Riots (2013)

In the wake of Baroness Thatcher's demise, there is consensus among politicians and commentators of all persuasions that she was the most divisive British Prime Minister in living memory. Call it irony, call it hypocrisy, call it what you will, but it is the same Conservative Party that unceremoniously ousted her from power when she became an electoral liability that is now heaping praise on her and honouring her with a state funeral in all but name.

To my mind, Thatcher was a ruthless class warrior for the ruling class. Her ignominious achievement was the tearing up of the post-Second World War 'settlement', clawing back the gains the working class had won. Her cross-party admiration stems from the fact that she is regarded as the architect of the neo-liberal orthodoxy to which they all subscribe, notwithstanding the dire straits to which the free-market dogma has taken the British economy.

How did Thatcher's rule impact the black population? In 1979, when the Conservative Party won the general election, black people were still being treated as third-class citizens, if citizens at all. By then we had been engaged in a three decades long struggle against racial oppression and marginalization and for racial equality. Although our parents had arrived in Britain as colonial subjects, we were still being treated as aliens. The Thatcher years saw an intensification of our struggle for racial justice. Thatcher will be remembered by many black people of my generation as a bigot and a xenophobe who fanned the flames of racial hatred, giving succour to the fascists who were emboldened to carry out terrorist attacks against black and Asian people. When she ranted on about Britain being swamped by alien cultures, it was sweet music to the ears of the National Front/British National Party brigade. As we approach the thirty-second anniversary of the Brixton riots this month, my mind goes back to January 1981 when thirteen young black people died in a racist arson attack on a birthday party in New Cross, south-east London. I remember how the atrocity was covered up by the police and the coroner at the hastily convened inquest. I remember how the parents of the deceased were thwarted by the authorities in their quest for justice. I remember the Black People's Day of Action when an estimated twenty thousand people took to the streets to demand justice, and the Brixton riots that came a month later. I recall the Tottenham riots of 1985 which, like the Brixton riots of '81 and those of 2011, spread throughout inner-city areas. I recall that back in the eighties, for young black people, living in an inner-city area was like living in a police state.

The 1980s, the Thatcher decade, was one of class struggle and racial conflict. It was the decade when black people had to resort to riots, uprisings and insurrection in order to integrate ourselves into British society; a time when we had to organize

A publicity photo of LKJ with his friend Raymond Lawrence,
taken in 1980.

and agitate for justice. By the beginning of the nineties Thatcher had to go, stabbed in her back by her own cabinet, and black people began to make some progress in our struggle against marginalization and for racial equality and social justice.

There are some first- and second-generation black people who will agree with David Cameron's assertion that Thatcher not only saved Britain from ruin, but that she also put the 'great' back into Great Britain. My late Jamaican barber was one of her more fanatical supporters and I discovered that my mother had voted for the Tories in 1979. I asked her why and she replied that, at the time, she felt a woman deserved a chance and could not do worse than the Labour administrations of Harold Wilson and Jim Callaghan. She quickly added that, in her twenty-seven-year sojourn in England, it was the first and last time she ever voted in a general election.

LKJ Records blog, 14 April 2013

South African Connections (2017)

The Chancellor of Rhodes University, the Hon. Judge Lex Mpati; the Vice-Chancellor, Dr Sizwe Mabizela, Chairperson of Council; Mr Vuyo Kahla, Members of the Council of Rhodes University, the Executive Management and Senate of the University; my fellow graduands and family members; staff, students and friends of the university, distinguished guests, ladies and gentlemen, good afternoon. I would like to say a few words about my South Africa connections.

Notwithstanding the controversy surrounding the statue of Cecil Rhodes in Oxford, and the indignation the name evokes in young and old alike, it would have been churlish of me not to accept an honorary degree from a venerable institution such as Rhodes University. In any event, my ego would not allow such folly. Indeed, it is with humility that I accept this honour. Several eminent Jamaicans were Rhodes scholars. They include the poet, novelist and educator Neville Dawes; cultural theorist and sociologist Stuart Hall; Jamaica's Poet Laureate, Professor Mervyn Morris; and Rex Nettleford, the late Vice-Chancellor of the University of the West Indies.

I am proud of my Jamaican heritage, proud of the fact that Jamaica was the first country to refuse to have anything to do

LKJ and the Dennis Bovell Dub Band performing
at an anti-apartheid festival in 1983.

with apartheid South Africa; proud of the fact that one of Jamaica's most revered public intellectuals was the South African-born novelist Peter Abrahams. From the time of Marcus Garvey in the early twentieth century, Jamaicans have been known for our African consciousness. 'If Africa noh free, black man can't free'. That is the opening line from a 1976 reggae recording by the Twinkle Brothers, titled 'Free Africa'. Reggae music is replete with such expressions of African consciousness. And it is the power and ubiquity of reggae music that has brought me here today. For, although I am a published poet, reggae music is the vehicle that has afforded me a global audience for my verse.

My first visit to Rhodes was in 2009, and I have fond memories of the occasion. It was during my first and last mini-tour of South Africa with the Dennis Bovell Dub Band, organized by Hazel Walton of Purple Haze Productions. We had concerts in Cape Town, Durban, Grahamstown and Johannesburg. We were well received everywhere. However, with the exception of Cape Town, which was a sold-out show, the tour was a flop. In fact, it was a financial disaster for Hazel who, to my astonishment, fully honoured her contractual obligations. I would like to take this opportunity to publicly thank her for her integrity. The evening after the concert in Grahamstown, we were invited to a reception here at Rhodes. We were wined and dined in fine style. Given such wonderful hospitality, the least I could do was to sing for our supper, so I gave a short poetry recital after dessert. Hazel told me that it was someone called Maurice who linked us up with the university and I would like to take this opportunity to thank him for his initiative.

My South Africa connections go back further than the 2007 concerts. When I became politically conscious in my late teens, I joined the Black Panther Movement. Three South African exiles who had nothing to do with the Panthers were involved in my personal struggle for justice against the racist police force in Brixton, south London, where I grew up.

One Saturday afternoon in November 1972, I was walking through Brixton Market when I saw three plain-clothes policemen arresting a black youth, with excessive force. I asked the youth for his name and address and wrote it down on a piece of paper. The police took the youth to a 'Black Maria' police van parked on the busy market street on Railton Road where there were other uniformed police. I wrote down their numbers. I intended to pass the information to the relatives of the youth. This is what we were trained to do in the Black Panthers, because the police would often arrest black youths and lock them up in remand centres without informing their next of kin. The police saw me writing down the details. Four of them grabbed me and threw me into the police van along with the youth. There were already two young black women in the van. I managed to slip the piece of paper I had been writing on to a comrade. It proved to be a crucial piece of evidence during my subsequent trial. During the short drive to Brixton police station, in the darkened van, the police shone their torches on us and beat and kicked us while racially abusing us. The three young people were charged with 'sus' – that is, loitering with intent. I was charged with two counts of assault and one count of actual bodily harm.

What we in the black communities of urban Britain called

the 'sus' law was the Vagrancy Act, a piece of nineteenth-century legislation used in Queen Victoria's time to control the movement of the unemployed. Notwithstanding the fact that some black youth were engaged in minor criminal activities, this dormant piece of legislation was revived and used by racist police officers to criminalize many black youth of my generation. You would be charged with 'attempting to steal from persons unknown', and it would be your word against the police. And you can guess whose word the magistrate would accept as the truth.

Within minutes of my arrest, a crowd gathered outside Brixton police station demanding my release. As soon as I was locked up I asked to see a doctor. I made sure I saw my own doctor after I was bailed so that there would be documentary evidence of the police brutality. That was also part of my training as a Black Panther. The case was tried in June 1973. All four of us were acquitted of all charges, thanks to the presence of two black people on the jury. How do I know this? The black bus conductor on a bus I was travelling on one day happened to have been a member of the jury. He gave me an account of what had happened.

During the trial, I was represented by a barrister from South Africa of Indian descent named Barney Desai. He was born in Durban in 1932, and was reclassified as 'coloured' in 1957. He was active in the 'defiance campaign', was Vice-President of the South African Coloured People's Congress, and had been elected to the Cape Town City Council but was prevented from taking his seat by the government. He went into exile soon after. During his exile in London, where he became an eminent lawyer, he was associated with Pan Africanist Congress. He is the father of the filmmaker Rehad Desai.

I couldn't have asked for a better barrister than Barney Desai. His cross-examination of the police was clinical. He was able to demonstrate to the court that the police were liars; that they had fabricated the charges against me. After my acquittal he advised me to press charges against the police for assault and malicious prosecution. But, due to the ordeal of the court proceedings and the fact that I was preparing for university, I declined. However, I made an official complaint to the police about my treatment. My complaint was investigated by the police who, needless to say, found no grounds for further action.

Before the trial, I had complained to the local Community Relations Council (CRC) in Brixton, an institution set up by the Home Office to mediate the struggles of black people in urban Britain against racial oppression. Naturally the CRC couldn't do anything, but I got a sympathetic hearing from another South African exile named Lionel Morrison. At the time he was involved in the race relations industry but later became known for his journalism. He became the first black president of the National Union of Journalists, of which I was a member when I worked in television.

I don't know if Barney Desai or Lionel Morrison had anything to do with it, but shortly after my trial, an article about my case with the headline 'Why Blacks In Brixton Are Blowing Their Tops' appeared in the *Sunday Observer* newspaper. It was written by yet another South African, a novelist and academic named Lewis Nkosi. Not long after the article appeared, Bloom, Farr and Levers, the three police officers who had brutalized and fabricated the charges against me and the three youths, were transferred from Brixton police station.

So my connection with South Africa began with three distinguished South African exiles in London: Barney Desai, Lionel Morrison and Lewis Nkosi. That period of ordeal – November 1972 to June 1973 – was an important turning point in my life. It was then that, as an aspiring poet, I made a number of decisions about language, orality and music, choices which determined the formation of my poetics. Having heard blues and jazz poetry, I decided that I wanted to write reggae poetry. My verse would be a cultural weapon in the black liberation struggles.

Thanks to Roshnie Moonsammy of Urban Voices and Arts Exchange, my first visit to South Africa was in 1994. I gave a sold-out poetry recital to an enthusiastic audience in Newtown, Johannesburg. In 1995 I had a reggae concert in Alexandra township. Since than I have done a number of poetry recitals, including one for Poetry Africa at the University of Kwa Zulu Natal, the Bat Centre in Durban, and the Baxter Theatre in Cape Town in 2004 to celebrate ten years of democracy in South Africa. I also took part in a special event in 2015 in Johannesburg to celebrate the life of African-American poet Jayne Cortez, organized by Arts Alive. My most treasured memory of my visits to South Africa was meeting Albertina and Walter Sisulu in Soweto in 1995. In 2013 I was given a Lifetime Achievement in Writing Award, the Golden Pen, by English PEN. The president of English PEN at the time was the South African novelist Gillian Slovo. I don't know what I have done to deserve it, but South Africans have been very kind to me. Thank you.

Honorary doctorate acceptance speech at Rhodes University, April 2017

4.

'TINGS AN TIMES' –
PLACES AND MOMENTS

Race Today Review (1986)

INTRODUCTION

During the last year or so, no single subject of international importance dominated news reports more than the political ferment in South Africa. By their continuous mass protest, acts of civil disobedience and revolt, the black masses of South Africa have served notice on Botha's regime that the days of apartheid are numbered, that the struggle for freedom and democracy is on and that there can be no turning back now. All are involved, from grandmothers to schoolchildren. After decades upon decades of remarkable endurance, South Africa's black majority are now showing an equally remarkable resolve to endure no more.

History has shown that the artistic creations of an oppressed people are not only sources of spiritual and moral fortitude for the people, but are also powerful cultural weapons in their struggle for freedom. So it is in South Africa. Poets, novelists, short story writers, dramatists, musicians and visual artists consistently reflect, analyse and criticize, through their artistic creations, the social relations that constitute apartheid. Needless to say that, for the most part, they create under the most severe conditions of constraint with the omnipresent shadow of the censor hovering over them. Those whose work falls foul of the authorities will be lucky to get away with being banned; some are forced into exile; others not so lucky are imprisoned, tortured and murdered.

This issue of *Race Today Review* focuses on some aspects of South African literature and theatre. Novelist and short story writer R. R. R. Dhlomo is regarded as a pioneer of the modern black South African short story. His story 'Juwawa', first published in 1930, shows that a revolutionary tradition has long been evident in modern black South African literature. Amelia House's short story 'Awakening', in a different way, reflects that same tradition, laying bare the bestiality of the police state; the arbitrariness and pervasiveness of its terror. In his essay 'Commitment and Writing in Theatre: The South African Experience', Zakes Mda traces the development of black theatre in South Africa from the apolitical 'township theatre movement' of the 1960s to the revolutionary one of today. Some of the most powerful artistic acts against apartheid have come from the poets. We also include in this issue a selection of South African poetry.

After twenty-five years as Tanzania's head of state, Africa's elder statesman Julius Nyerere last year gracefully stepped down from office. We include here extracts from an interview with Tariq Ali and Darcus Howe which was televised last October on Channel 4. The former president talks candidly about the achievements and disappointments in realizing the goals set out in the Arusha Declaration in 1967, and the failure to build socialism in a poor, backward African country.

The eighties boom in literary works by black American

24 ON THE BOX
Review of "Viv" the Channel
Four Portrait

25 Review of "Black Silk"
A BBC 2 Television Series

26 SHORT STORY
The Awakening by
Amelia House

30 POETRY

31 VISUAL ART
The Marginalisation of
Black Art
by Eddie Chambers

34 BOOK REVIEWS
politics, poetry, novels,
history

45 PROTEST
Greater London Arts
Association
Black Artistic Activity

Jayne Cortez photo: Val Wilmer

Eddie Chambers

Kwame Nkrumah

Contents listing for *Race Today Review*,
February 1986.

women writers continues unabated. Writer Maya Angelou and poet Jayne Cortez, in separate interviews, talk about their lives, their work and some of the influences which have shaped their respective arts.

Although black visual artists in Britain are still struggling to establish an independent footing in the highly competitive and exclusive 'art world', still struggling to win recognition and adequate funding for their work, they have undoubtedly made significant strides over the last four years. However, Eddie Chambers, one of the new generation of Britain's increasingly vociferous black artists, argues in a polemical piece that patronage of black art by white institutions like the Institute of Contemporary Arts and funding bodies like the ill-fated Greater London Council is leading to the marginalization of black art in Britain.

Finally, as well as our review of books and our protest column, we also include critical appraisals of two significant black programmes shown last year on British television: the BBC 2 series *Black Silk*, based on a black lawyer, and Channel 4's *Viv*, a profile of West Indies cricket captain, Vivian Richards.

Race Today Review, 1986

Race Today Review (1987)

INTRODUCTION

In his introduction to the 1982 *Race Today Review*, Darcus Howe asserted that there was a 'dearth of powerful creativity' in the black community. He advanced two reasons why: firstly, the 'crippling bankruptcy which pervades the world of art in Britain today' and, secondly, 'the stifling effects of the uncertainty of our existence here'. Howe went on to suggest that the black uprisings of 1981 would accelerate 'the process through which our uncertainty is brought to an end'. That is precisely what has been taking place over the last five years.

The black uprisings of the last decade, which intensified during the first half of the eighties, unleashed a new wave of black creativity in the arts, throwing up new talents in most areas of artistic expression. In the wake of the riots, many of the fetters on black creativity have been removed. Akua Rugg was able to observe in the 1984 *Race Today Review* that 'the ground has been cleared and the space created for black artists' as a consequence of the struggles that blacks had waged.

In this new period of black creativity, independent cultural organizations like The International Book Fair of Radical Black and Third World Books and Creation For Liberation have emerged to provide an intellectual and cultural base from which to transcend the 'crippling bankruptcy' about which Howe wrote. Moreover, journals like *Artrage*, *New Beacon Review*, our own *Race Today* and *Race Today Review* have sought to forge a critical tradition to assist the movement forward.

This last year has been particularly vibrant; art exhibitions, poetry recitals, theatrical productions, festivals, concerts and seminars abounded. There are some events which stood out. The *C. L. R. James – Man of the People* exhibition at the Riverside Studios was a fitting tribute. The exhibition was accompanied by a series of lectures on different aspects of James' work by John Archer, Marty Glaberman, Grace Lee Boggs, Tim Hector and Wilson Harris.* There were also films of James talking on subjects as diverse as cricket, Shakespeare, Poland and the Caribbean.

The Fifth International Book Fair of Radical Black and Third World Books was another important landmark in black independent publishing in Britain. The book fair and its organizers have over the years helped to stimulate interest in, and the market for, black literature. There was, during 1986, a deluge of reprints and new publications of African, Afro-American and Caribbean literature. Heinemann, Longman, Virago and Faber

---

* John Archer was a veteran of the early British Trotskyist movement; Marty Glaberman was an American socialist comrade of C. L. R. James who later became an academic; Grace Lee Boggs was an American author, social activist, philosopher and feminist who collaborated with C. L. R. James in the 1940s and 1950s; Tim Hector was the left-leaning Antiguan political leader and cricket administrator; Wilson Harris was the Guyanese author of poetry, fiction and essays.

The Race Today Review '87

EDITED BY LINTON KWESI JOHNSON

1·50

BLACK BRITISH CULTURE

THE TOTTENHAM INSURRECTION AND THE STRUGGLE FOR CHANGE IN BRITAIN
JOHN LA ROSE

AND THEN THE WEST END
NORMAN BEATON

BREAKING NEW GROUND
COURTNEY PINE

LINTON KWESI JOHNSON IN CONVERSATION WITH
CARYL PHILLIPS

SHORT STORIES POETRY VISUAL ARTS BOOK REVIEWS FILM SPORT

Magazine cover for *Race Today Review*, 1987.

and Faber were prominent among those publishing houses who sought a piece of the action.

The state made its intervention too. There was the Commonwealth Institute's ambitious nine-month-long Caribbean Focus whose aim was, presumably, to bring Caribbean culture to the British public at large and blacks in particular. In spite of the hard work and resources that went into it, Caribbean Focus was at times in danger of ending up as a Caribbean fiasco. They had their successes, but the combination of the popular, the anthropological and the intellectual failed to generate the desired level of response from the black communities up and down the country.

BBC television, too, had its own sort of Caribbean Focus, allotting some fourteen hours of viewing time to the Caribbean. *Arena*'s Caribbean Nights offered a crash course in Caribbean art, culture and society. Ali Mazrui's documentary series *The Africans* gave a broad sociological view of Africa. It was both educational and informative.

Our focus in this issue of *Race Today Review* is on black artistic expression in Britain today. John La Rose's article, 'The Tottenham Riots and the Struggle for Change in Britain', gives an incisive analysis of the political context in which the current spate of black creativity is taking place.

In the world of theatre, the last year was definitely one for the Caribbean productions. The Commonwealth Institute, as part of their Caribbean Focus, staged a number of these. The Jamaican all-women's theatre group Sistren brought their riveting musical *Muffet Inna All a We*. The reformed Pan-Caribbean Theatre Company did Dennis Scott's *Dog* and Rawle Gibbons' *I, Lawah*, and the St Lucia National Theatre performed Derek

Walcott's *Ti-Jean and His Brothers* and Roderick Walcott's *Banjo Man*. The Theatre Royal Stratford East continued their successful run of plays by Jamaican playwright Trevor Rhone with *School's Out*. They also staged *Moon on a Rainbow Shawl* by the Trinidadian playwright Errol John. Finally, the Talawa Theatre Company broke new ground with their impressive production of C. L. R. James' *The Black Jacobins* at The Riverside Studios and Dennis Scott's *An Echo In The Bone* at the Drill Hall.

A major literary talent to have surfaced in the eighties is the writer Caryl Phillips. His plays and novels have the depth and power which Howe saw lacking in Britain's black communities five years ago. We publish here an interview with him [page 115] talking about his work and the experiences which have shaped his characters. Another powerful talent to emerge in the eighties is British-born saxophonist Courtney Pine. He belongs to a new generation of blacks, some of whom have embraced jazz music as a part of their heritage. Pine sees himself in the tradition of Afro-American jazz innovators like John Coltrane, Sonny Rollins and Wayne Shorter. We also carry an interview with him.

Black Britain has so far not produced many short story writers. The recent publication of a collection, *Incidents at the Shrine*, by Ben Okri, and Archie Markham's *Something Unusual*, hopefully, are indications that things are changing. We publish a story from each.

Over the last two decades, through his work in theatre, television and films, Norman Beaton has rightly earned the reputation of being Britain's leading black actor. We include here an extract from his recently published autobiography, *Beaton But Unbowed*.

TIME COME

One of the most prominent art exhibitions of works by black visual artists was the Whitechapel Gallery's *From Two Worlds*. The exhibition displayed works by some fifteen black artists. Eddie Chambers, himself a leading young artist, takes issue with the assumptions underlying the exhibition. Jamaican painter Errol Lloyd reviews another important exhibition, the Commonwealth Institute's *Caribbean Art Now*.

Finally, sports writer Clayton Goodwin offers an overview of our impact in the world of sport during the last year.

Race Today Review, 1987

South London Calling (2000)

Having lived in and around Brixton (on and off) for over thirty-six years, I feel qualified to call myself a Brixtonian. I love Brixton. That love is today more rooted in memory, familiarity and nostalgia than anything else. Three years ago, I found the perfect house on Railton Road and moved back to the neighbourhood where I had lived and worked for many years. Railton Road is the location of the infamous 'front line' where blacks and the police did battle during the 1970s and 1980s.

I have witnessed many a change in the neighbourhood over the years. However, it was not until recently, when I attended a meeting at the Railton Methodist Church (called by a local councillor and Member of Parliament to discuss the implications of a proposed waste-disposal site in the area), that I realized how far-reaching the changes had been. You could count the number of blacks attending the meeting on two hands. It was by no means evidence of apathy on the part of local blacks, but a stark reflection of the demographic changes that have taken place locally during the last twenty years.

Looking back, in many ways the days of the front line were my halcyon days. Those were exciting times, full of laughter and tension, hope and apprehension, confrontation and celebration.

The front line began at the junction of Atlantic Road and stretched about four hundred yards about a third of the way up Railton Road. It consisted of a row of old derelict two-storey houses and shop fronts with damp basements and peeling plaster. In addition to the mostly black residents, the front line was peopled by workers, the unemployed, hustlers, pimps and prostitutes, rude boys, rebels, Rastas, con artists and police informers. Out of that motley mix emerged 'generals' who commanded respect. Swords, knives, hatchets and broken bottles would come into play and, from time to time, blood would flow. But I do not recall a single shot being fired or anyone being murdered. The front line was the centre of black street life in Brixton, an oasis of Caribbean cultural identity, resistance and rebellion. People came from all over – blacks and whites – looking for thrills and excitement or just to score some dope. Most self-respecting blacks avoided the place like the plague and forbade their children to venture there, such was its notoriety.

The hub of the front line during its heyday was Peggy's cafe, a local 'institution' if ever there was one. Run by a small, wiry, good-natured Jamaican woman with a reputation for sweet fingers when it came to Jamaican cuisine, Peggy's attracted customers from all over London. You could meet visiting reggae stars from Jamaica there, local black celebrities, famous gangsters, locals and down-and-outs whom Peggy would take pity on and feed. The other eating place was Chins, run by an Afro-Chinese Jamaican with martial arts lessons going on in his basement. Then there was Bishop's and Con's shebeens where you could listen to D'unis or Soprano B sound systems until daybreak; and gambling houses in basements where huge

LKJ in Brixton, captured for *Time Out*'s 23 March 2000 edition.

sums of money passed hands during para pinto dice games or card games like kaluky, seventy-nine or koon kan and dominoes. If you were coming from a blues dance in the wee hours of the morning you got salt fish and fried dumpling from Eggy's or Tumpa's. The youth had Railton Road Methodist Church youth club (Shepherd's) further up Railton Road, where they danced away Friday nights to Neville King's sound system. And in the summer months, if the weather was good, the pavement would be full of people just hanging out listening to sweet reggae music from car stereos, reasoning about this and that. At times there would almost be a carnival-like atmosphere with vendors selling sugar cane, mangoes, roast corn or snow balls (shaved ice with syrup).

Then came the riots in April 1981, largely sparked by the blatantly racist behaviour of the local police during Operation Swamp 81. Those riots marked the beginning of the demise of the front line. In its wake came Lord Scarman's inquiry into policing and urban decay and the then Tory government's initiatives on inner-city regeneration. Some of the houses were demolished and later rebuilt. The rebels and rude boys were able to secure a building called the 'white house' on the corner of Leeson Road and Railton Road for themselves and later a prefab building at the junction of Atlantic and Railton Roads, called 'the hut'. Peggy's cafe was relocated nearby. By the time of the second Brixton riots in 1985, the old front line had all but disappeared. The hut was closed down by the police after Operation Condor and Peggy died in 1987. Her death was symbolic of the final nail being driven into the coffin of the front line.

During the eighties the local dealers were squeezed out by a new breed of Jamaican hustlers, who came with a ruthlessness and viciousness never before seen on the front line, plying a different trade. This was also a period when the black exodus from Brixton to greener pastures accelerated. By the end of the eighties street activity had shifted to Coldharbour Lane and Atlantic Road.

The nineties were a period of gentrification with young middle-class professionals moving into the area. Peggy's cafe still exists on Atlantic Road, run by Peggy's husband Choppy, catering to a different clientele and in competition with Jamaican takeaways, sushi and satay bars, noodle houses and internet cafes and the like. Gone are the shebeens, gambling dens, late-night blues and the hustle and bustle of the line. Now we have Lord David Pitt House, Marcus Garvey Way and Bob Marley Drive. An important chapter in Black British life is now closed. That's progress for you.

Time Out, **23 March 2000**

Reunited: Shocking with Such Glee (2004)

Last year I attended my first graduation ceremony at my alma mater, Goldsmiths College, University of London, some twenty-seven years after I had graduated. Back in 1976 I was too poor to attend. Our warden, the late Ben Pimlott, made an eloquent speech in which he summed up the college's ethos. 'Goldsmiths is an idea working around a tradition that I would call bloody-minded anti-orthodoxy,' said Professor Pimlott. 'A tradition of attacking stuffy traditions that need to be attacked, a tradition of providing an environment where new ideas flourish.' Sitting among the dignitaries on the stage, waiting nervously to receive an honorary fellowship, I remembered how cool a school Goldsmiths had been when I had studied there.

Three decades on, the college has lost none of its cool, but there have been changes. I was struck by two. Firstly, neither the academic nor the non-academic staff were all white, as they had seemed to be during my student days. Secondly, and more amazingly, the proportion of Asian and black students had multiplied at least tenfold. Professor Pimlott proudly boasted that 35 per cent of Goldsmiths students were from ethnic minorities. Moreover, the college has opened its doors to the local community in Lewisham where it is located. If 'cool' is one word that characterizes Goldsmiths, then 'inclusive' has to be another.

After graduating in 1976, penniless, unemployed, with a wife and three children, I wondered if I had made the right decision when I had opted to do a degree in sociology. After all, economics had been my favourite 'A' Level subject. When I enrolled I was a twenty-one-year-old political and cultural activist dedicated to changing the world, thirsting for knowledge, searching for answers.

Looking back, I have no doubt that sociology was the right choice for me. Goldsmiths had an enviable reputation for sociology, with several lecturers there, including my tutor, Paul Filmer, being the leading exponents of 'ethnomethodology'. I did not find the answers to all the questions that haunted my young mind, but I left Goldsmiths armed with ways of making sense of the world around me.

Back in the 1970s when I was a student, I didn't have to worry about tuition or top-up fees and I received a small grant. But those were still hard times. With a young family and as the only breadwinner, I would do any part-time work I could find to supplement our meagre income. Given the same circumstances, I don't know if I could manage such a feat today, but I am sure that, in spite of the hardship and privation, the shared sacrifice was more than worthwhile.

I was further honoured by my alma mater when I was asked to give the inaugural Richard Hogarth Lecture last year. I was generously introduced by the warden. I spoke about the post-*Windrush* black experience in Britain, albeit mostly in verse. The lecture was very well attended and equally well received. On my way home I remembered Professor Pimlott talking about Goldsmiths' capacity 'to shock with glee' at the graduation ceremony, and it made me smile.

Times Higher Education Supplement, 24 September 2004

Amsterdam: Places, People
and Beginnings (2014)

In the neighbourhood where I live in London, I am sometimes greeted in the street as 'poet', sometimes as 'musician' by people I have known a long time. For some I am one or the other, never both. The truth is that, over the last four decades, I have straddled two worlds of creativity: poetry and popular music, a feat which, sometimes looking back, I find astounding and, in some ways, fortuitous.

My earliest performances in Europe outside the United Kingdom were in cities such as Amsterdam, Brussels, Stockholm, Copenhagen, Oslo, West Berlin, Rome and Paris. In those days I had no backing musicians. My musical accompaniment was provided on a pre-recorded backing tape and I was joined on stage by three male dancers. They were Winston Curniffe and Vivian Weathers, who played drum and bass respectively on the recordings, and Percival Blake, a school friend who loved dancing to reggae. We had all migrated to Britain as children to join our parents and attended the same secondary school. The most memorable of those early reggae performances was in Paris in 1979 at the Palace Theatre. It was just after the release of my second album, *Forces of Victory*. I was the opening act for the premiere of the movie *Rockers*. My debut in France began inauspiciously. At the beginning of the show the Revox tape machine had not been cued properly and the music began about six bars from the start. I was petrified, panicked and began to chant the words completely out of time with the music. To make matters worse, Chris Blackwell, the boss of Island Records to which I was signed, was in the audience. Somehow I managed to get through the first tune and the rest of my set was fine, but by the end I was a nervous wreck, even though the performance was well received by the audience and Chris Blackwell seemed pleased.

Last month [August 2014], thirty-five years later, accompanied by the Dennis Bovell Dub Band, who have been my backing musicians since 1982, I performed at the No Logo Festival at a place called Fraisans near Besançon in France. The audience, an estimated fifty thousand patrons, was one of the largest we have ever performed for at a reggae festival. It was certainly larger than Sunfest in Germany or Rototom in Italy and Spain. Jimmy Cliff, doyen of reggae music, Luciano and I were among the headliners. I am known throughout Europe and elsewhere as a reggae artist and, indeed, that has been my profession. However, many of my fans are ignorant of the fact that nearly all my reggae recordings began life as published poems. In 1978 when I recorded my first album, *Dread Beat An' Blood*, I was virtually unknown as a poet outside the UK. By the beginning of the 1980s people began to know of my poetry as literature in certain parts of Europe, and it all began right here in Amsterdam.

When I think of Amsterdam, three names come to mind:

LKJ in Amsterdam in 1981.

Leidseplein, C. L. R. James, the Trinidadian historian and intellectual, and Ben Posset. I remember Leidseplein for the Milky
Way and the Paradiso, two venues where I did poetry readings
and reggae concerts, the museums and art galleries, and a
seafood restaurant where I had oysters for the first time. I
remember way back in the eighties sitting at C. L. R. James'
bedside talking with him about an upcoming reading I had in
Amsterdam. He implored me to visit the Rijksmuseum to have
a look at Rembrandt's famous painting *The Night Watch*, and I
did. He extolled the virtues of Bols gin, which he said was the
finest in the world. In those days C. L. R. was living above the
office of the *Race Today* journal, edited by his great-nephew
Darcus Howe, and I was a member of the Race Today Collective.
The first time I visited Amsterdam, I performed at the Paradiso
with my backing tape and dancers. It was a sold-out gig. When
I came off stage there was this tall man with large bulging eyes
and a wide grin on his face waiting for me in my dressing room.
I thought to myself who the hell is this guy and how did he
get in here. He offered his hand and said, 'My name is Ben
Posset. That was a great gig. I would like to do some work
with you.' I reluctantly shook his hand. He told me about the
organization he ran called One World Poetry and mentioned
the names of some poets he worked with. I was impressed
enough to take him seriously and, soon after that meeting,
began to work with him. Some years later, when the Crossing
the Border festival began in Den Haag after Ben's death, I
thought of him, because it is in some ways the continuation of
a legacy left by him.

One World Poetry was the leading organization for

alternative poetry events in Holland. Ben was a squatter and a beatnik at heart who was in the thrall of the Beat poets of the USA. Working with One World Poetry, I got to meet and read with poets like Allen Ginsberg, Lawrence Ferlinghetti, Gregory Corso, Amiri Baraka and William S. Burroughs. With One World I did a couple of extensive poetry reading tours in the Netherlands and parts of Belgium in the 1980s. It was through Ben Posset that I met the French anarchist, sound poet and artist Jean-Jacques Lebel, whose Paris-based organization, Polyphonix, also put on poetry readings and avant-garde events in France and other parts of Europe. Jean-Jacques and I became buddies, and through him I met Édouard Glissant, who also became a good friend. There were times when I wondered what on earth was I doing sharing a stage with a bunch of bohemians with whom, at a superficial level, I had nothing in common. Commonalties only became apparent later as my limited knowledge of the world of poetry grew and things became clearer.

As I have stated on a number of occasions, in my creative endeavours I began with the word but somehow music was there too. As a teenager I was a reggae enthusiast and later a student of the music. However, it was not inevitable that the two would combine in my verse. The beat and rhythm of reggae found its way into the language and structure of the verse I was writing. Perhaps I had always been a 'wannabe' reggae performer, and when the opportunity came for me to record my verse with music, I didn't have to think about it. It was not difficult for me to rationalize moving from book to record. Very few people are interested in poetry and not many buy books, I reasoned. By combining verse with music, I stood a

LKJ and the Dennis Bovell Dub Band performing at
the One World Poetry Festival in Amsterdam, 1981.

better chance of reaching a wider audience. Moreover, the kind of verse I was writing was suitable for the page and the stage. It was not a forced marriage but, rather, an organic meeting of forms. The precedent had been set with blues and jazz poetry, and I was going to do the same with reggae. I called my verse 'reggae poetry'.

Unlike so many poets I've met over the years, I hadn't been surrounded by books in my childhood. My father was illiterate and my mother semi-literate. As a boy in Jamaica the only poetry that I read on a regular basis was the Psalms, a favourite of my maternal grandmother, some of which had seeped in to Jamaica's oral culture. And it was through my grandmother and my socialization that I absorbed much of the oral culture of the folk. There were the ring games, word games and nonsense rhymes of children's play; riddles, duppy stories, proverbs of folk wisdom and biblical sayings; folk songs, hymns from the Sankey hymnal and gospel songs. As a schoolboy in Jamaica, I was good at English, but I loved Jamaican talk: its musicality, its expressiveness, its capacity to convey derision and menace. So it is no accident that the verse I write is located in the oral tradition of Caribbean poetry.

Yet, it all began with the written word. My inspiration to write poetry began after I read a book borrowed from the library of the Black Panther Movement called *The Souls of Black Folk* by W. E. B. Du Bois, African-American scholar and pioneering Pan-Africanist. The beautiful prose poetry of that book had such a profound impact on me that it changed my life. It made me want to write about the black experience in Britain; to articulate the thoughts and feelings of the generation to which I belong as we struggled against racial discrimination and oppression. *The Souls of Black Folk* also whetted my appetite for literature. New Beacon Books, Britain's first independent black publishing house and bookseller, enabled me to sate my hunger. After reading books of poetry like Aimé Césaire's *Notebook of a Return To My Native Land* and Christopher Okigbo's *Labyrinths*, I became intoxicated with words in my head. It was also in the Panthers that I came across some recordings of the Last Poets, a group of radical poets who employed the spoken language of African-Americans, sometimes accompanied by percussion, for their discourse on the black struggle in the USA. My first collaboration with musicians was with a group of Rastafarian drummers called Rasta Love. It was the recordings of Count Ossie and the Mystic Revelation of Rastafari on an album called *Grounation*, a combination of oration, poems, jazz, reggae and drumming, that brought us together.

Another decisive influence in the formation of my poetics was the talking tunes from Jamaica and the emerging art of the early reggae deejays, whose urgings on the microphone in the dancehall to the revellers were transferred to the recording studio and developed into a distinct lyrical genre of reggae music. I was inspired by the talking tunes of Prince Buster, the dread lyricism of Big Youth and the jive talk of U-Roy. The chants and intoned narratives of the deejays offered commentary on and insight into contemporary Jamaican society and culture, as well as verbalizations of protest and dissent, some of which found echoes of the black experience in Britain.

My resolve to create verse for the eye and the ear, grounded in a Caribbean tradition of orality, was strengthened by the encouragement I got from people like Sam Selvon, Mervyn Morris, John La Rose, Andrew Salkey and Kamau Brathwaite. The latter three had founded the Caribbean Artists Movement back in 1966. The Caribbean Artists Movement gave me an aesthetic orientation; reggae music provided a vehicle to reach audiences most poets could only imagine.

Amsterdam event speech, September 2014

Acceptance Speech to the University of the West Indies (2021)

Good morning. Chancellor, Vice-Chancellor, Pro-Vice-Chancellor, Mona Campus Principal, other officers of the university, members of academic staff, distinguished guests, my fellow graduands, members of the graduating class, ladies and gentlemen. I cannot find words adequate enough to describe how delighted I am to be participating in this graduation ceremony. After all, I began life as a barefoot peasant boy from the hills of Clarendon. My maternal grandmother, who had a hand in raising me, and my father were both illiterate; my mother semi-literate. However, my uncle, Sylvester Johnson, who taught at Edwin Allen High School, was a UWI graduate.

I grew up in a Caribbean working-class community in London, became active in the struggle for racial equality and social justice, earned a reputation as a poet, and am lucky enough to have had a successful career as a reggae artist. It is my verse that enabled me to have that career. There are quite a few people to whom I owe gratitude. The most obvious is of course Louise Bennett-Coverley, Miss Lou, who cleared a path for others to follow, championing Jamaican speech as a legitimate vehicle for poetry and so much more. I am a child of the Caribbean Artists Movement founded by Kamau Brathwaite, John La Rose and Andrew Salkey, a loose grouping of writers and visual artists who felt it more important to find their own Caribbean aesthetics for their artistic creativity instead of seeking validation from their former colonial masters. I am especially thankful to Andrew Salkey and John La Rose who were my mentors. It would be remiss of me not to mention Jamal Ali, Lindsay Barrett, Yvonne Brewster, Nadia Cattouse, Errol Lloyd and Sam Selvon, whose words of encouragement made me feel that I could be a poet. Respect is due to Eric and Jessica Huntley, founders of Bogle-L'Ouverture Books, who published my first collection of poems; and Kenneth Ramchand, the first Caribbean critic to give my verse any attention. Thanks to the Calabash International Literary Festival and the Jamaica Poetry Festival for giving me a plat-form in Jamaica. Thanks to Eddie Baugh and Carolyn Cooper for their friendship over the years and, last but not least, thanks to Mervyn Morris for a lifetime of nurturing. The late Jean 'Binta' Breeze and Michael Smith, Mutabaruka and Oku Onuora made me feel that I belong to a community of poets from yard. Respect is also due to Herbie Miller for introducing my music to Jamaica and Elise Kelly for playing my records on Irie FM.

I feel a kind of affinity to Mona, something akin to a distant relative of an eminent family. Although I live in London, I am no stranger to the campus; I have family and friends from Papine, some of whom worked on campus and some who taught there. Over the years when in Jamaica, I've attended various events on campus and have had the honour of giving the

LKJ in his University of the West Indies honorary doctorate
apparel getting ready to record his thank you speech,
October 2021.

occasional talk, poetry reading or workshop. Moreover, the University of the West Indies has been an invaluable source of learning for me, through its books and journals; good nourishment that has helped to sustain my Caribbean consciousness.

Ladies and gentlemen, I already have two honorary doctorates, one from Rhodes University in South Africa and another from Solent Southampton University in the UK. But to receive such an honour from a top-ranking, world-beating institution like UWI is beyond my wildest dreams. It is with humility and profound gratitude that I accept. Vice-Chancellor, this one really sweet. Thank you very much, sir.

Honorary doctorate acceptance speech, 19 October 2021

5.

'BEACON OF HOPE' – PEOPLE

Martin Carter: Give Thanks
(1997)

Contribution to
All are Involved: The Art of Martin Carter,
edited by Stewart Brown

About twenty years ago, I had the honour of sharing a stage with Martin Carter. I 'warmed up' the audience for him at a lunchtime reading at the Soho Poly Theatre in London. I recall being reasonably well received by the predominantly white, literary-type audience, but just being asked to open for Martin Carter was in itself an enormous boost to my ego as a budding poet. Looking back, that reading must have provided the audience with quite a contrast – the rhythmic rage of the young Black British apprentice and the quiet eloquence of the Caribbean revolutionary master.

I had been familiar with some of Martin Carter's poetry from the early 1970s. I have the late Jamaican poet and novelist Andrew Salkey to thank for that. Andrew had the habit of using every opportunity he had to promote other people's poetry. One of the poets whose work he took great delight in exposing was Martin Carter. It was on one of those occasions, a reading at the Keskidee Centre, that I heard Andrew reading Carter's 'On the Fourth Night of a Hunger Strike', 'This is the Dark Time My Love' and the immortal 'Death of a Comrade' amongst others. That recital, hearing those poems, had a profound impact on me.

In the early 1970s I was a young political and cultural activist armed with unlimited idealism and total commitment to the black liberation struggle. I had not long discovered black literature and was already harbouring ambitions of being a poet. It was through my political engagement that I discovered poetry and I was drawn towards political verse. When I heard Andrew Salkey recite those poems by Martin Carter, I was at once inspired, because they epitomized for me what I thought committed revolutionary poetry ought to be like. A few years later, when the Trinidadian publisher/activist John La Rose gave me a mint copy of the paperback edition of *Poems of Succession* in 1977, I realized that there was much more to the poetry of Martin Carter than the 'political' dimension. His 'Poems of Shape and Motion' (1 and 2) remain all-time favourites of mine, as do 'Death of a Comrade' and 'A Mouth is Always Muzzled'.

On the one and only occasion that I met him, Martin Carter was just as I had imagined him to be. He was tall, quietly spoken and dignified, with an aura about him. Needless to say, after that encounter I was in even greater awe of him. I still have that copy of *Poems of Succession*. It is now in a tattered state. I go back to it from time to time and I am rewarded every visit. Martin Carter is one of those poets to whom I feel indebted. As a way of acknowledging my indebtedness, I have recorded a rendition of 'Poems of Shape and Motion' on my new album, *More Time*. I give thanks for the inspiration and the example.

Contribution to *All Are Involved: The Art of Martin Carter*, edited by Stewart Brown (Leeds: Peepal Tree Press, 2000). Written in Montego Bay, Jamaica, 12 December 1997

Remembering Michael Smith:
Mikey, Dub and Me (2005)

The late Jamaican poet Michael Smith was, to my mind, one of the most interesting and original poetic voices to emerge from the English-speaking Caribbean during the last quarter of the twentieth century. He was the quintessential performance poet, gifted with an unrivalled talent to mesmerize his audience. With an actor's sense of the dramatic and a musician's acute sense of rhythm, Mikey enthralled audiences from the Caribbean to Europe with his electrifying performances.

He was a gifted wordsmith who could deftly negotiate the verbal contours of Jamaican speech, creating memorable poetic discourse that spoke to the conditions of existence for the 'oppressed' and 'dispossessed' in their everyday language. He drew from a wide range of oral sources, always on the lookout for the ironic and the paradoxical. Mikey was essentially a political poet, a people's poet, who wrote about the dehumanization of the poor and their struggle against poverty and injustice. He wrote with conviction and performed with passion.

Contemptuous of the main political parties in Jamaica, Mikey was identified with the radical left. He was not averse to engaging people in high places in heated verbal combat. He

Jamaica, 2018. LKJ and Mervyn Morris, Mikey Smith's editor, at Calabash.

once told his editor, Mervyn Morris, that he had 'anarchist tendencies' and that he was 'close to rasta'.[1] For Mikey, writing poetry was, to quote him, 'a means of giving hope, building awareness . . . as a part of the whole process of liberation'.

Michael Smith was born in 1954. He came from a working-class background. His father was a mason and his mother a factory worker. He attended various schools and graduated from the Jamaica School of Drama in 1980 with a diploma in theatre arts. He began writing poems at the age of fourteen when he was hospitalized with a broken leg which left him with a permanent limp. Soon he began reciting his verse at various youth clubs in Kingston and by the end of the seventies he had earned a reputation as one of the most dynamic performers on the Jamaican poetry scene.

In 1978 Michael Smith represented Jamaica at the eleventh World Festival of Youth and Students in Cuba. That year saw the release of his first recording, a twelve-inch 45 titled 'Word', followed by another, 'Mi Cyaan Believe It/Roots', accompanied by Count Ossie's Rastafarian drummers, both on the Light of Saba label in Jamaica. In 1981 Mikey performed in Barbados during Carifesta and was filmed by BBC Television performing 'Mi Cyaan Believe It' for the documentary *From Brixton to Barbados*. In 1982 Mikey took London by storm with performances at the Camden Centre for the International Book Fair of Radical Black and Third World Books, and also at the Lambeth Town Hall in Brixton for Creation For Liberation.[2] Whilst in Britain, together with Oku Onuora, he also did a successful poetry tour and recorded a reggae album, which Island Records released under the title *Mi Cyaan Believe It*. And the story did not end there. The BBC's Anthony Wall made a television programme about Mikey for the flagship arts series *Arena*. Entitled *Upon Westminster Bridge*, the programme was broadcast that year on BBC2 and again after Mikey's death in 1983. In November of 1982 Mikey performed in Paris for UNESCO and went on to do another reading in Milan. He returned to Jamaica briefly and then came back to London for another tour, this time as an opening act for the reggae band Black Uhuru, to promote his recently released album. He returned to Jamaica soon after.

What Michael Smith had achieved in such a short space of time was nothing if not remarkable. His untimely death on 17 August 1983 brought to an abrupt end the promise that had so excited those of us who had witnessed his meteoric rise to fame. The circumstances of his death have been shrouded in controversy. As far as I understand the facts, Mikey had attended a meeting in Stony Hill where the ruling Jamaica Labour Party's (JLP) Minister of Education, Mavis Gilmour, was speaking, and had heckled her. The following day he was confronted by three party activists. An argument ensued. Stones were thrown and Mikey died from a blow to his head.

It was I who, upon hearing of Mikey's death and getting an account on the phone from journalist John Maxwell, mobilized the international poetry community to send telegrams and letters of protest demanding that Mikey's killer or killers be brought to justice. I was also instrumental in the organization of a demonstration outside the Jamaican High Commission in London, supported by Creation For Liberation and the alliance of the Black Parents Movement, the Black Youth Movement and the Race Today Collective. I handed a letter to Herbert Walker, Jamaica's High Commissioner at the time, demanding justice. There was also a demonstration in Jamaica, organized by Dr Freddie Hickling, Mikey's friend. Two people were eventually arrested but nothing came of the case for lack of independent witnesses.

A couple of years later I was verbally chastised for my response by Babsy Grange from the then JLP Prime Minister's office when I met her in Jamaica. She said that I had been used by the JLP's enemies for political purposes. More significantly, I discovered from friends that Mikey's mental health had deteriorated not long after his return to Jamaica. Looking back, I remember that on his first visit to London, Mikey's behaviour at times had seemed strange. He would be suspicious of people for no good reason, would be almost paralysed with fear before a performance and was aggressive towards me on a couple of occasions. After his death I learned that he had assaulted Honor Ford-Smith, his former drama tutor and friend.

Between 1984 and 1986 a number of poetic tributes to Michael Smith were published in *Race Today* magazine and *Race Today Review* in London. These were: 'For Michael Smith' by Bob Stewart and 'Godfather's Sermon and Mikey Smith' by Archie Markham in *Race Today Review* 1984; and in the December 1986 issue of *Race Today*, 'I and I (For Michael Smith)' by Jayne Cortez and 'Stone for Mikey Smith' by Kamau Brathwaite. Abdul Malik recorded a reggae rendition of 'Instant Ting', written in 1985 and published in his collection, *The Whirlwind*, in 1988. There was also a tribute in prose by John La Rose titled 'Fallen Comet', published in *The Guardian* (UK) newspaper on 2 September 1983 and also in *Race Today Review* in 1984. *It A Come*, Michael Smith's only collection of poems, edited by Mervyn Morris, was published in 1986 by Race Today Publications and in 1989 by City Lights in the USA. A memorial tribute for Mikey was held on 3 November 1983 at Lambeth Town Hall in Brixton where Afro-American poet Amiri Baraka, Mutabaruka and Oku Onuora from Jamaica and I read. There were a number of tributes to Mikey from novelist and writer Farrukh Dhondy, cultural activist from Benin William Tanifeani, and Kenyan novelist Ngũgĩ wa Thiong'o among others.

The Trinidadian poet and publisher John La Rose locates Michael Smith's poetry in the post-colonial revival and renewal of orality in Caribbean poetry.[3] Mikey belonged to a school of Jamaican oral poetry called 'dub poetry', which came into currency towards the end of the 1970s. Dub poetry was largely associated with a group of poets at the Jamaica School of Drama and, apart from Mikey, included Noel Walcott, M'bala, Jean 'Binta' Breeze and Oku Onuora, dub poetry's main exponent and explainer. Other dub poets in Jamaica at the time included Malachi Smith, Mutabaruka – who had not attached that label to himself then – and a group of poets called Poets-In-Unity. My own work has also been dubbed dub poetry, in spite of my attempts to distance myself from the term, which I actually coined. As a student of reggae music, I had been trying to analyse its lyricism in a sociological context. In an essay I wrote in 1975 entitled 'Jamaican Rebel Music', published in *Race & Class* in 1976, and another entitled 'The Politics of the Lyrics of Reggae Music' published in *The Black Liberator* in 1977, I used the terms 'dub-lyricism' and 'dub poetry' to describe the art of the reggae deejay. Recently I re-read what I had written in the essay in *The Black Liberator* and discovered that I had written, and I quote, 'dub poetry that "scatter matter shatter shock"'. The 'scatter matter shatter shock' is a line from my poem 'Bass Culture', about reggae music. What I was doing there, whether consciously or not, was identifying my own verse with the art of the reggae deejay. And yet by then I had already defined my verse as reggae poetry.

What is this dub poetry in which Michael Smith so excelled? A survey of some of what has been written on the subject turned up some interesting, if at times unhelpful, answers. In his essay 'Dub Poetry?' Professor Mervyn Morris offers, perhaps, the most clinical definition. He writes:

The word 'dub' in 'dub poetry' is borrowed from recording technology, where it refers to the activity of adding or removing sounds. 'Dub poetry', which is written to be performed, incorporates a music beat, often a reggae beat. Often, but not always, the performance is done to the accompaniment of music, recorded or live. Dub poetry is usually, but not always, written in Jamaican language; in Jamaican Creole/dialect/vernacular/nation language. By extension, it may be written in the informal language of people from anywhere. Most often it is politically focused, attacking oppression and injustice. Though the ideal context of dub poetry is the live performance, it also makes itself available in various other ways: on the radio, on television, in audio recordings, video recordings and on film. Many dub poets also publish books.[4]

There is an echo of Mervyn Morris' definition in the observation by Professor J. Edward Chamberlin that:

> dubbing words over a musical background became common enough that dub poetry came to include any rendition incorporating reggae musical rhythms, and any verse combining reggae rhythms with local speech . . . But musical accompaniment is not as important to dub poetry as hearing the reggae rhythm in the poem.[5]

Pamela Mordecai tells us that the voice of the dub poet is 'a voice meant to be propelled from the page onto the stage and into the sound studio where reverb, sound separation, amplification etc. would enhance its statement'.[6]

Professor Gordon Rohlehr has written extensively on popular culture and the literary arts in the English-speaking Caribbean. He has outlined four categories of dub poetry: 'Dread Talk, Dub Sermon, Prophet Sight and Prophesy, which have grown out of the speech and music rhythms of reggae and rastafari'. Rohlehr asserts that 'dub poetry is, at its worst, a kind of tedious jabber to a monotonous rhythm. At its best it is the intelligent appropriation of the manipulatory techniques of the DJ'.[7]

Although Professor Kwame Dawes sees some merit in some dub poetry, he says that 'in its dogged adherence to the reggae backbeat, quite often phrasing in ways which are counter to the natural rhythms of speech, [it] can sound as if it has been stretched awkwardly to find a way into the grooves of the music'. For Dawes, dub poetry is only interesting when it points to the possibilities for a reggae aesthetic. He writes: 'Perhaps it has taken the exploration of a reggae sensibility in other forms (in fiction, in poetry which is concerned with the written as well as the performance, dance, drama and painting and sculpting) to enable us to recognise that there is an aesthetic which crosses forms'.[8]

The Oxford Companion to Twentieth Century Poetry quotes London-based Jamaican poet James Berry OBE describing dub poetry as 'over-compensation for deprivation'. The definition goes on to tell us that 'rage and belligerent overstatement are its keynotes, but also optimistic vitality, energy and exuberance'.[9] I will end my review with this quote from Pamela Mordecai in which she captures the real significance of dub poetry: 'If nothing else does, "dub" [poetry] lays to rest the notion that Jamaican poetry is still "copying" the forms and devices of any other literature'.[10]

What my brief survey of commentators on dub poetry suggests is that there is mostly unanimity about its content and form. There is also agreement among the most informed critics about the structural integrity of Michael Smith's poetry. Professor Chamberlin points to Mikey's use of language to create 'a poetic style that sustains the plain-as-life qualities of speech and the heightened sense of and highly structured intensity of personal revelation that is the business of certain kinds of poetry, especially lyric poetry, to achieve'.[11] Kamau Brathwaite, who was a seminal influence for most of the prominent dub poets, rightly asserts that they are inheritors of the revolution (that he led) against the dominating influences of the English poetic canon on Caribbean poetry. He states that, in Mikey's case, 'a quite remarkable voice and breath control, accompanied

by a decorative S90 noise . . . becomes part of the sound structure and meaning of the poem' – the S90 noise being that of
a motorbike.[12] Morris, too, asserts that in Mikey's poetry:

> one can hardly fail to notice his firm sense of structure and
> of rhythmic patterning. The rhetoric of the preachers and
> politicians, the cries of the [street] pedlars, allusions to prov-
> erbs, nursery rhymes, children's games [...] – and to flashpoints
> in Jamaican and international news – they are all pulled
> together or set against each other in what are usually well
> articulated rhythmic structures.[13]

Michael Smith was clearly a serious poet whose work has been
taken seriously.

What was the relationship between Michael Smith and myself?
I did not know Mikey well enough for long enough to say that
we were close, but I think I can get away with saying we were
friends. Thanks to Mervyn Morris, we had knowledge of and
admiration for each other's work by the time we first met in
Kingston in 1980. I had been in correspondence with Mikey
from 1979. Mikey was very striking in appearance. Tallish, dark,
with nascent locks, beard, protruding front teeth and a winning
smile, he impressed me with his sincerity, and I concluded after
our first meeting that we were kindred spirits. We saw each other
on a number of occasions during my stay in Jamaica. I remember
accompanying him to the Gun Court, where I sat in on one of
his regular workshops which he held with a group of prisoners.
The Gun Court was instituted in the 1970s by Michael Manley's
PNP government to deal with rising gun crime, fuelled by

political warfare. Possession of guns or ammunition meant indefinite incarceration in the specially built jail.

As far as Mikey was concerned, I was this big-time poet and reggae artist from London who was involved in the struggle and, therefore, had an obligation to lend a helping hand to a struggling poet from yard committed to the same ideals. The moral blackmail was not necessary, because I admired his poems and had already decided that I would try to do whatever I could to promote his work. In those days I was a member of the Race Today Collective and our magazine, *Race Today*, had an international circulation. I was Poetry Editor and as soon as I returned to London I arranged for the publication of Mikey's celebrated poem, 'Mi Cyaan Believe It', in the December issue of *Race Today Review*, our annual publication devoted to arts and culture.

In 1980 I established LKJ Records and the label's first release was Mikey's recording of 'Mi Cyaan Believe It' and 'Roots'. As luck would have it, the following year I received a telephone call from Alan Yentob, who was the then editor of the BBC television arts programme *Arena*. Yentob asked me if I knew anything about Carifesta, a Caribbean regional cultural festival, and I said yes. The next thing I knew, I was off to Barbados with director Anthony Wall and an American film crew, as researcher, interviewer and presenter of a documentary about the festival, which was broadcast that year under the title *From Brixton to Barbados*. I was surprised to meet Mikey there and suggested to Anthony Wall that Mikey was someone who had to be included in the programme.

The next time I met Mikey was in London in 1982. As a

member of the *Race Today* editorial board, I was a member of the organizing committee of the first International Book Fair of Radical Black and Third World Books, organized jointly by New Beacon Books, Race Today Publications and Bogle-L'Ouverture Books. It was I who suggested that Mikey and Oku Onuora be invited to participate in the Book Fair Festival. Creation For Liberation, an organization of which I was a founder member, had already arranged for Oku Onuora and Mikey to come to Britain for a poetry tour. I was also involved in the making of the film *Upon Westminster Bridge* which Anthony Wall made for BBC television.

Mikey was keen to record a reggae album and had brought with him a demo tape of three or four of his poems, which had been done with the assistance of Ibo Cooper, then a member of the reggae band Third World. I agreed to co-produce the album with Dennis Bovell and persuaded Chris Blackwell of Island Records to sign Mikey to his label. Later that year I received an invitation from Édouard Glissant, the Martiniquan poet and novelist, who was then editor of UNESCO's *Courier*, to take part in poetry events in Paris and Milan. The events were to be held in November. I knew I would be in Jamaica then, researching my BBC radio series on the history of reggae, *From Mento to Lovers' Rock*, and suggested Mikey as an alternative. Édouard agreed.

The Michael Smith Memorial Committee that was formed in Jamaica by Freddie Hickling and others has ceased to function. Len Dyke of Dyke & Dryden in London and myself wanted to donate some money for a plaque or something permanent in memory of Mikey. Mervyn Morris suggested that the money be donated to some kind of student fund at the Jamaica School of Drama. Between us we donated £1,000 to this end and agreed to top up the fund from time to time. This was only a couple of years after Mikey's death. I do not know what became of the fund. The person who was then Principal of the School of Drama hadn't even heard of Michael Smith, the college's most famous past student at the time. It is unfortunate that Michael Smith's only collection of poems, *It A Come*, is no longer available in Britain with the demise of Race Today Publications. Neither is his only reggae album, *Mi Cyaan Believe It*. His poetry continues to be taught in schools in Jamaica and at the University of the West Indies. The people's poet has left a lasting legacy to Caribbean literature.

Notes

1 Morris, Mervyn, 'Building Awareness: Mikey Smith Interviewed' in *Making West Indian Literature* (Kingston, Jamaica and Miami: Ian Randle Publishers, 2005), pp. 100–5. First published in *Jamaica Journal* 18, no. 2 (May–July 1985).

2 Creation For Liberation was an organization founded in the late 1970s in London, UK, linked to the Race Today Collective (publishers of *Race Today* magazine). It was engaged in promoting cultural activities. Linton Kwesi Johnson was a founding member.

3 La Rose, John, 'Fallen Comet' in *The Race Today Review* (1984), pp. 4–5.

4 Morris, Mervyn, 'Dub Poetry?' in *Is English We Speaking and Other Essays* (Kingston, Jamaica: Ian Randle Publishers, 1999), p. 36.

5 Chamberlin, J. Edward, *Come Back to Me My Language: Poetry*

and the West Indies (Urbana and Chicago, Illinois: University of Illinois Press, 1993), p. 235.

6 Mordecai, Pamela, 'Introduction' in From Our Yard: Jamaican Poetry Since Independence, ed. Pamela Mordecai (Kingston, Jamaica: Institute of Jamaica Publications, 1987), p. xxiii.

7 Rohlehr, Gordon, 'Introduction' in Voice Print: An Anthology of Oral and Related Poetry from the Caribbean, ed. Stewart Brown, Mervyn Morris and Gordon Rohlehr (Harlow: Longman, 1989), p. 18.

8 Dawes, Kwame, Natural Mysticism: Towards a New Reggae Aesthetic in Caribbean Writing (Leeds: Peepal Tree Press, 1999), pp. 82–3.

9 Berry, James, 'dub poetry' entry in Oxford Companion to Twentieth Century Poetry In English, ed. Ian Hamilton (Oxford: Oxford University Press, 1994).

10 Mordecai, Pamela, 'Introduction' in From Our Yard, op. cit., p. xxiii.

11 Chamberlin, J. Edward, op. cit., p. 238.

12 Brathwaite, Kamau, History of the Voice: The Development of Nation Language in Anglophone Caribbean Poetry (London and Port of Spain: New Beacon Books, 1984), p. 46.

13 Morris, Mervyn, 'Editor's Notes' in It A Come: Poems By Michael Smith, ed. Mervyn Morris (London: Race Today Publications, 1986), p. 10.

Michael Smith Bibliography

Poems by Michael Smith published by Race Today *(London, UK)*
'Mi Cyaan Believe It', Race Today Review (December 1980/January 19981).
'Mi Feel It Yuh Si', Race Today Review (1983).
'Say Natty', Race Today (February/March 1982).

Books by Michael Smith
Morris, Mervyn, ed., It A Come: Poems by Michael Smith (London: Race Today Publications, 1986).

Morris, Mervyn, ed., *It A Come: Poems by Michael Smith* (San Francisco, USA: City Lights, 1989).

Michael Smith Discography

Smith, Michael, 'Word', 12 inch 45 (Jamaica: Light of Saba, 1978).
Smith, Michael, 'Mi Cyaan Believe It/Roots', 12 inch 45 (Jamaica: Light of Saba, 1978).
Smith, Michael, 'Mi Cyaan Believe It/Roots', 12 inch 45 (London: LKJ Records Ltd, 1981).
Smith, Michael, *Mi Cyaan Believe It*, LP album (London: Island Records, 1982).

Other Bibliographical Reading

Dawes, Kwame, ed., *Wheel and Come Again: An Anthology of Reggae Poetry* (Leeds: Peepal Tree and Fredericton, Canada: Goose Lane Editions, 1998).
De Coteau, Delano Abdul Malik, *The Whirlwind* (London: Panrun Collective, 1988).
Habekost, Christian, ed., *Dub Poetry: Nineteen Poets from England and Jamaica* (Neustadt: Michael Schwinn, 1986).
Johnson, Linton Kwesi, 'Jamaican Rebel Music', in *Race & Class* (Spring 1976).
Johnson, Linton Kwesi, 'The Politics of the Lyrics of Reggae Music', in *The Black Liberator* (1977).

Lecture, 4 August 2005

Mutabaruka: Cutting Edge
of Dub (2005)

Jamaican dub poet Mutabaruka is visiting these shores this month, but he won't be staying long. I once had the dubious honour of a Mutabaruka poem being dedicated to me. I say 'dubious' because of the poem's refrain: 'it no good fi stay inna white man country too long'. The poem, 'White Man Country', Muta told me, was inspired by 'Inglan is a Bitch', my poem about the Caribbean migrant experience of my parents' generation in Britain. 'Mi seh, but – how de bredrin inna Inglan a seh Inglan is a bitch; why him no leff di bitch?' In another poem, 'My Great Shun', Muta mocks the illegal immigrant, the 'Jamaican body' with the 'foreign mind': 'but yu neva know tings was like dis/ in de lan of opportunity an bliss'. But to be fair to Muta, in the later poems 'H2 Worka' and 'Old Cut Bruk', he empathizes with the immigrant.

Muta belongs to a tradition of Rastafarian oratory, exemplified by elder Rasta poets like Mortimo Planno, Sam Brown, Sam Clayton, Joseph Ruglass and Bongo Jerry. His name is known throughout Jamaica; his weekly late-night talk show *The Cutting Edge* on Irie FM has made Muta a national figure, albeit a controversial one, and through the internet, his show now has an international audience. The internationally renowned dub poet, reggae artist, actor, Rasta philosopher, broadcaster and entrepreneur found his adopted name in a book of poems as a schoolboy. He later discovered that, in Rwanda, the name means 'one who is always victorious'. Muta is a charismatic, loquacious, bare-footed Rasta man who oozes self-confidence. A strict vegan, he does not imbibe opiates of any kind.

I first came across the name Mutabaruka in 1974 when I saw a poem of his, 'Nursery Rhyme Lament', in a Jamaican magazine called *Swing*. The poem wittily employs colonial nonsense rhymes to comment on post-colonial conditions of life for Jamaica's working class. It made me laugh and I remember liking the poem, and still do. I was a young poet then of Muta's age, trying to find my own voice. We eventually met in the early eighties in Kingston. In 1985 we read together with Amiri Baraka and Oku Onuora at a tribute for the late Mikey Smith at Lambeth Town Hall in Brixton.

Recently we both read at the fifth Calabash Literary Festival in Treasure Beach, Jamaica. I took the opportunity to ask him about his new book of poems, *The Next Poems*, published in Jamaica by Paul Issa and introduced by the poet and literary critic Mervyn Morris. *The Next Poems* is an upside-down book with two distinctive covers. It is, in fact, two books in one as his earlier collection, *The First Poems*, published twenty-five years ago, is also included. *The First Poems* section of the book consists of poems written between 1970 and 1979, including poems previously published in *Twenty-Four Poems* (1972), *Outcry* (1973) and *Sun and Moon* with Fabienne Miranda (1976). These poems reflect the emerging consciousness of a young mind grappling with issues of blackness, belief and belonging, influenced by the black power movement of the late sixties and early seventies. Of the forty-one poems in this section of the book, only four are in Jamaican Creole, the rest in English.

The Next Poems section are poems written from the 1980s onwards, after Muta began recording. Many of these were recorded with reggae accompaniment but not published. The poems are neatly arranged chronologically in decades. There is a continuity of themes from *The First Poems*, but the canvas is now widened to include poems that focus on environmental concerns, hard drugs, junk food and other issues; as Mervyn Morris observes, 'the protest element predominates [. . .]: protest against poverty, inequality, racism, class prejudice, oppression, political deceit and the wickedness of powerful nations'.

Unlike earlier works, more than half of the thirty-one poems are written in Jamaican Creole. I asked Muta if that had anything to do with the fact that they were written after he started making records. He replied: 'No . . . mi couldn't answer that. You would haffi find a Mutabaruka analyser fi analyse that. Ah don't have a preference . . . mi know mi write how mi feel an mi use the kind a music mi feel fi use. That is why the dub poetry reggae poetry ting kind a get to be a way. Because sometimes I don't even hear reggae inna di poem. I hear all jazz an hear funk and house.' Whether his poems are written in English or Creole, Muta's voice is unmistakably Jamaican.

Named Alan Hope at birth, Mutabaruka was born in Kingston in 1952. He grew up in a working-class neighbourhood and attended Kingston Technical High School. He has fond memories of his time there. 'We was very fortunate that

Marcus Garvey son, Marcus Garvey Junior, teach me; and we did have a bredrin name Locksley Comrie who was part a the staff.' Through these two well-known radicals Muta was able to access the black power literature of the day. This at a time when Hugh Shearer's Jamaica Labour Party government had banned black power literature and had barred Guyanese radical historian Walter Rodney from returning to his post at the University of the West Indies. Muta read books by H. Rap Brown, Stokely Carmichael and Eldridge Cleaver. He heard the *Message to the Grassroots* album by Malcolm X, recordings by the Last Poets, and read poetry by Sonia Sanchez and Don L. Lee.

After leaving school he worked for the Jamaica Telephone Company and became involved in a black power organization. His poems were being published regularly in *Swing* magazine and elsewhere and Muta began reciting his poems at small gatherings and bookshops. Sometimes he was accompanied by percussionist Larry McDonald of Taj Mahal fame. Muta was drawn to Rastafari and became a member of the Twelve Tribes of Israel, where he met Peter Phillips, Jamaica's current Minister of National Security, and the Rasta poet Bongo Jerry. Now having fully embraced Rastafari, in 1974 Muta abandoned city life and retreated to the hills of Potosi in St James.

It was during this period of retreat that Muta became involved in the tourist industry, working for the father of Paul Issa, his publisher. Based at the Negril Village Beach hotel, Muta's job was to 'explain bout Rasta an expose people to that part a Jamaica an the culture.' Although he had withdrawn from the poetry scene, Muta continued to write. Meanwhile, Cedric

Brooks' band of jazz musicians, Count Ossie's Rasta drummers and poets recorded a rendition of Muta's poem 'Outcry' on their *Light of Saba* album.

By the late seventies a new movement of poetry, associated with students of the Jamaica School of Drama, had emerged. Dub poetry was the name given to the new style of verse which reflected a revival of orality in Caribbean poetry, influenced by reggae music. Oku Onuora (dub poetry's chief exponent and explainer), the late Mikey Smith, Malachi Smith, Poets-in-Unity, M'bala and Jean 'Binta' Breeze were among the new voices of the movement.

Muta had known about the dub poets, but it was not until after Michael Smith had recorded his classic poem, 'Mi Cyaan Believe It', and Oku Onuora had recorded 'Reflections in Red' that Muta boarded the dub poetry train. He was persuaded by some Rasta elders, including Mortimo Planno, to recite a poem at a Jimmy Cliff concert, accompanied by Cliff's backing musicians. He recited 'White Sound' at one of the earliest Reggae Sunsplashes, Jamaica's first music festival, and the enthusiasm with which his performance was received persuaded Chinna Smith, band leader of the High Times Players, to record the poem. It was released in Jamaica in 1981 under the title 'Everytime I Hear the Sound', and was an instant success, marking the beginning of Muta's successful career as a reggae artist. He has released several albums including *Check It* (Alligator, 1983), *Outcry* (Shanachie, 1984), *The Mystery Unfolds* (Shanachie, 1988), *Any Which Way Freedom* (Shanachie, 1989) and *The Ultimate Collection* (Shanachie, 1996). Muta has toured all over the world performing his poetry with and without reggae accompaniment. I put it to Muta that he had initially kept a discreet distance from the dub poetry movement, only to emerge as the ruler of the roost in Jamaica with the death of Mikey Smith and the migration of Oku Onuora and Jean 'Binta' Breeze. Muta smiles wryly, tells me that he was a Rasta man and had not been into poetry per se. He reminds me that it was he who produced Jean 'Binta' Breeze's first record, the single 'Slip'. He also produced the first anthology album of Jamaican dub poets, *Word Soun' 'Ave Power: Reggae Poetry* (Heartbeat, 1983), and *Womantalk* (Heartbeat, 1986) featuring female dub poets, including Louise Bennett, the mother of Jamaican poetry. I remind Muta that I was in Jamaica when *Word Soun' 'Ave Power* was being recorded and had helped him out with a couple of bass lines. He couldn't recall my presence until I described the guitarist who had made insulting remarks about me being there.

Mutabaruka's sound system, Black Music, provided musical entertainment at Calabash. Black Music has a reputation for playing the music of the diaspora. It was Muta's reputation as a sound system operator that got him into radio broadcasting. Muta is also regularly invited to participate in television debates on religious topics. He was given a fellowship by the University of the West Indies and was the resident Folk Philosopher at the Mona Campus for eighteen months.

Many years ago I saw Muta performing in the USA and realized that, although he hadn't been to drama school like some of the dub poets, he was not lacking in a sense of the theatrical. On that occasion he performed a poem bare-chested, with his hands manacled in chains. At Calabash Muta was suitably attired in colourful robes with matching turban. A performer with great presence on stage, Muta's often incisive and witty comments in between poems are integral to his performance. At Calabash he had two powerful Jamaican performers to follow: Stacyann Chin and Joan Andrea Hutchinson. He did not disappoint.

The Guardian, 27 August 2005

Obituary: John La Rose
(2006)

John La Rose, who has died aged seventy-eight, was the elder statesman of Britain's black communities. Like Marcus Garvey, C. L. R. James, George Padmore, Fidel Castro and Frantz Fanon, John belongs to a Caribbean tradition of radical and revolutionary activism whose input has reverberated across continents. The depth and breadth of his contribution to the struggle for cultural and social change, for racial equality and social justice, for the humanization of society, is unparalleled in the history of the black experience in Britain. He was a man of great erudition whose generosity of spirit and clarity of vision and sincerity inspired people like me. John was not only my mentor, friend, comrade, he was like a father to me. He was the most remarkable human being I have ever known.

A poet, essayist, publisher, filmmaker, trade unionist, cultural and political activist, John was born in Arima, Trinidad, where his father was a cocoa trader and his mother a teacher. At nine he won a scholarship to St Mary's College, where he later taught before becoming an insurance executive. He also taught in Venezuela. Culture, politics and trade unionism were central to his vision of change. He was an executive member of the

Val Wilmer's photograph used to accompany LKJ's obituary of
John La Rose which appeared in *The Guardian*, 4 March 2006.

Youth Council in Trinidad and produced their fortnightly radio programme, *Noise of Youth*, for Radio Trinidad. In the mid-1950s he co-authored, with the calypsonian Raymond Quevedo ('Atilla the Hun'), a pioneering study of calypso entitled *Kaiso: A Review*, republished in 1983 as *Atilla's Kaiso*.

One of John's favourite sayings was 'we didn't come alive in Britain', an allusion to the struggles that had been waged by Caribbean peoples in the Caribbean against colonialism and for workers' and people's power. In the 1940s in Trinidad, he helped to found the Workers Freedom Movement and edited their journal, *Freedom*. He was an executive member of the Federated Workers Trade Union, later merged into the National Union of Government and Federated Workers. He became the General Secretary of the West Indian Independence Party and contested a seat in Trinidad's 1956 general election after being banned from other West Indian islands by the British colonial authorities. He was also involved in the internal struggle of the Oilfield Workers Trade Union, siding with the 'rebel' faction who wanted a more radical and democratic union, with one member, one vote. The rebels prevailed in the 1962 union election and John became their European representative, a position he held until his death.

Soon after he arrived in Britain in 1961 he was once again engaged in activism. In 1966 he co-founded (with Sarah White) New Beacon Books, the first black publishing house, bookshop and international book service. In that same year, together with the Jamaican writer and broadcaster Andrew Salkey and the Barbadian poet and historian Kamau Brathwaite, he co-founded the Caribbean Artists Movement, providing a platform for

Caribbean artists, poets, writers, dramatists, actors and musicians. In 1972–3 he was Chairman of the Institute of Race Relations and Towards Racial Justice, which published the radical campaigning journal *Race Today*, edited by Darcus Howe.

John was also involved in the Black Education Movement in the 1960s, particularly in the struggle against banding, and the placing of West Indian children in schools for the educationally sub-normal. He founded the George Padmore Supplementary School for West Indian children in 1969 and was one of the founders of the Caribbean Education in Community Workers Association. That organization published Bernard Coard's ground-breaking *How the West Indian Child is made Educationally Subnormal in the British School System* (1971). He was also instrumental in the founding of the National Association of Supplementary Schools in the 1980s and was its chairman for a couple of years.

In 1975, after a black schoolboy was assaulted outside his school by police in the London borough of Haringey, John, together with concerned parents, founded the Black Parents Movement to combat the brutalization and criminalization of young blacks, and to agitate for youth and parent power and decent education. By then the *Race Today* journal had severed links with the Institute of Race Relations and was now the journal of the Race Today Collective. The Black Parents Movement formed an alliance with them and with the Black Youth Movement.

This alliance became the most powerful cultural and political movement organized by blacks in Britain, winning many campaigns for justice against police oppression, agitating for better state education and supporting black working-class struggle. It was the alliance who formed the New Cross Massacre Action Committee in response to the arson attack which resulted in the death of thirteen young blacks in 1981, and mobilized twenty thousand black people and their supporters in March 1981 to protest the death of the young people and the failure of the police to conduct a proper investigation. John was the chairman of the New Cross Massacre Action Committee and gave tremendous support to the bereaved families.

In 1982, John was again instrumental in the founding of Africa Solidarity, in support of those struggling against dictatorial governments and tyranny in Africa. That year he also became chairman of the Committee for the Release of Political Prisoners in Kenya, whose founding members included the Kenyan novelist and critic Ngũgĩ wa Thiong'o. In response to the rise in fascism and xenophobia, John La Rose helped to found European Action for Racial Equality and Social Justice, bringing together anti-racists and anti-fascists from Belgium, Italy, France and Germany. He made a short film on the Black Church in Britain for a special Caribbean edition of *Full House*, which he produced for BBC Two in 1973, and co-produced and scripted Franco Rosso's documentary film *Mangrove Nine*, about the resistance of the black community to police attacks in the popular Mangrove restaurant.

One of John's greatest achievements was the International Book Fair of Radical Black and Third World Books (1982–95), organized jointly with Bogle-L'Ouverture Books and Race Today Publications. He was joint director with Jessica Huntley of the Book Fair and, after the withdrawal of Bogle-L'Ouverture, its sole director. In the call to the first Book Fair, John wrote, 'This First International Book Fair of Radical Black and Third World Books is intended to mark the new and expanding phase in the growth of the radical ideas and concepts and their expression in literature, politics, music, art and social life'. The Book Fair was indeed 'a meeting of the continents for writers, publishers, distributors, booksellers, artists, musicians, film-makers, and people who inspire and consume their creative productions'.

The George Padmore Institute, a library and educational research centre housing materials relating to the black community of Caribbean, African and Asian descent in Britain and continental Europe, was established in 1991 and chaired by John. He was also the editor at New Beacon Books and of their journal, *New Beacon Review*, and published two volumes of his own poetry, *Foundations* (1966) and *Eyelets of Truth Within Me* (1992).

John La Rose could have been anything he wanted, but he was without ambition. He preferred to stay in the background and make things happen. He was the man who dreamed to change the world.

John La Rose leaves behind his first wife, Irma La Rose, and their sons Michael and Keith; and Sarah White, his partner, and their son Wole.

John La Rose, born 27 December 1927, died 28 February 2006

The Guardian, 4 March 2006

Obituary: Louise Bennett, Voice of the People (2006)

Louise Bennett-Coverley, also known as Miss Lou, a legend in her lifetime who earned iconic status in her native Jamaica, died on 26 July 2006 aged eighty-six. Actress, comedian, broadcaster, poet, folklorist, teacher and social commentator, she was a household name in Jamaica and celebrated abroad. With the exception of Marcus Garvey, I cannot think of any other Jamaican who has had a greater impact on the shaping of the nation's identity. Her influence on Jamaican culture is phenomenal. She has made a significant contribution in helping the Jamaican people come to terms with their African heritage, valorizing the culture of the folk.

Her greatest achievement was to rehabilitate, elevate and validate the spoken language of the people, Jamaican Creole, through her poetry. As Mervyn Morris asserts:

> She was a patriot committed to correcting the colonial legacy of self-contempt and she cleared the way for others by demonstrating that Jamaican Creole could be the medium of significant art. (*The Guardian*)

She used irony disguised in laughter to offer Jamaican people a mirror in which they could see themselves. Her impact was not limited to Jamaica; she is regarded as the most influential Caribbean writer for bringing Creole 'into the foreground of West Indian cultural life' (Morris, *The Guardian*) and is recognized as a poet of international significance.

Louise Simone Bennett, an only child, was born on 7 September 1919 in Kingston, Jamaica. Her mother, Kerene Robinson-Bennett, was a dressmaker, and her father, Augustus Cornelius Bennett, a baker who died when she was seven years old. Her love of Jamaican talk and her talent for performing were nurtured by her mother and grandmother Mimi. She attended Calabar Elementary School, St Simon's College and Excelsior High School in Kingston and Friends' College in Highgate, St Mary. At school she liked literature and tried her hand at writing verse in English. She wrote her first Jamaican 'dialect' poem, 'On a Tram Car', when she was fourteen years old. The poem was well received by schoolmates so she continued to write more in her native tongue and began performing them at free concerts. In 1938 she received her first professional fee from local impresario Eric 'Chalk Talk' Coverley, who in 1954 became her husband. In 1943 her poems began to appear regularly in the *Jamaican Gleaner*. Her best-known publications are *Jamaica Labrish* (1966), *Anancy and Miss Lou* (1979), *Selected Poems* (1982) and *Aunty Roachy Seh* (1993).

Although she had been publishing books since 1942, it was not until 1963 when Mervyn Morris wrote his seminal essay, 'On Reading Louise Bennett Seriously', that Miss Lou began to receive critical attention and acclaim. Other academics who have looked at her work include Gordon Rohlehr, Carolyn Cooper, Lloyd Brown and Rex Nettleford. A decade after Morris' essay, Louise Bennett began receiving numerous awards and honours, including the MBE, the Order of Jamaica and, most recently, the Order of Merit from the Jamaican government in 2001 and becoming a Fellow of the Institute of Jamaica in 2003.

An accomplished actress and comedian, Miss Lou brought laughter into the lives of three generations of Jamaicans. She was regarded as the first lady of Jamaican theatre. She made a significant contribution to the Jamaicanization of the Little Theatre Movement's national pantomime as actress, writer, lyricist and director, and performed in twenty-five productions between 1943 and 1975. A British Council scholarship allowed her to hone her theatrical talent at the Royal Academy for the Dramatic Arts (RADA) in Britain from 1945 to 1947, and she performed with repertory companies in Amersham, Coventry and Huddersfield. After a brief sojourn in the USA between 1953 and 1955, during which she worked in radio, sang folk songs and married Eric Coverley, they returned to Jamaica where they resided for the next three decades. In the early 1980s they migrated to the USA and eventually settled in Canada.

It was largely through radio and later, television, that Miss Lou became a household name in Jamaica. Her broadcasting career began when she was a student at RADA and was given her own programme by the BBC. After graduating in 1947 she went back to Jamaica and returned to England in 1950 to work on the BBC radio programme *West Indian Guest Night*. Jamaicans will remember her local radio shows *Laugh with Louise*, the *Aunty Roachy Seh* series and *The Lou and Ranny Show*. Her television show *Ring Ding* captivated and delighted children during the 1970s.

Louise Bennett was a scholar of Jamaica's folklore and oral culture which she had begun to study whilst a student at Friends College and continued during the 1950s when she worked as Drama Officer for the Jamaica Social Welfare Commission, travelling all over the island. She was consulted by lexicographers and scholars and lectured on drama and folklore for the Extramural department of the University of the West Indies.

It was in her capacity as a scholar that I first met Miss Lou in 1981 when I was doing research for my BBC radio series, *From Mento to Lovers' Rock*, on the history of modern popular Jamaican music. Miss Lou was very accommodating, warm, charming and hospitable. The information I got from her was invaluable in putting the series together. Then in 1983, I couldn't believe my luck when Miss Lou invited me to do a couple of items with her on stage during a rare performance in London at the Lyric Theatre in Hammersmith. Together we performed the folk song 'Under the Coconut Tree' and the word game 'Mawnin Buddy'. The show was recorded and released as the album *Yes M'Dear – Miss Lou Live* by Island Records. Some of Miss Lou's other recordings include *Jamaica Singing Games* (1953), *Listen to Louise* (1968) and *The Honourable Miss Lou* (1981).

Several Caribbean artists, including the Jamaican dub poets, have acknowledged the enormous debt owed to Louise Bennett. In Britain we have our own Miss Lou in the poet Valerie Bloom.

Mervyn Morris tells us in his essay 'Miss Lou, Some Heirs and Successors' that:

> Joan Andrea Hutchinson and Amina Blackwood Meeks, distinctly talented writers and precisely effective performers, have absorbed and, in their differing ways, have begun to extend the creative legacy of Louise Bennett. (82)

Louise Bennett was given the state funeral that her creative accomplishments, her life's work, merited, and was buried at Heroes Circle in Kingston, Jamaica, with her husband. I am sure I am not the only Jamaican who hopes that it will be just a matter of time before Miss Lou joins Nanny of the Maroons to become Jamaica's second national heroine.

Works Cited and Select Bibliography

Bennett, Louise, *Jamaica Labrish* (Kingston, Jamaica: Sangster's, 1966).

Bennett, Louise, *Selected Poems*, ed. Mervyn Morris (Kingston, Jamaica: Sangster's, 1982).

Bennett, Louise, *Yes M'Dear – Miss Lou Live*, album (London: Island Records, 1983).

Morris, Mervyn, 'Miss Lou, Some Heirs and Successors', in *Making West Indian Literature* (Kingston, Jamaica and Miami: Ian Randle Publishers, 2005), pp. 75–83.

Morris, Mervyn, 'Obituary: Louise Bennett-Coverley', *The Guardian*, 1 August 2006.

Wasafiri, October 2006

Remembering Andrew Salkey
(2014)

I am sitting at the dining table looking ahead, my face turned slightly to my left, and there they are, Sam Selvon, John La Rose and Andrew Salkey, standing together staring at me. The black and white photo, taken by Trinidadian-British filmmaker and photographer Horace Ové, is an exterior shot of them standing against a brick wall. It is one of three in a landscape frame given to me as a fiftieth birthday present; a treasured possession. The camera is focused on Andrew from an angle that makes his two friends seem much smaller. He is looking straight at the camera through large, square-framed glasses. He is wearing an olive-green bush jacket and hat and sports a huge Fidel Castro style beard.

When I was first introduced to Andrew by John La Rose at New Beacon Books in 1971, he didn't look like that. His hair was combed back, his beard neatly shaped and he had on round, gold-rimmed glasses. Andrew greeted me with a warm smile, a firm handshake and a glint in his eyes. When he spoke with his BBC accent, his mellifluous voice sounded sweet to my ears. I was as equally awestruck by him as I was when I had first met John. My spirit took to Andrew at once and I think the feeling was mutual.

It is impossible for me to write about Andrew without mentioning John. They were very close friends and comrades committed to changing the world. I consider myself very fortunate to have been mentored by these two remarkable Caribbean men. I was a young activist in the Black Panther Movement when I met them. In the Panthers I got a glimpse into the world of black literature. John opened the doors wide and recommended books by poets whose work I've grown to love. Andrew took me under his wing, diligently nurturing my interest in poetry. They both ensured that I was exposed to the activities of CAM – the Caribbean Artists Movement – which they co-founded together with Kamau Brathwaite. My political activism and peripheral involvement with CAM were life-changing experiences. Just being around or simply meeting people like George Lamming, Errol Lloyd, Emmanuel Jegede, Ronald Moody, Sam Selvon and others was amazing. The ambience was stimulating and inspirational.

Like so many young aspiring poets, I was anxious to see my work in print. Andrew recommended a couple of journals, which returned the verse I'd sent with terse notes of rejection. I was disappointed but not disheartened because once I started reciting in public, I was encouraged by the reception I received. At one of those early readings Sam Selvon, a friend of Andrew and John, gave me the proverbial pat on the back and told me to keep on writing my Jamaican verse. On another occasion I took part in a reading at the Keskidee Centre in Islington. George Lamming was in the audience. He sat leaning forward, his head tilted sideways, his brow knitted with his face wearing what seemed like a frown throughout my recital. This heightened my nervousness. I said to Andrew after the reading, 'Did you see the look on George Lamming's face during my reading? He didn't like my poems.' 'No, man, he was just concentrating. We all enjoyed your reading,' was Andrew's reassuring reply.

Andrew was a brilliant reader of poetry. Whenever CAM organized a reading at the West Indian Students Centre in Earls Court or at the Keskidee Centre, he would be one of the readers alongside younger poets like Jamal Ali, Frank John, Jimi Rand, Rudi Kizerman and, occasionally, me. Andrew would have words of encouragement for the young poets full of revolutionary ardour. He would advise us to try and write about revolution without using the word 'revolution' in the poem. He would invariably use his allotted time to introduce the audience to the work of revolutionary poets and recite maybe one or two of his own poems at the end. It was a treat to hear him read poems by Nicolás Guillén, Martin Carter, Bongo Jerry, Marc Matthews and other poets whose work was not widely known in the UK.

I visited Andrew a few times at his flat in Bayswater, where I met his wife Pat and his two young sons Elliot and Jason. At one of those visits the Jamaican actress Yvonne Brewster was there. She and Andrew were putting together an evening of poetry and prose at the Commonwealth Institute in Kensington which showcased new writing from the Caribbean published in *Savacou* 3/4, edited by Kamau Brathwaite. I was included among the readers. Later, in 1977, I would have two of my first 'reggae poems' published in *Savacou* 9/10, edited by Andrew and John. In 1973, when Nigel Williams commissioned John

La Rose to produce a Caribbean edition of the BBC2 television arts programme *Full House*, Andrew and John made sure that I was included. Again in 1974, it was through Andrew that I was able to recite my verse on national radio in Jamaica when Jeremy Verity invited me to go on *Poetry Now*, hosted by Elaine Wint.

Andrew was very well connected in the literary world and the Caribbean diaspora in Britain. He seemed to know just about everybody. He introduced me to the Jamaican High Commissioner Arthur Wint, who in turn invited me to become a trustee for the short-lived Marcus Garvey Memorial Trust. While at university I was able to cut my teeth in broadcasting, doing an occasional short report for *Caribbean Magazine*, broadcast on the BBC World Service. That, too, was Andrew's doing. He was de facto editorial advisor at Bogle-L'Ouverture Publications, Britain's second publisher of black literature and booksellers, established in 1968 by Eric and Jessica Huntley. Andrew persuaded the Huntleys to publish my second book of verse, *Dread Beat and Blood*, in 1975 and wrote a generous introduction. It was with that book that my reputation as a reggae poet was built.

After he left to teach at Amherst College in the USA there was not much communication between us. If I got a letter from him, it would invariably begin, 'My dear brother' and end with the words 'venceremos' or 'keep on keeping on'. I may have seen him once or twice when he came home; I can't remember. But I do remember being grateful for the chance to say a few words at a tribute organized for him at the Commonwealth Institute. I remember sitting between him and John and having a moan to them about a couple of mutual acquaintances. I will never forget what Andrew said to me in response, 'My brother, in the ebb and flow of life, there is always the froth and the foible. When you are gasping for that last breath all these will pale to insignificance.'

The last time I saw Andrew was at a dinner in a Brazilian restaurant somewhere in north London where I was among a few invited friends. I recall him choosing from the menu food he said his doctor had advised against: belly of pork with rice and black beans. I will always remember him for his loving ways, his kindness, intellect and revolutionary spirit.

Speech for the University of Glasgow, October 2014

Don Mattera and James Matthews:
A Tribute (2019)

I consider it a tremendous honour to have been invited to participate in this reading in tribute to James Matthews and my friend Don Mattera, these two freedom fighters, veteran journalists and doyens of the movement of cultural resistance against apartheid; both award-winning distinguished men of letters. In Britain, it was not until the 1980s that we began to learn of the potency of the poetry of black writers in South Africa. You would get an idea of the names of some of the poets and what they were writing only if you could find the magazines *Drum* and *Staffrider*. I was one of the organizers of the International Book Fair of Radical Black and Third World Books between 1982 and 1995, held in London, Manchester and Bradford. The anti-apartheid struggle was very much in focus during those book fair years. South African exiles supported the book fair and some, like Mongane Wally Serote and Mandla Langa, were participants. In the book *A Meeting of the Continents*, which documents the book fairs, you can find the names James Matthews and Don Mattera in the index, not as participants, but as writers published by Ravan Press and Index on Censorship respectively.

Back in the early nineties, the Dennis Bovell Dub Band and I were booked by a company called Joyful Noise to do a reggae concert at the Queen Elizabeth Hall at the Southbank Centre in London. I was happy to do the show, partly because the promoter was black. We normally have a variety of alcohol and other refreshments in our dressing rooms, provided by the promoter. When I went backstage after soundcheck, I realized that the promoter had not even provided water. When I confronted him, he said to me, 'You're a poet; you must suffer for your art.' James and Don are two poets who know what it means to suffer, not only for their art, but also – to borrow a phrase from Barack Obama – for their audacity of hope and their activism. Harassed, imprisoned, banned, they have been resolute in asserting their freedom of creative imagination.

The last time I was here I read alongside the late South African poet laureate Bra Willie* at a tribute to the African-American poet Jayne Cortez. I felt a certain affinity to Bra Willie because of the similarity in our poetics, based on the relationship between language and music. I share some affinity with James and Don too. Like them I eschewed the aristocratic notion of art for art's sake. Like them, for me writing verse was a political act and poetry a weapon in the black liberation struggle.

One of my most treasured possessions is a signed copy of *Azanian Love Song*, Don Mattera's collection of poems written between 1960 and 1982. It is a fine collection, full of revolutionary fervour and passion, with poems of resistance, defiance,

---

* Originally known as Keorapetse Kgositsile.

despair, hope, love and spirituality. One the poems is titled 'The Poet Must Die, For James Matthews and Gladys Thomas, After Their Poems Were Executed'. In the dedication to me, Don writes, 'To a brother, Linton Kwesi Johnson. May Babylons crumble! Brixton, 18 December, 1986'. I've wracked my brain, but simply cannot recall the occasion when I received the book. However, I suspect that it may have been when Don was on his way back to South Africa from Sweden where he had won an award and spent some time.

Another treasured gift I have is a copy of James Matthews' *Gently Stirs My Soul*, a present from Robert van Niekirk, Director of the Institute of Social and Economic Research at Rhodes University. I don't know if Derek Walcott's assertion that 'the destiny of poetry is the elegiac' is true. It seems to be the case with James' poetry. *Gently Stirs My Soul* is a deeply moving, beautiful work of art.

Finally, I would like to say to these two living legends, poets of love and compassion, maximum respect. May your rich legacies reverberate through the ages.

Speech in South Africa, May 2019

Jean 'Binta' Breeze, 1956–2021:
A Tribute (2021)

My sister poet and recording artist, Jean 'Binta' Breeze MBE, passed away last night in Jamaica. She had been suffering from COPD, a lung disease, for some time. I first met Jean in the late 1970s when she was a part of the 'dub poetry' movement based at the Jamaica School of Drama alongside Michael Smith and Oku Onuora. Her poetry went beyond that genre after she settled in Britain from 1985. Her poem 'Riddym Ravings' ('The Mad Woman Poem') is considered a classic of modern Caribbean poetry.

She made her debut as a performer in London at the International Book Fair of Radical Black and Third World Books in 1985, and went on to establish a solid reputation as one of the most popular poets on the reading circuit. Her books include *Riddym Ravings* (Race Today Publications, 1988), *Spring Cleaning* (Virago, 1992), *The Fifth Figure* (Bloodaxe, 2006), *Third World Girl* (Bloodaxe, 2011) and *The Verandah Poems* (2016).

I signed Jean to LKJ Records in 1991 and, together with Dennis Bovell, produced her album *Tracks*. Her other recordings include *Riddym Ravins* (ROIR, 1987), *Riding on de Riddym* (57 Productions, 1997) and *Eena Me Corner* (Arroyo Records, 2010).

LKJ with Jean 'Binta' Breeze and Dennis Bovell. On tour in Pisa, 1990.

I have wonderful memories of Jean on tour with me and the Dennis Bovell Dub Band all over Europe and North America. There were times when I thought she would steal the show. The band loved having her on the road with us.

In 2003 Jean was awarded a Nesta Fellowship; in 2012 an MBE. Her other awards include a Silver Musgrave Medal from the Institute of Jamaica, a Lifetime Achievement Award from the Jamaica Poetry Festival and honorary Doctor of Letters from the University of Leicester.

Jean is survived by her son Gareth, daughters Imega and Caribe and two grandchildren.

For the George Padmore Institute website, 21 June 2021

Linton Kwesi Johnson's prose in chronological order

1970s

The Swamp Dwellers by Wole Soyinka (*Race Today*, September
    1975)
Jamaican Rebel Music (*Race & Class* XVII 4, 1976)
The Reggae Rebellion (*New Society*, 10 June 1976)
The Year of Reggae (*Melody Maker*, 25 December 1976)
Marley at the Polls (*Melody Maker*, 5 February 1977)
Caribbean Chronicles (*Times Literary Supplement*, 25 March
    1977)
Bob Marley and the Reggae International (*Race Today*, June/
    July 1977)
Echo by Orlando Wong (aka Oku Onuora) (*Race Today*,
    September 1977)

1980s

'Blackbeard' in Profile: Laying the Foundations (*Race Today
    Review*, December 1981/January 1982)
Language as Power: *Decolonising the Mind* by Ngũgĩ wa
    Thiong'o (*Race Today*, December 1986)
Introduction (*Race Today Review*, 1986)

TIME COME

Introduction (*Race today Review*, 1987)

Searching for Answers: Caryl Phillips in Conversation (*Race Today Review*, 1987)

1990s

Speaking in Tongues: *Dictionary of Caribbean English Usage* (*The Guardian*, 19 April 1996)

Martin Carter: Give Thanks (Essay in *All are Involved: The Art of Martin Carter*, ed. Stewart Brown, 2000, written 1997)

2000s

South London Calling (*Time Out*, 23 March 2000)

Jamaica Uncovered: *Life and Debt* (*The Guardian*, 28 February 2002)

Reunited: Shocking with Such Glee (*Times Higher Education Supplement*, 24 September 2004)

Remembering Michael Smith: Mikey, Dub and Me (Lecture, 4 August 2005)

Mutabaruka: Cutting Edge of Dub (*The Guardian*, 27 August 2005)

Obituary: John La Rose (*The Guardian*, 4 March 2006)

Obituary: Louise Bennett, Voice of the People (*Wasafiri*, October 2006)

Exodus: The Poetry of Exile (*The Independent*, 1 June 2007)

PROSE IN CHRONOLOGICAL ORDER

2010s to date

Writing Reggae: Poetry, Politics and Popular Culture (*Jamaica Journal*, December 2010)

We Have Not Forgotten (Prologue to *The New Cross Massacre Story*, 2011)

I & I: The Natural Mystics by Colin Grant (*Wasafiri*, July 2011)

Riots, Rhymes and Reason (Speech, 24 March 2012)

Thatcher and the Inner-City Riots (LKJ Records blog, 14 April 2013)

African Consciousness in Reggae Music: Some Examples (Lecture, July 2013)

Amsterdam: People, Places and Beginnings (Amsterdam event speech, September 2014)

Remembering Andrew Salkey (Speech for the University of Glasgow, October 2014)

The People Speak (Introduction to *So Much Things to Say* by Roger Steffens, 2017, written 2015)

South African Connections (Honorary doctorate acceptance speech, April 2017)

Don Mattera and James Matthews: A Tribute (Speech in South Africa, May 2019)

Jean 'Binta' Breeze: A Tribute (For the George Padmore Institute website, 21 June 2021)

The Upsetter (Introduction to *People Funny Boy* by David Katz, 2021, written 8 September 2021)

Acceptance Speech to the University of the West Indies (Honorary doctorate acceptance speech, 19 October 2021)

Acknowledgements
and permissions

With thanks to all the people – writers, artists, filmmakers, activists, publishers, friends, family – who have been part of this fifty-year journey.

The Swamp Dwellers by Wole Soyinka (*Race Today*, September 1975)

Jamaican Rebel Music (*Race & Class* XVII 4, 1976)

The Reggae Rebellion (*New Society*, 10 June 1976)

The Year of Reggae (*Melody Maker*, 25 December 1976)

Marley at the Polls (*Melody Maker*, 5 February 1977)

Caribbean Chronicles (*Times Literary Supplement*, 25 March 1977)

Bob Marley and the Reggae International (*Race Today*, June/ July 1977)

Echo by Orlando Wong (aka Oku Onuora) (*Race Today*, September 1977)

'Blackbeard' in Profile: Laying the Foundations (*Race Today Review*, December 1981/January 1982)

Language as Power: *Decolonising the Mind* by Ngũgĩ wa Thiong'o (*Race Today*, December 1986)

Introduction (*Race Today Review*, 1986)

Introduction (*Race Today Review*, 1987)

Searching for Answers: Caryl Phillips in Conversation (*Race Today Review*, 1987)

Speaking in Tongues: *Dictionary of Caribbean English Usage* (*The Guardian*, 19 April 1996) Copyright © Guardian News and Media Ltd 2022

Martin Carter: Give Thanks (*All are Involved: The Art of Martin Carter*, ed. Stewart Brown, 2000, written 12 December 1997)

South London Calling (*Time Out*, 23 March 2000)

Jamaica Uncovered: *Life and Debt* (*The Guardian*, 28 February 2002) Copyright © Guardian News and Media Ltd 2022

Reunited: Shocking with Such Glee (*Times Higher Educational Supplement*, 5 July 2004)

Remembering Michael Smith: Mikey, Dub and Me (Lecture, 4 August 2005)

Mutabaruka: Cutting Edge of Dub (*The Guardian*, 27 August 2005) Copyright © Guardian News and Media Ltd 2022

Obituary: John La Rose (*The Guardian*, 4 March 2006) Copyright © Guardian News and Media Ltd 2022

Obituary: Louise Bennett, Voice of the People (*Wasafiri*, October 2006)

Exodus: The Poetry of Exile (*The Independent*, 1 June 2007)

Writing Reggae: Poetry, Politics and Popular Culture (*Jamaica Journal*, December 2010)

We Have Not Forgotten (Prologue to *The New Cross Massacre Story*, George Padmore Institute, 2011)

I & I: The Natural Mystics by Colin Grant (*Wasafiri*, July 2011)

Riots, Rhyme and Reason (Speech, 24 March 2012)

Thatcher and the Inner City Riots (LKJ Records blog,
14 April 2013)

African Consciousness, Reggae and the African Diaspora
(Lecture, July 2013)

Amsterdam: People, Places and Beginnings (Amsterdam
speech, September 2014)

Remembering Andrew Salkey (Speech for the University of
Glasgow, October 2014)

The People Speak (Introduction to *So Much Things To Say* by
Roger Steffens, 2017, written 2015)

South African Connections (Honorary doctorate speech, April
2017)

Don Mattera and James Matthews (Speech in South Africa,
May 2019)

Tribute: Jean 'Binta' Breeze (George Padmore Institute
website, 21 June 2021)

The Upsetter (Introduction to *People Funny Boy* by David
Katz, 2021, written 8 September 2021) Reproduced with
permission of the Licensor through PLSclear.

Acceptance Speech to the University of the West Indies
(Honorary doctorate speech, 19 October 2021)

Picture acknowledgements

Endpapers: Promotional poster, courtesy of Linton Kwesi
Johnson.

Page 7 'The Year of Reggae' from *Melody Maker*; page 18
Island Records portrait of LKJ © Dennis Morris; pages 50

and 54 from *Race Today* June/July 1977; page 59 LKJ with
Dennis Bovell, aka 'Blackbeard' © John Kpiaye; page 66 from
Race Today Review December 1981/January 1982; page 101
from *Race Today* September 1975; page 113 from *Race Today*
December 1986; page 117 from *Race Today Review* 1987; page
147 Goldsmiths College NUS pass, courtesy of Linton Kwesi
Johnson; page 154 LKJ at seventeen, courtesy of Linton Kwesi
Johnson; page 177 from *The New Cross Massacre Story* © Chris
Abuk; page 191 LKJ in 1980 © Adrian Boot; page 182 LKJ
Brixton portrait © Jim Varney; page 194 LKJ performing at
an anti-apartheid festival 1983, courtesy of Linton Kwesi
Johnson; page 205 from *Race Today Review* February 1986;
page 209 from *Race Today Review* 1987; page 215 LKJ in south
London, photography by Nick Wilson/Camera Press London;
page 225 LKJ in Amsterdam 1981 © Phil Bayly; page 228
LKJ performing at the One World poetry festival, Amsterdam
1981 © Phil Bayly; page 235 Celebrating LKJ's honorary
doctorate from the University of the West Indies © Sharmilla
Beezmohun; page 242 LKJ with Mervyn Morris © Sharmilla
Beezmohun; page 266 John La Rose © Val Wilmer; page 288
LKJ with Jean 'Binta' Breeze © John Kpiaye.

Index

57 Productions 287

A. C. McClurg 162
Abrahams, Peter 195
Abyssinians, The 38, 82, 83
Achebe, Chinua 99–100
Africa Solidarity 269
African Union 79
Africans, The (TV series) 210
Agee, Philip 172
Ah Who Se? God De! (album) 61
Albany Theatre, Deptford 178
Ali, Jamal 234, 279
Ali, Tariq 204
Allah, Ras 39
Allfrey, Ellah 134
Alligator (record label) 261
Allsopp, Richard 129–31
Amber Lane Press 115
André Deutsch (publishers) 104
Andy, Bob 80, 82
Anancy and Miss Lou (book) 272
Angelic Upstarts 62
Angelou, Maya 206
Anti-Nazi League 178
Any Which Way Freedom (album)
   261
Archer, John 208

Arena (TV programme) 210, 244,
   251
Arroyo Records 287
Arthur Ravenscroft Memorial
   Lecture 133–62
Artrage (magazine) 208
Arts Alive 199
Arusha Declaration 1967 204
Ashanti record label 27
Aswad 39, 85
'Atilla the Hun' (aka Raymond
   Quevedo) 267
Atilla's Kaiso (also called *Kaiso: A
   Review*) 267
Atlantic Road, Brixton 214, 216,
   217
Augustus Buchanan (record label)
   26 (n. 4)
Aunty Roachy Seh (book) 272
Aunty Roachy Seh (radio
   programme) 273–4
Azanian Love Song (book) 284–5

B, Anthony 138
Babylon (film) 62
Baldwin, James 128
Banjo Man (play) 210–11
Banton, Buju 138, 173

Baraka, Amiri (aka LeRoi Jones) 148, 153, 227, 246, 258
Barbara and the Originates 63
Barrett, Aston 52, 167
Barrett, Carlton 52, 167
Barrett, Lindsay 234
Bat Centre, Durban 199
Baugh, Eddie (Edward) 234
Baxter Theatre, Cape Town 199
BBC 124, 135, 146, 184, 206, 210, 243, 244, 251, 252, 269, 273, 274, 280
BBC World Service 280
'Beat Down Babylon' (song) 24–5, 93, 146
Beaton, Norman 211
Beaton But Unbowed (book) 211
Bennett, Augustus Cornelius 272
Bennett, Louise (aka Louise Bennett-Coverley or Miss Lou) xix, 141, 157, 223, 262, 271–5
Berry, James 249
Berry Street Studio 60
Betjeman, John 135
Bionic Dread (album) 44–5, 47
Big Youth 46, 47, 105, 109, 137–8, 152, 230
BIM (journal) 155, 156, 157
Black, Stephanie 171–4
Black Ark studio 95
Black Education Movement 268
Black Jacobins, The (book) 157
Black Jacobins, The (play) 211
Black Liberator, The (journal) 246–7
Black Music sound system 262
Black Panther Movement (UK) 152, 153–5, 157, 196–7, 229, 230, 278

Black Parents Movement xvi, 183, 244, 268–9
Black People's Day of Action 175–6, 177, 179, 184, 190
Black Poetry (book) 153
Black Power Movement (USA) xvii, xviii, 47, 81, 84, 260
Black Reconstruction in America (book) 157
Black Silk (TV show) 206
Black Star Line 15, 80
Black Star Liners (album) 38, 80, 81
Black Swan (record label) 44
Black Uhuru 244
Black Wax (record label) 44
Black Workers Movement 157
Black Youth Movement xvi, 183, 244–5, 268
Blackheart Man (album) 40
Blackwell, Chris 88, 165–6, 224, 252
Blake, Percival 223
Blair, Tony 145
Bloodaxe Books 134, 287
Bloom, Valerie 274
Bob Marley: Lyrical Genius (book) 73
Boggs, Grace Lee 208
Bogle, Paul 16, 70
Bogle-L'Ouverture Books 134, 156, 234, 252, 269, 280
Bongo Jerry xix, 133, 155, 156–7, 257, 260, 279
Bontemps, Arna 153
Book of Rule (album) 26
Booker, Cedella 91
Boothe, Ken 58
Bovell, Dennis ('Blackbeard')

xviii, 57–67, 93, 184, 252, 287, 288

Bra Willie (aka Kgositsile, Keorapetse) 284

Bradford Black Collective 183

Brain Damage (album) 67

Brathwaite, Kamau (Edward) xix, 78, 155, 159, 231, 234, 245, 249–50, 267, 278, 279

Breaklight (book) 157

Breakspeare, Cindy 91

Breese, Caribe 289

Breese, Gareth 289

Breese, Imega 289

Breeze, Jean 'Binta' xix, 234, 246, 261, 262, 287–9

Brewster, Yvonne 234, 279

Bristol riots 1980 183

British Council 273

British Movement 178

British National Party (BNP) 190

Brixton, London – or Brixton riots 1981 127, 146, 154, 176, 182, 183–4, 186, 190, 196–8, 207, 213–17, 243, 258

Broadside Press 162

Brodber, Erna 78

Brooks, Cedric 33, 82, 260–1

Brooks, Gwendolyn 153

Brown, Castro 60

Brown, H. Rap 260

Brown, James 146

Brown, Lloyd 273

Brown, Sam 257

Brown, Stewart 239

Brown Sugar 60

Bull Head Mountain, Jamaica 136

Burchell, Thomas 16

Burke, Vanley 124

Burnin (album) 137, 160

Burning Spear (aka Winston Rodney) 13–14, 20, 24, 33, 81–2, 146

Burning Spears 82

Burning Spears, The (album) 43

Burroughs, William S. 227

Burtons (*see also* Carib Club) 93

Bushay, Clem 60

Bustamante, Alexander 16

Byles, Junior 24–5, 93, 146

Cadogan, Susan 95

Caesar, Imruh 100

Calabar Elementary School, Kingston 272

Calabash (International) Literary Festival 234, 242, 258, 262–3

Callaghan, Jim (James) 192

Camden Centre, London 243

Cameron, David 192

Cann, Patrick 60

Capitalism and Slavery (book) 157

Capleton 84

Carib Club, Cricklewood (*see also* Burtons) 93n

Carib Gems (record label) 160

Caribbean Artists Movement (CAM) xvii, 155–6, 158, 231, 233–4, 267–8, 278, 279

Caribbean Artists Movement: A Literary and Cultural History, The (book) 155–6, 162

Caribbean Education in Community Workers Association 268

Caribbean Magazine (radio
    programme) 280
Carifesta 243, 251
Carmichael, Stokely 260
Carter, Martin 155, 157, 239–40,
    279
Castro, Fidel 172, 265
Catch A Fire (album) 24, 49, 51, 161
Cateforis, Theo 88n
Cattouse, Nadia 234
CB 200 (album) 36, 37, 47
Césaire, Aimé 155, 230
Chamberlin, J. Edward 248, 249
Chambers, Eddie 206, 212
Channel One Studio 36, 45
Chapelton, Jamaica 136
Chapelton All Age School 138
Charles, Ray 64
Check It (album) 261
Chin, Stacyann 263
Chung, Geoffrey 38
CIA (Central Intelligence Agency)
    87, 172
Cimarons, The 39, 42
City Lights Publishers 246
Clarendon, Jamaica 136, 233
Clarke, Johnny 36, 58, 81
Clayton, Sam 12, 257
Cleaver, Eldridge 260
Cliff, Jimmy 224, 261
Coard, Bernard 268
Cochrane, Kelso 178
Cold War xvii, 87
Cole, Alan 'Skill' 91
Column 88 178
Coltrane, John 211
Come Back to Me My Language
    (book) 254
Committee for the Release of

Political Prisoners in Kenya
    269
Commonwealth Institute 210, 212,
    279, 280
Community Relations Council
    (CRC) 198
Comrie, Locksley 260
Congos, The 82
Continent of Black Consciousness, The
    (book) 78
Cooper, Carolyn 234
Cooper, Ibo 252
Coore, Cat 91
Corso, Gregory 227
Cortez, Jayne 199, 206, 245, 284
Count Nick's sound system 93
Count Ossie and the Mystic
    Revelation of Rastafari 158,
    230, 243, 261
Courier (journal) 252
Coverley, Eric 'Chalk Talk' 272, 273
Coxsone, Lloyd 60
Coxsone Records 27, 28
Creation For Liberation 207, 243,
    244, 252
'Cricklewood Twelve' 93
Cullen, Countee 153
Curniffe, Winston 223
Cutting Edge, The (radio show)
    257–8

Daily Telegraph 135
Dalí, Salvador xviii, 93
Dam X (aka Stephen Hall) 158
Darnell, Larry 148
Dawes, Kwame 73, 164, 248–9
Dawes, Neville 193
Declaration of New Cross 179
Decolonising the Mind: The Politics of

INDEX

Language in African Literature (book) 111–14

Dekker, Desmond 80

Dennis Bovell Dub Band 59, 184, 194, 195, 224, 228, 284, 289

Desai, Barney 197–8, 199

Desai, Rehad 197

Development of Creole Society in Jamaica 1770–1820, The (book) 78

Dhlomo, R. R. R. 204

Dhondy, Farrukh 246

Dictionary of Caribbean English Usage (book) 129–31

Dillinger 4n, 36, 37, 44, 45, 46, 47, 108, 152

DIP Studios 60

Dr Alimantado 108

Dodd, Clement 'Sir Coxsone' 90, 94

Dog (play) 210

Dove, Robert 16

Downie, Tyrone 52

Dread Beat An' Blood (album) 224

Dread Beat and Blood (book) 88, 156, 280

Dread Locks Dread (album) 28

Drifters, The 64

Drill Hall, London 211

Drum (magazine) 283

Drummond, Don 79

Du Bois, W.E.B 153, 157, 229

Dub Poetry: Nineteen Poets from England and Jamaica (book) 255

Duffy, Carol Ann 160n

Duggan, Mark 185

Dunbar, Sly 30

D'unis sound system 214

Dunkley, Errol 60

Dyke, Len 252

Dylan, Bob 58, 164

Earth and Fire 36

Echo (book) 105–9, 152

Echo in The Bone, An (play) 211

Educationally Sub-Normal Schools (ESNs) 145, 268

Edwin Allen High School, Jamaica 233

Eena Me Corner (album) 287

Elizabeth I 12

EMI Records 58

English PEN 199

Enwonwu, Benita 100

Equality and Human Rights Commission 186

Ethiopians, The 82

European Action for Racial Equality and Social Justice 269

European Tribe, The (book) 115, 128

Excelsior High School, Kingston 272

Exodus (album) 49–56, 69–73, 87

Exodus (book) 87

Eyelets of Truth Within Me (book) 270

Faber & Faber (publishers) 115, 208

Fabulous Greatest Hits (Prince Buster) (album) 161

Fanon, Frantz xvii, 8–9, 157–8, 265

Fashion Records 161

Federated Workers Trade Union 167

Ferlinghetti, Lawrence 227

INDEX

Fiammenghi, Gioia 103
Fifteen, Sixteen and Seventeen 60
Fifth Figure, The (book) 287
Filmer, Paul 220
Final Passage, The (book) 115,
    122–5, 128
First Poems, The (book) 258–9
Fischer, Stanley 173–4
Flamingo, The (club) 65
Forces of Victory (album) 223
Ford, Laxton 11
Ford-Smith, Honor 245
Foundations (book) 270
Fox Records 27
Free Press 162
Freedom journal 267
Friends' College, St Mary 272
From Brixton to Barbados
    (documentary) 243, 251
From Mento to Lovers' Rock (radio
    series) 252, 274
*From Our Yard: Jamaican Poetry
    Since Independence* (book) 254
'front line', Brixton 213–17
Front Line, The (album) 37
Full House (TV programme) 269

G7 countries 171
Gardiner, Boris 45–6
Gardiner, Robert 16
Garvey, Marcus 25, 55, 70, 71, 75,
    79, 80–1, 163, 167, 195, 217,
    260, 265, 271, 280
Garvey, Marcus Jnr. 260
Gently Stirs My Soul (book) 285
George Padmore Institute 179,
    270, 289
George Padmore Supplementary
    School 268

Gibbons, Rawle 210
Gilmour, Mavis 244
Ginsberg, Allen 227
Glaberman, Marty 208
Gladiators, The 37
Glissant, Édouard 227, 252
Goldsmiths College, London 146,
    147, 219–21
Goodwin, Clayton 212
Goose Lane Editions 255
Gooseberry Studios 60
Grange, 'Babsy' Olivia 245
Grant, Colin 81, 163–8
Great British MCs (album) 161
Greater London Council 206
Grounation (album) 158, 230
Groundings With My Brothers (book)
    27
Grove Press 162
Guardian 174, 187, 245, 263, 266,
    270, 271, 272
Guevara, Che 88
Guillén, Nicolás 279
Gun Court (Kingston) 29, 250–1

Hall, Stephen (aka Dam X) 158
Hall, Stuart 77, 84, 193
Hamish Hamilton (publishers)
    162
Harker, Joseph 187
Harris, Dennis 60
Harris, Wilson 156, 208
Harry J Music (record label) 26
Hart, Richard 16
Hawkins, John 12
Heartbeat (record label) 262
Hector, Tim 208
Heinemann (publishers) 208
Heptones, The 5, 33, 40–1

INDEX

Heroes Circle, Kingston 275
Heritage, Morgan 84
Hickling, Freddie 245, 252
Higgs, Joe 33, 41–2, 90, 165
High Times Players, The 261
History of the Voice (book) 254
Hit the Road Jack (album) 37
Honourable Miss Lou, The (album) 274
Hoo Kim, Jo Jo 36, 45
Hope, Alan (aka Mutabaruka) xix, 82, 234, 246, 257–63
House, Amelia 204
How the West Indian Child Is Made Educationally Sub-Normal in the British School System (book) 268
Howe, Darcus 204, 207–8, 211, 226, 268
Hughes, Langston 148, 153
Huntley, Eric 156, 234, 280
Huntley, Jessica 156, 234, 269, 280
Hussey, Dermot 90
Hutchinson, Joan Andrea 263, 275
Hutchinson (publishers) 27

I & I The Natural Mystics (book) 163–8
I Roy 4n, 10–11, 58, 60, 152
I Sus (album) 35, 39
Ian Randle Publishers 253, 275
Iguana's Tail: Crick Crack Stories from the Caribbean, The (book) 103–4
I, Lawah (play) 210
Impressions, The 72, 146
Incidents at the Shrine (book) 211
Independent Police Complaints Commission 185

Index on Censorship (publishers) 283
Inglan Is A Bitch (book) 160, 257
Institute of Contemporary Arts, London 206
Institute of Jamaica 273, 289
Institute of Jamaica Publications 254
Institute of Race Relations 268
Inter-America Development Bank 173
International Book Fair of Radical Black and Third World Books 207–8, 252, 269–70, 283, 287
International Monetary Fund (IMF) 84, 171–4
Irie FM 234, 257
Is English We Speaking and Other Essays (book) 253
Isaacs, Gregory 21–2
Island Records 18, 35, 40, 61, 88, 165–6, 224, 243, 252, 274
Issa, Paul 258, 260
It A Come (book) 246, 253

J & L Records 161
Jackson, Pipecock (aka Lee 'Scratch' Perry) xviii, 36, 45–6, 93–6, 148
Jaguar record label 26
Jah Lion (aka Jah Lloyd) 143
Jah Ted 27
Jah Woosh 37
Jah Youth 25, 37
Jamaica, a long historical poem (book) 27
Jamaica Journal 162
Jamaica Labrish (book) 272
Jamaica Poetry Festival 234, 289

Jamaica School of Drama 243, 246, 252–3, 261, 287
Jamaica Singing Games (album) 274
Jamaica Social Welfare Commission 274
Jamaican Gleaner 272
Jamaican Labour Party (JLP) 16, 24, 30, 31–2, 43–4, 53, 84, 244, 245
James, C. L. R. 157, 208, 211, 226, 265
James Currey 114
James Hill, Jamaica 136
Jamrec Music 28
Jeffreys, Garland 62
Jegede, Emmanuel 278
Jericho record label 28
Jim Daddy sound system 65
John, Errol 211
John, Frank 279
John, Gus 186–7
Johnson, Howard 99, 102
Johnson, Sly 146
Johnson, Sylvester 233
Jonathan Cape (publishers) 168
Jones, Evan 157
Jones, LeRoi (aka Amiri Baraka) 148, 153, 227, 246, 258
Joyful Noise 284
Junior Ross & The Spears 39
Justice League record label 28

Kahla, Vuyo 193
Kaiso: A Review (also called *Atilla's Kaiso*) 267
Kalonji, Sizzla 82
Kartel, Vybez 76–7
Katz, David 93, 95–6

Kay, Janet 60
Kaya (album) 70
Kelly, Elise 234
Kelly, Pat 58
Kelso, Beverley 90
Keskidee Centre xvii, 99, 156, 158, 239, 278, 279
Kgositsile, Keorapetse (aka Bra Willie) 284
Kim, Jo Jo Hoo *see* Hoo Kim, Jo Jo
Kincaid, Jamaica 173
King, Peter 151
King Emmanuel 84
Kizerman, Rudi 279
Köhler, Horst 171

La Rose, Irma 270
La Rose, John xvii, 155, 175–6, 179, 184, 186, 210, 231, 234, 240, 245, 246, 265–70, 277, 279–80
La Rose, Keith 270
La Rose, Michael 270
La Rose, Wole 270
Labyrinths (book) 230
Lambeth Town Hall 243, 246, 258
Lamming, George 133, 156, 278–9
Langa, Mandla 283
Last Poets, The 155, 230, 260
Laugh with Louise (radio programme) 274
Lawrence, Stephen 186
League of Nations 77
Lebel, Jean-Jacques 227
Lee, Don L. 108, 153, 260
Legalise It (album) 40, 41
Leggo! A Fi Wi Dis (album) 61
Leidseplein, Amsterdam 226

INDEX

Lenin, Vladimir Ilyich Ulyanov 158

Levy, Andrea 76

Lewin, Olive 79

Lewisham Way Centre, London 178

Life and Debt (film) 171–5

Life of Contradiction (album) 41–2

Light of Saba, The 33

Light of Saba record label 243

Lindsay, Jimmy 60

Listen to Louise (album) 274

Little Theatre Movement, The 273

Living Music record label 27

Livingston, Bunny (aka Bunny Wailer) 29–30, 40, 52, 83, 88, 90, 164

LKJ Records 192, 251, 287

Lloyd, Errol 156, 212, 234, 278

Locks, Fred 38, 80–1

Long Song, The (book) 76

Longman (publishers) 208

Lord Brynner 83

Lord Koos sound system 93

Lou and Ranny Show, The (radio programme) 274

Lyric Theatre, Hammersmith 141, 274

Mabizela, Sizwe 193

Macca B 85

McDonald, Larry 260

McGough, Roger 160n

McKay, Claude 136, 153

McNeil, Tony 157

Macpherson Inquiry 186

Making of the English Working Class, The (book) 157

Making West Indian Literature (book) 253, 275

Malcolm X 260

Malik, Abdul 245

Mango record label 161

Mangrove Nine (film) 269

Mangrove restaurant 269

Manley, Michael xvii, 32, 44, 52, 87, 171–2, 173, 250–1

Manley, Norman Washington 16

Mao Zedong 158

Marcus Garvey (album) 27, 161

Mark, Louisa 60

Markham, Archie 211, 245

Marley, Bob 11, 21, 23, 29, 32, 33–4, 35, 39, 40, 42, 43–4, 49–56, 69–73, 77, 82, 83–4, 85, 87–91, 95, 137, 146, 163–8, 217

Marley, Damien 'Junior Gong' 91

Marley, Rita 90

Maroon Wars (1729–39, 1760–96) 16, 78, 81, 275

Marvin, Julian 52

Marx, Karl 158

Mattera, Don 283–5

Matthews, James 283–5

Matthews, Marc 279

Matumbi 39, 58, 85

Maxwell, John 244

Mayfield, Curtis 73, 146

Mazrui, Ali 210

M'bala xix, 246, 261

Mda, Zakes 204

Meeks, Amina Blackwood 275

Meeting of the Continents, A (book) 283

Melody Maker (magazine) xv, 7, 42, 47, 55

Metro youth club, Notting Hill 62

Mi Cyaan Believe It (album) 243, 251, 253, 261
Mi Revalueshanary Fren (book) 134
Michael Joseph (publishers) 160
Michael Schwinn (publishers) 255
Micron Music record label 161
Milky Way club, Amsterdam 226
Mighty Diamonds, The 36, 37, 42, 82
Mighty Sparrow, The 64
Miller, Glenn 58
Miller, Herbie 234
Miłosz, Czesław 160
Miranda, Fabienne 258
Miss Lou (aka Louise Bennett) xix, 141, 157, 223, 262, 271–5
Mr Foundation 31–2
Misty in Roots 85
Mitterrand, François 128
Mixed Blood (journal) 161
Moody, Ronald 156, 278
Moon on a Rainbow Shawl (play) 211
Moonsammy, Roshnie 199
Moonshot community centre 178
Morant Bay Rebellion (1865) 16
Mordecai, Pamela 248, 249
More Intensified Volume Two – Original Ska 1963–67 (album) 161
More Time (album) 240
Morgan, Derrick 79
Morrison, Lionel 198–9
Moses, Pablo 38, 82–3
Mpati, Lex 193
Muffet Inna All a Wi (musical) 210
Mundell, Hugh 83
Munroe, Trevor 16
Murvin, Junior 36

Mutabaruka (aka Alan Hope) xix, 82, 234, 246, 257–63
My Green Hills of Jamaica (book) 136
Mystery Unfolds, The (album) 261

Nanny of the Maroons 81, 275
Nash, Johny 90
National Association of Supplementary Schools 268
National Front 178, 190
National Union of Government and Federated Workers 267
National Union of Journalists 198
Natty Carnival Dread (album) 37
Natty Dread (album) 40, 52, 88
Natty Passing Thru (album) 44–7
Natural Mysticism: Towards a New Reggae Aesthetic (book) 164
Negril (album) 33
Negro With a Hat (book) 81, 163
Nettleford, Rex 193, 273
Neville King's sound system 216
New Beacon Books (bookshop and publisher) 155, 156, 230, 252, 267, 270, 277
New Beacon Review (magazine) 208, 270
New Cross fire 175–9, 183, 190, 269
New Cross Massacre Action Committee (NCMAC) 175–9, 183–4, 269
New Cross Massacre Story: Interviews with John La Rose, The (book) 175–9
New Society xv, xviii, 34
Next Poems, The (book) 258–9

Night Food (album) 40–1
Nkosi, Lewis 198–9
No Logo Festival 224
Non-Aligned Movement 172
Notebook of a Return To My Native Land (book) 230
Notting Hill Carnival riots (1976, 1977) 181–2
Notting Hill race riots (1958–9) 121, 145, 177–8
Nottingham race riots (1958–9) 145, 177–8
Nyerere, Julius 204

Obama, Barack 284
O'Brien, Sean 135
Oilfield Workers Trade Union 267
Okigbo, Christopher 155, 230
Okri, Ben 211
One World Poetry 226–7, 228
Onuora, Oku (aka Orlando Wong) xix, 105–9, 152, 234, 243, 246, 252, 258, 261–2, 287
Operation Black Vote 187
Operation Swamp 81 216
Outcry (album) 261
Outcry (book) 258
Ové, Horace 277
Oxford Companion to Twentieth Century Poetry, The (book) 249
Oxford University Press 131, 254

Padmore, George 265
Pan Africanist Congress 197
Pan-Caribbean Theatre Company 210
Panther Collective 255
Paradiso club, Amsterdam 226
Patterson, P. J. 79

p'Bitek, Okot 155
Peepal Tree Press 164, 239
Penguin (publishers) 134, 160n
Penguin Modern Classics 134, 160n
People Funny Boy (book) 93–6
Perkins, Wilmot 75
Perkins on Line (radio show) 75, 76
Perry, Lee 'Scratch' (aka the 'Upsetter' or Pipecock Jackson) xviii, 36, 45–6, 93–6, 148
People's National Party (Jamaica) (PNP) xvii, 16, 30, 32, 43–4, 52–3, 84, 171, 250–1
Phillips, Caryl 115–28, 211
Phillips, Peter 260
Phillips, Trevor 186
Phonogram (record label) 67
Pierre, Marie 60, 67
Pimlott, Ben 219–20, 221
Pine, Courtney 211
Pitt, Lord David 217
Planno, Mortimo 257, 261
Playing Away (film) 127–8
Pleasures of Exile, The (book) 133
Poems of Succession (book) 240
Poetry Now (radio show) 280
Poets-In-Unity 246, 261
Pop Group, The 62
Politics of Constitutional Decolonization: Jamaica, 1944–62, The (book) 27
Polyphonix 227
Positive Vibrations (album) 40
Posset, Ben 226, 227
Powell, Enoch 178
Prescod, Colin 54
Presenting I Roy (album) 27

INDEX

Pressure Drop: Volume Three (album) 161

Prince Buster 44, 79, 148–51, 230

Prince Far I 138

Prince Jazzbo 4n, 44–7, 151, 152

Prince Pampado 108

Psalms For I (album) 160

Purple Haze Productions 195

Pyramid record label 28

Queen Ifrica 82

Quevedo, Raymond (aka 'Atilla the Hun') 267

Raas Claut Dub (album) 36

Race & Class journal xviii, 26, 246

Race Today (magazine) xv, 50, 54, 56, 88, 101, 102, 109, 113, 114, 152, 208, 226, 245–6, 251, 268

Race Today Collective xvi, 183, 226, 244–5, 251, 268

Race Today Publications 134, 246, 252, 253, 269, 287

Race Today Review 66, 67, 117, 128, 203–6, 207–12, 245–6, 251

Radio Trinidad 267

Railton Road, south London 196, 213–17

Rainbow Theatre, London 51

Ram Jam Club, London 65

Ramchand, Kenneth 234

Randall, Dudley 153

Ras Michael & The Sons of Negus 41, 42

Rasta Love 158–9, 230

Rastafari (album) 41

Rastaman Vibration (album) 51–2

Ravan Press 283

Redding, Otis 41

Reggae's Got Soul (album) 41

Rembrandt 226

Revolutionaries, The 36

Revolutionary Dream (album) 36–7

Rhodes, Cecil 193

Rhone, Trevor 211

Richard Hogarth Lecture 220

Riddym Ravings (book) 287

'Riddym Ravings' (poem) 287

Riding On De Riddym (album) 287

Right Time (album) 36, 37, 82

Rijksmuseum, Amsterdam 226

Ring Ding (television show) 274

Riverside Studios, London 208

Roach, Eric 157

Roaring Twenties, The (club) 65

Robinson-Bennett, Kerene 272

Rock History Reader, The (book) 88n

Rockers (film) 223–4

Rockers Time Now (album) 36

Rocket 69 sound system 65

Rodney, Walter 17, 260

Rodney, Winston (aka Burning Spear) 13–14, 20, 24, 33, 81–2, 146

Rodriguez, Rico 60

Rohlehr, Gordon 10, 23, 138, 157, 248, 273

Rollins, Sonny 211

Romeo, Max 36

Rosso, Franco 62, 269

Rototom Festival 224

Routledge (publishers) 88

Royal Academy for the Dramatic Arts (RADA), London 273

Royals, The 27, 28

Rugg, Akua 207

Ruglass, Joseph 17, 257

INDEX

St Lucia National Theatre 210–11

St Jude's Junior school, south London 143

St Simon's College, Kingston 272

Salkey, Andrew xvii, 13, 155, 156–7, 159, 231, 234, 239–40, 267–8, 277–81

Salkey, Elliot 279

Salkey, Jason 279

Salkey, Pat 279

Sanchez, Sonia 108, 153, 260

Sandy River, Jamaica 136, 138, 139, 144

Sangster's 109

Satta Massagana (album) 38, 83

Savacou (journal) 155, 156–7, 279

Scarman, Leslie, Lord 216

Schmidt, Michael 135

School's Out (play) 211

Scientific, Higher Ranking Dubb (album) 61

Scott, Dennis 157, 210, 211

Screaming Target (album) 26

Seaga, Edward 89

Selassie, Haile 76–7, 150, 158

Selected Poems (of Louise Bennett) (book) 272

Selvon, Sam 156, 159, 231, 234, 277, 278

Serote, Mongane Wally 283

Shabazz, Menelik 116

Shakespeare, William 208

Shanachie (record label) 261

Sharpe, Sam 16

Shearer, Hugh 17, 24, 260

Shelter, The (play) 115, 120–1

Clapham's Youth Club (Railton Road Methodist Church youth club) 216

Sherlock, Philip 103–4

Shorter, Wayne 211

Shorty the President 4n

Sibbles, Leroy 3, 5–6

Silk, Garnett 84

Simpson-Miller, Portia 79

Sims, Danny 90

Sir Lord Comic 148, 151

Sir Niney 33

Sistren 210

Sisulu, Albertina 199

Sisulu, Walter 199

Slits, The 62

Slovo, Gillian 199

Smith, Earl 'Chinna' 261

Smith, Malachi 246, 261

Smith, Michael (Mikey) xix, 143, 234, 241–53, 258, 261, 262, 287

Soho Poly Theatre, London 239

So Much Things to Say: The Oral History of Bob Marley (book) 87–91

Something Unusual (book) 211

Soprano B sound system 214

Souls of Black Folk, The (book) 229–30

Sounds of Music record label 28

South African Coloured People's Congress 197

Southbank Centre, London 284

Soyinka, Wole 99–102

Spring Cleaning (book) 287

Staceyville All Age School 138

Staceyville Baptist church 136–7

Staffrider (magazine) 283

State of Independence, A (book) 115, 119 7

Steel Pulse 85

INDEX

Steffens, Roger 89–91
Stewart, Bob 245
Strange Fruit (play) 115, 118–19, 124
Studio 80 61
Studio One 90, 165
Sufferer's Hi Fi/sound system 62, 93
Sun and Moon (book) 258
Sunday Observer 198
Sunfest Festival 224
Super Ape (album) 36, 46, 95
Survival (album) 70
'sus' law (aka Vagrancy Act) 196–7
Swamp Dwellers, The (play) 99–102
Swing magazine 258, 260

Taj Mahal 260
Talawa Theatre Company 211
Tanifeani, William 246
Tate & Lyle 166
Taylor, George 16
Techniques, The 72
Teenagers, The 165
Temptations, The 146
Thatcher, Margaret 176, 183, 189–92
Theatre Royal Stratford East 211
Them A Mad Over Me (album) 161
Things Fall Apart (book) 99
Thiong'o, Ngũgĩ wa *see* wa Thiong'o, Ngũgĩ
Third World (album) 41
Third World (band) 33, 41, 83, 252
Third World Girl (book) 287
Thomas, Gladys 285
Thompson, E. P. 157

Thompson Twins, The 62
Ti-Jean and his Brothers (play) 210
Time (magazine) 69, 87
Time Out (magazine) 217
Times Higher Education Supplement (THES) 221
Times Literary Supplement (aka *TLS*) 104, 135
Tings an Times (book) 134
Toomer, Jean 153
Toots and the Maytals 6–8, 34, 41, 42
Torch of Freedom (album) 33
Tosh, Peter 33, 51–2, 78, 88, 146, 164–8
Tottenham riots (1985) 190, 210
Tottenham riots (2011) 184–5, 190
Towards Racial Justice 134, 268
Tracks (album) 287
Trench Town, Jamaica 44, 51, 143, 165
Trenchtown Mix-up (album) 37
Trojan Records 161
Tuff Gong Records 88
TuffGong Films 171
Tutu, Desmond 128
Twenty-Four Poems (book) 258
Twinkle Brothers, The 83, 195

U Tam'si, Tchicaya 155
Ultimate Collection, The (album) 261
UNESCO 244
Universal Negro Improvement Association (UNIA) 80
University of Illinois Press 254
University of Kwa Zulu Natal 199
University of Leeds 162

INDEX

University of Leicester 289
University of North Carolina Press
162
University of the West Indies 17,
193, 233, 236, 253, 260, 262, 274
Upon Westminster Bridge (TV
programme) 244, 252
Upsetter, The (aka Lee 'Scratch'
Perry or Pipecock Jackson)
xviii, 36, 45–6, 93–6, 148
Urban Voices and Arts Exchange
199
U-Roy 4n, 37, 42, 46, 47, 152, 230

Vagrancy Act (aka 'sus' law) 196–7
van Niekirk, Robert 285
Verandah Poems, The (book) 287
Verity, Jeremy 280
Victor Gollancz (publishers) 162
Victoria (queen) 197
Vintage (publishers) 162
Virago (publishers) 208
Virgin Records 35, 36–7, 40
Viv (TV documentary) 206
*Voice Print: An Anthology of Oral and
Related Poetry* (book) 254
Voices of the Living and the Dead
(book) 158
Vulcan Records 41

W. W. Norton (publishers) 91
wa Thiong'o, Ngũgĩ 111–14, 246
Wailer, Bunny (aka Bunny
Livingston) 29–30, 40, 52, 83,
88, 90, 164
Wailers, The (first known as the
Wailing Wailers) 23, 29, 31, 32,
33–4, 35, 39, 40, 42, 43–4,
49–56, 69–73, 88, 90, 95, 163–8

Walcott, Derek 155
Walcott, Noel xix, 246
Walcott, Roderick 211
Walker, Herbert 245
Walker, Margaret 153
Walker Brothers, The 63
Wall, Anthony 244, 251, 252
Walmsley, Anne 155–6
Walton, Hazel 195
War in A Babylon (album) 36
Wasafiri magazine 168, 275
Washington, Delroy 35, 39, 42
Weathers, Vivian 223
Weidenfeld & Nicolson
(publishers) 87
West Indian Guest Night (radio
programme) 273
West Indian Independence Party
267
West Indian Students Centre
279
*Wheel and Come Again: An
Anthology of Reggae Poetry* (book)
265
Where There Is Darkness (play) 115,
119–21, 123–4
Whirlwind, The (book) 245
White, Sarah 155, 267, 270
Whitechapel Gallery, London 212
Whylie, Marjorie 79
Wildflower record label 27
Williams, Aubrey 156
Williams, Eric 157
Williams, Joan 75, 76
Williams, Lari 100
Williams, Nigel 279
Williams, Richard 87n
Wills, Viola 62
Wilson, Harold 192

INDEX

Wint, Arthur 280
Wint, Elaine 280
World Tonight (radio programme)
    135
Womantalk (album) 262
Woolley, Simon 187
*Word Soun' 'Ave Power: Reggae
    Poetry* (album) 262
Workers Freedom Movement 267
World Bank 171–3
World Festival of Youth and
    Students 243
Wong, Orlando (aka Oku Onuora)

xix, 105–9, 152, 234, 243, 246,
    252, 258, 261–2, 287
Wretched of the Earth, The (book)
    157–8

Yabby-U and the Prophets 33
Yellowman 151
Yentob, Alan 251
Yes M'Dear – Miss Lou Live (album)
    274
Youth Council (Trinidad) 267

Zukie, Tapper 37, 83